A Philosopher Looks at The Bible

A Critical Review Of What's Actually In It

Vol. 1: The Old Testament

Bangs L. Tapscott, Ph.D.
Emeritus Professor of Philosophy
University of Utah

DEDICATION

To the hundreds of students who have taken my Philosophy courses over the years –especially those who actually learned a thing or two.
(You know who you are.)

Copyright © 2013 by Bangs L. Tapscott
All Rights Reserved
All Wrongs Disavowed

PREFACE

This is neither a religious book nor an anti-religious book. It's a commentary book, with similarities to both a journal and a long book report. It came about when I decided, one day, to read The Whole Bible –not for spiritual reasons, but to see what's actually in it. I regard The Bible as a book to be read, not as Holy Writ. As it turns out, I rather like the Bible

As I read along, I would stop and write about what I had read, I called each segment a "chapter." My chapters vary in length, depending on how much I wrote on that particular day. (They have nothing to do with the chapter divisions in the Bible itself. Those are the work of long-ago authors and editors.)

It is written in conversational language, the way people talk. I wanted to bring the content of the Bible to the reader, especially without the archaic phrasing in the King James translation, which tends to turn people away at the outset.

I'm told that what I've written is both enjoyable reading and thought-provoking. I hope you find it so.

For reasons of my own, I refer to the deity throughout by his name, "Yahweh", rather than his title of office, "God",

Bangs L. Tapscott
January 3, 2017

ABOUT THE BIBLE

"The Bible" consists of the **Old Testament** and the **New Testament**. The Old Testament chronicles the history of the Jews over several thousand years, beginning with the Creation. The New Testament chronicles early stages in the development of Christianity, beginning with the birth of Jesus.

The **Old Testament** contains 39 books, written by various authors over centuries. Some are narratives, relating legends and stories; some are directives, laying down laws for proper conduct; some are sermons, generally prophesying disasters for disobedience. Some are poetry; some are personal ruminations. They are arranged roughly in the order in which they were written, with a few notable deviations. The earliest books were written around 1500 B.C; the latest around 400 BC

The first five books-- Genesis, Exodus, Leviticus, Numbers. and Deuteronomy-- are called the **Pentateuch** or the **Five Books of Moses.** Legend has it that they were written by Moses, although they almost certainly were not.

The **New Testament** contains 27 books. The first four, the **Gospels of Matthew, Mark, Luke, and John**, concern the life and activities of Jesus. The fifth, **Acts of the Apostles**, concerns the activities of Jesus' followers in the time immediately following his death and resurrection. The final book, **Revelation**, or **The Apocalypse**, is a prophecy of what is to come. The remaining books are letters, or epistles, written by early church leaders to congregations here and there. Most were written by Paul; a few were written by others.

The books of the New Testament aren't arranged in the order they were written. The earliest are the letters of Paul, written beginning around 48 AD; the latest is Revelation, written sometime between 70 AD and 97 AD.

Table of Contents

Title	page
About The Bible	4
The Books of the Old Testament	8
The Book of Genesis	10
The Book of Exodus	43
The Book of Leviticus	60
The Book of Numbers	63
The Book of Deuteronomy	67
The Book of Joshua	81
The Book of Judges	87
The Book of Ruth	101
The First Book of Samuel	104
The Second Book of Samuel	123
The First Book of Kings	143
The Second Book of Kings	167
The First Book of Chronicles	183
The Second Book of Chronicles	188
The Book of Ezra	195
The Book of Nehemiah	200
The Book of Esther	208
Commentary	223
The Book of Job	225
The Book of Psalms	233
The Book of Proverbs	237
The Book of Ecclesiastes	244
The Song of Songs	250
The Book of Isaiah	255
The Book of Jeremiah	265
The Book of Lamentations	296
The Book of Ezekiel	298

The Book of Daniel	320
The Book of Hosea	344
The Book of Joel	352
The Book of Amos	356
The Book of Obadiah	365
The Book of Jonah	368
The Book of Micah	377
The Book of Nahum	384
The Book of Habakkuk	386
The Book of Zephaniah	390
The Book of Haggai	399
The Book of Zechariah	377
The Book of Malachi	411
Some Apocrypha:	
About the Apocrypha	417
The Book of Tobit	418
The Book of Judith	435
The Book of 1 Maccabees	460
Final Commentary	463
Appendix I:	
Early History of the Jewish People	469
Appendix II:	
Kings of Israel and Judah	473
Appendix III:	
Prophets of the Old Testament	475

The Old Testament

The Books of the Old Testament

1) **GENESIS**: Early history of the Hebrews, beginning with the Creation. Adam & Eve;
Noah's flood; Abraham; Jacob/Israel; Migration into Egypt.
2) **EXODUS**: Moses; Departure from Egypt; Mt. Sinai & the 10 Commandments; Arrival at the Promised Land.
3) **LEVITICUS**: Named for the Levites, the tribe assigned priestly duties. A book of laws
governing all aspects of life.
4) **NUMBERS**: An administrative journal of the Journey to the Promised Land.
5) **DEUTERONOMY**: A review of the Draconian laws and penalties for Yahweh's chosen people.
6) **JOSHUA**: Joshua succeeds Moses as leader. The siege of Jericho. Conquest of the Promised Land
7) **JUDGES**: A time of no central government; rule by tribal chieftains called Judges. The story of Sampson. War with Benjaminites.
8) **RUTH:** A simple tale of love & faithfulness. No bloodletting.
9) **1 SAMUEL:** The first Kings of Israel. Prophet Samuel; King Saul; David shows up.
10) **2 SAMUEL:** King David. Various wars; Bathsheba; Absalom; The Combined Kingdom of Israel and Judah.
11) **1 KINGS**: David succeeded by King Solomon. Solomon's harsh rule; The building of the first Temple; the Queen of Sheba; Solomon's death; Breakup of the Combined Kingdom;
Successive kings of each; the prophet Elijah; Various wars.
12) **2 KINGS**: Elisha succeeds Elijah; Elisha's miracles.
13) **1 CHRONICLES**: The list of generations from Adam on down; the David story rehashed.
14) **2 CHRONICLES**: The kings of Israel and Judah; Babylonian conquest.
15) **EZRA**: Babylonian conquest; Nebuchadnezzar; Persians take over Babylonian Empire. Jews return to Jerusalem.
16) **NEHEMIAH**; Rebuilding the Temple.
17) **ESTHER**: A self-contained story of Babylonian Jews.

Exciting reading.
18) **COMMENTARY**.
19) **JOB**: The story of a righteous man, tormented just to see whether he'd break.
20) **PSALMS**: A book of poems.
21) **PROVERBS**: A book of sayings.
22) **ECCLESIASTES**: A dissertation on the Meaninglessness of Everything.
23) **SONG OF SONGS**: A long love poem.
24) **ISAIAH**: A long sermon on Yahweh's impending punishments of his Chosen People.
25) **JEREMIAH**: Another long sermon on Yahweh's impending punishments.
26) **LAMENTATIONS**: A series of poems about the general awfulness of things.
27) **EZEKIEL**: Surrealistic visions by the Prophet.
28) **DANIEL**: Life in Babylon; The Fiery Furnace; The Den of Lions; The Moving Finger.
29) **HOSEA**: The strange story of Hosea; A lot of preaching.
30) **JOEL:** Locust hordes; a prophecy about Judah.
31) **AMOS:** Condemnation of the surrounding kingdoms, plus Judah, and Israel. Conversations with Yahweh.
32) **OBADIAH:** Making war on Edom.
33) **JONAH:** The Big Fish Story.
34) **MICAH:** A prophecy about Samaria and Jerusalem
35) **NAHUM:** The destruction of Nineveh.
36) **HABAKKUK:** Yahweh and the Babylonians
37) **ZEPHANIAH:** Yahweh is mad at Judah, as well as its neighbors.
38) **HAGGAI:** Yahweh complains about Judah's stinginess.
39) **ZECHARIAH:** A series of visions.
40) **MALACHI:** Yahweh complains some more.
41) **FINAL COMMENTARY.**

The Bible, Chapter One

The Book of Genesis

part 1

The Book of Genesis is the oldest book of the Old Testament. It is the first of the five Books of Moses. Tradition says they were written by him, but current scholarship indicates that they could not have been. Almost certainly, several writers contributed to Genesis. There is no certainty as to when it was written, but historical study suggests a date around 1450 b.c.

IN THE BEGINNING, Yahweh created.

We first have to give Yahweh credit for his inventiveness. He created a whole bunch of stuff without having anything prior to base it on. He just made nearly all of it up, out of whole cloth.

In the beginning, the cosmos was a formless hodgepodge consisting mainly of water. Yahweh decided to do something about it, and the first thing was to invent a thing called Light. He did it, and liked it so he did some more inventing. He invented Darkness to contrast with Light, and he called Light "Day" and Darkness "Night".

At this point "day" and "night" don't signify periods of time; they signify states of illumination or lack thereof. However, pretty soon night went away and day came along again. Yahweh called that period of time The First Day. The period of a Day had no connection to sunrises or sunsets because there wasn't any sun to rise or set. There wasn't anything except alternating episodes of Light and Dark in the formless watery tangle of the universe.

Then Yahweh decided to separate the lower water from the upper water with a dome-shaped dry space in the middle. The roof of the dome he called Sky. The floor of the dome didn't get a name right then. It took him the same amount of time as before, so he called that the Second Day.

Then he got the watery floor of the dome to sort itself out into areas of dry land and other areas of water. He called the land Earth and the water Sea. Then he put his imagination to work and set about inventing an incredible number of different kinds of flora ranging from seaweed to rose-bushes to Venus flytraps, moss, and oak trees, which he called "plants", and invented a reproductive method for them using seeds. That occupied the Third Day.

Next --and here's where many perceive a paradox— he invented sources of light in the Sky, including the Sun in the morning and the Moon at night along with stars and whatnot. It seems paradoxical because there would have been no place for the earlier light to have come from before the Sun existed. *Since I have no solution to the paradox, I intend to ignore it.*

It isn't mentioned specifically, but he also set up the diurnal motions of the sun and moon so they would travel across the sky from east to west at regular intervals. How fast should they go? Well, Yahweh already had one unit of time to work with: the Day. So he set the time from one sunrise to the next to correspond to the Day. *Which shouldn't surprise us, since Yahweh originally got his notion of a Day from the period when Light came and went before there was a sun or stars. We aren't told what determined THAT period. It certainly wasn't sunrise and sunset. Maybe it just happened. Or maybe Yahweh just made it up.*

Anyhow, that took up the Fourth Day.

Then he set his imagination to work again and invented fish and birds and oysters and crabs and jellyfish and whales and chickens and blue-footed boobies and eagles and buzzards and maybe bats. And invented ways for them to reproduce and told them to go do it. But no land animals yet. *Amphibs like frogs are in some sort of limbo.*

That took up the Fifth Day.

I need to mention here that there are two separate accounts of what happened next, and they are seriously different.

The First Account: Then Yahweh invented all of the terrestrial animals from cockroaches to mastodons and sent them off to populate the Earth.

And then he invented Humans. But here it wasn't out of whole cloth. He had a pattern to follow: Himself. He created humans, male and female, in his own likeness, and gave them dominion over all other living things. And he told them to get out there and start reproducing so they could subdue nature. And he told them that all of the plants of the Earth were meant for their food, so eat hearty.

That occupied the Sixth Day.

And on the Seventh Day, Yahweh didn't do anything. He kicked back and rested from his labors...not surprising, since he had to be tired out after doing all that stuff in just six days. Then he laid his blessing on the seventh day of the week, making it special because that's the day when he rested after creating the universe.

Notably absent is any suggestion that he wanted to prohibit everybody from working on that day. That comes up a lot later.

The Second Account: After Yahweh created everything, there were no plants. The seeds hadn't sprouted because he hadn't provided any rain for them; and besides, there was nobody to till the soil to help them grow.

So Yahweh took some mud and formed it into an effigy of himself. Then he blew into its nose to bring it to life, and called it Man...the only human on earth.

(From this, we know what Yahweh looks, or looked, like. He looked like Adam, because Adam was a living effigy of himself.

We know, for example, that Yahweh had arms and legs and nipples, and a navel, and various unmentionables, and buttocks and toenails and eyes, nose, mouth, and hair. And fingerprints.

*We know Yahweh had all of these external features, because his effigy had them. But what we don't know about is his insides. We don't know whether he had a liver or spleen or lungs or bones. We are left in the dark about that, because the mud effigy had only an **external** structure identical with that of Yahweh. Internally, it was just a uniform amorphous mass of mud.)*

Then he created a garden in Eden for the man to live in, and invented fruit trees and other beautiful plants for his surroundings. Among then was the **Tree of Life** and **the Tree of Knowledge of Good and Evil**. If somebody ate the fruit of the Tree of Life, he would live forever. If somebody ate the fruit of the other tree, he would become aware of a difference between good and bad, right and wrong...and would be able to recognize which was which. Without that knowledge, a man would be like the other animals (which didn't exist yet) --innocent of any moral concepts, without conscience, just doing whatever came naturally.

Yahweh put the man in the garden, and named him Adam, and told him he was free to eat the fruit of any of the trees except those two --they were poison, and if he ate them he would die immediately.

Then, so the man wouldn't be lonely, Yahweh took some more mud and created all of the birds and animals. *We aren't told how he brought them to life... presumably not by blowing into their nostrils, since invertebrates have no nostrils to blow into.*

After he had created them all , he paraded them all past Adam, and Adam assigned names to them. *Given the number of species created, that should have taken a long time, and Adam should have been a very old man before he got through. But somehow, he named them all rather quickly.*

Alas! none of them would make a suitable partner for him.

So Yahweh put Adam into a trance, and removed one of his ribs, and formed it into a woman, and brought her to life. When Adam saw her, he approved of what he saw, and maybe said something like "Come to Papa!". Because they were of the same flesh, the bond between them was special...and represented the bond thereafter between a man and his wife. And that was that.

In this Second Account, there's no indication of how long anything took, no mention of days at all. There's no suggestion that Yahweh needed a rest after creating Adam, and nothing about a special Sabbath day being recognized. Likewise, the first one says nothing about mud or ribs or forbidden trees or serpents They are wholly different stories.

We can take our choice of which account to accept; we can't have them both, no matter how hard we try. I rather suspect the hand of two different writers at work.

The Original Couple, and their dog Fido

The Bible, Chapter Two

The Book of Genesis
part 2

Adam and Eve and the Snake

Adam and Eve lived happily in the garden of Eden, in a complete state of nature. They were as naked as a jaybird or a frog, and quite unconcerned about it. They probably didn't even know what "naked" meant, since clothing hadn't been invented yet. They lived off the fruit of the trees in the garden, except for the forbidden two.

We are not told whether they Did It; but I wouldn't be surprised.

Among the animals in the garden was the serpent, and he was a sneaky creature. He slithered up to Eve and said, "Is it true that Yahweh has told you not to eat from certain trees?" Eve said," Yep, he told us that the Tree of Knowledge of Good and Evil had poisonous fruit, and if we ate it or touched it we would die."

The snake said, "He was putting you on. The real reason he said "Don't eat it" is because he doesn't want you to become like Yahweh and know stuff like good and evil. The fruit isn't poisonous...it's quite yummy."

So Eve took one and tried it, and it was indeed yummy. She gave one to Adam and he ate it and thought it was excellent. Yahweh had indeed been putting them on...it wasn't poison, and they didn't die like he said they would.

This gives us one of our first inklings that Yahweh may not be a person of complete honesty. He deliberately lied to Adam and Eve about the tree...and for the very reason the serpent mentioned. He didn't want them to develop a moral sense, and be able to judge right from wrong, justice from injustice, and thereby become different from the other animals in his zoo. How cool would it be to rule a people who have no conception of right or wrong? They'll do whatever you say.

But as soon as they ate it, their world-view changed; they realized "Good Lord! We're naked! And it's terribly wrong to go parading around naked!" *Although I'm not sure why they thought so, since they were the only two people, and were quite familiar with each other's bodies.* But that's what they thought. And they were embarrassed. So they sewed fig leaves together into loin cloths, to cover their naughty bits. *How did they know those bits were naughty? Well, they just knew.*

Later, when Yahweh was walking in the garden, they hid from him. Yahweh hollered "Why are you hiding?" and Adam answered "Because we're naked, and don't want you to see us." Yahweh: "I think you've been eating from the tree I told you not to eat from." Adam: "It's Eve's fault! She ate it first, and got me to try it." Yahweh: "How about it, Eve...why did you do that?" Eve: "The snake talked me into it." *They didn't say, "You lied to us about dying," even though, having eaten the fruit, they knew the difference between a lie and truth.*

So Yahweh punished the snake by making him crawl on his belly, even though that's probably what he'd been doing all along. And he punished the two humans by kicking them out of the garden where they'd had the easy life. No more handouts: from then on they'd have to work for a living. But rather than leaving them naked (except for fig leaves), he made them some coats out of animal skins, and sent them on their way. *This is the first reference I know of, to the killing of animals for any reason, since the humans had been living exclusively on fruits and vegetables and had no need for meat.*

Anyhow, that was that.

==============

Cain offs Abel

So Adam and Eve set up housekeeping, and he went in unto her and she had a baby boy named Cain, and a little while later another one called Abel. When they grew up, Cain became a dirt-farmer, raising wheat, and Abel became a shepherd, raising sheep. When it came time to make an offering to Yahweh, Cain brought a bunch of his wheat and Abel brought a lamb, which he butchered and gave the best parts as an offering.

Yahweh turned up his nose at the wheat, but was quite pleased with the lamb. *Which is another strike against Yahweh's character. Each had offered in good faith what he had grown. But that wasn't good enough for Yahweh. He wanted meat. (Apparently, there was some unwritten rule that Yahweh eats only meat.) and he came down on Cain for not having any.*

The rejection pissed Cain off, and he let everybody know it. Yahweh told him, "Quit your griping. You should have known better. If you'd done the right thing I would have been pleased, but you didn't." This did not make Cain feel any better. So first chance he got, he took Abel out in the field and beat him to death, reducing the human population from four to three. *Overreaction no doubt, since Abel hadn't done anything wrong. Of course, neither had Cain up to then. Yahweh was just being crabby.*

As punishment, Yahweh banished Cain from the family farm, so he went off to the land of Nod and married a woman and settled down on his own. *This isn't easy to accept since up to that point there hadn't been any people anywhere except Adam and Eve and Cain. There's no explanation where these Nod people came from. But that's what it says Cain did. Ambrose Bierce called the hypothetical pre-Adamites: "A race of people who antedated the Creation, and lived under conditions not easily conceived."*

Cain raised a family, had a couple of sons, and did a bunch of stuff, and dropped out of the narrative for good.

From Adam Down to Noah
Meanwhile, back at the ranch, Adam went in unto Eve some more and sired a couple more boys. And then we're given a long list of the many generations of descendants of Adam and Eve, ending up with Noah, who lived 500 years and THEN managed to beget three sons, which wasn't bad for somebody half a millennium old.
....

Yahweh's Sons Hanker After Girls
Then there's an episode clearly out of chronological order: At this point, we learn something remarkable but seldom mentioned: Yahweh had sons of his own. They were godlets or angels or something like that --it's not made clear. Nor whether he begat them from a Mrs. Yahweh, or just made them up like the rest of his creations. Anyhow, the godlets who were immortal like their daddy started taking up with human girls and going in unto them and begetting grandchildren for Yahweh. Some of these were giants. Others became great heroes. But none of this sat well with Yahweh. He wasn't about to let humans live forever, like his sons, so he set a limit and said that nobody of human descent could live longer than 120 years. *This must have taken effect several centuries later, because one of Noah's great-great grandsons lived to be 430, and his great-great-great-great-great-great-great-grandsons were still making it to 200 or so.*

Noah's Flood
The narrative then moves to a different time frame. The whole human race (almost) had become corrupt, and Yahweh began to regret having invented it. In fact, he came to regret having invented life on earth at all, and decided to wipe it out and start over.

But there were a small handful of people who weren't corrupt: Noah and his family. So Yahweh decided to spare them. And while he was at it, he decided to preserve the animal species he'd taken so much trouble to invent. So he told Noah to build a boat-like ark, and provision it for a long stay, for his family and the animals he would take with him. And he told Noah, "Take a male and female of every species on the ark with you, so they can propagate later."

Or else he told Noah, "Take seven pairs of every species of "clean" animals [those suitable to sacrifice to Yahweh's taste] and one pair of every species of unclean animals, and seven pairs of each kind of bird, on the ark with you." *We aren't told how Noah reacted to these conflicting instructions. Note that Yahweh wasn't concerned with the survival of plant species: just animals. Apparently, Yahweh wouldn't let plants drown.*

The Lion Seems Puzzled By It All

So Noah loaded his family and the animals and their provisions into the ark, and Yahweh unleashed a flood, from the skies and from underground, that lasted 40 days and covered up the earth and killed everything. At the time. Noah was 600 years old, so

20

his three boys were close to being centenarians. We have no word on the ages of the womenfolk.

At this point, we have a confused and garbled account of what happened next. The flood waters remained for another 150 days and then started to recede --presumably draining back into holes in the earth, since there was no place else for it to go. Eventually the ark settled on a mountaintop, while the water continued to go down. It took 3 months for other mountains to become visible.

Forty days after the ark settled, Noah sent out one of the ravens to see if dry land was visible yet, but the raven never came back. He then sent out a dove, which returned but with no news. A week later he sent out the dove again, and this time it came back with an olive leaf, showing that the waters had finally gone away.

The time discrepancy is troublesome. On the one hand, it took 3 months just for mountaintops to peep out of the waters. On the other hand, after just 47 days the earth was dry and doves were gathering olive leaves. One suspects the hand of different writers telling the same story, without bothering to coordinate them.

Anyhow, when the waters were gone, the people and animals left the ark and resumed their normal business. And Yahweh promised never to do it again, and invented the rainbow as a sign of his promise.

And then we're given a tiresome genealogy of the descendants of Noah's sons for about a dozen generations.

And that was that.

The Bible, Chapter Three

The Book of Genesis
part 3

Ham's Father's Nakedness

Noah's three sons were named Shem, Ham, and Japheth. After the flood, all people on earth descended from these three. In particular, the people of Canaan descended from Ham.

Noah planted himself a vineyard, and by and by he got a crop of grapes and made wine out of them and drank it and got blind drunk and staggered off to his tent and tore off his robe and flopped down, stark naked, and passed out.

Ham peeked into Noah's tent to see how daddy was doing, and saw that he was asleep naked. For reasons unexplained, a man seeing his father naked was an unspeakable offense, and Ham knew it. It wasn't intentional, but he couldn't un-see his naked

daddy so the offense was done. He told his brothers, "Don't go in there; Dad's naked and passed out." So the two took a robe, and walked into the tent backwards so they couldn't see Noah, and covered him up.

When Noah sobered up and learned that Ham had seen him naked, he cursed Ham and all his progeny in Canaan, and decreed that Ham and his people would always be subservient to his brothers and their people.

Hiding Daddy's Nakedness

This episode is unfathomable to me. It would be one thing for a son to sneak around trying to catch a peek at his naked parents. It's quite another to inadvertently get a momentary glimpse of a naked father and immediately retreat. Didn't matter to Noah. He didn't like being seen. Might have had something to do with the fact that he was getting along toward 700 years old, and probably wasn't an appealing sight with his clothes off.

After the flood, Noah lived 350 more years, and died at the ripe age of nine hundred and fifty. Without ever forgiving Ham for seeing him nekkid.

And that was that.

The Tower of Babel

The population continued to grow and everybody spoke the same language. A bunch of them came to a flat place and settled down and started making fired bricks. And one of them said, "Hey, let's use these bricks to build a tower to the sky! That will make us famous and allow us to stay together as a people!" *I'm not sure how a tower was supposed to have that effect, but that's what they thought.* Anyhow, they started building the tower.

Yahweh noticed what they were doing, and for some reason it bugged him. He said, "If these creatures can build a tower to the sky, there's no limit to what else they might do cooperatively as long as they all speak the same language! We can't have that!" *It's not clear why Yahweh didn't like what they were doing. Maybe he thought they were encroaching into his business of creating really big stuff.*

The Tower of Babel has a construction problem

So to break up that community, he made them speak a bunch of different languages and dispersed the various language groups around the country so they couldn't cooperate any more. And they named the place of the unfinished tower Babel, for obvious reasons. *Yahweh was the first union-buster. If you let those people organize, no telling what kind of trouble they'll cause.*

Abram Appears

Abram will play a central role in the narrative, as we will see. He was born in Ur of the Chaldees, a big city on the Euphrates in Mesopotamia near the Persian Gulf, a long way from Canaan. He was the Great x 8 grandson of Noah, but that's not why he's important: there were probably a gazillion other Great x 8 grandsons of Noah.

Abram married a lady named Sarai. One day, for reasons unknown, Abram's father decided to pull up stakes and migrate to Canaan, taking Abram, Sarai, and Abe's nephew Lot along with him. But when they got to a town called Haran he decided that was far enough, so the family settled there.

Then Yahweh took an interest in Abram, and told him to take his family and his stuff and continue on to Canaan. So they did. When they got there, Yahweh told him he would give the land to him and his descendants. Then Abram did a bunch of stuff I won't go into. His nephew Lot hung out with him for a long time, and Abram became quite wealthy. Lot was pretty well off himself, and because they both had large herds, there wasn't enough pasture where they were to support both herds, so Lot pulled up stakes and moved to a place called Sodom. A bunch of kings with unlikely names like Chedorlaomer got into a war, took over Sodom, and captured Lot.

When Abram heard of it, he rounded up 300 of his fighting men, went and kicked the various kings' butt, took the stuff they had looted, and freed Lot. *The kings and their armies were obviously nations of wimps.* Then Yahweh made a promise to look out for Abram, and more stuff happened.

Abram Dallies with The Servant Girl

Abram had a problem: his wife Sarai was barren, and hadn't produced a son to provide a family line for him. Sarai had a hot young slave girl named Hagar, and being an understanding wife, suggested that Abram get it on with Hagar in hopes of producing a son in Sarai's place. So he went in unto Hagar, and she gave birth to a son named Ishmael, who turned out to be an unruly kid.

Yahweh's Fixation with the Male Organ
Yahweh decided to make a covenant with Abram. He said, "I guarantee that you'll have many descendants and a long legacy. I'll give you a bunch of land, and I'll be your god and their god forever. In exchange, there's one thing you and they will have to do: Cut off the foreskin on the end of your penis. Do this to every adult male, and every slave you own, and to every little bitty baby when he's 8 days old. A man's denuded penis will be the sign that he accepts my covenant."

This is the sort of thing that gives one pause. Why should Yahweh want to dictate the condition of a man's dick? It is extremely creepy, but obviously is something that Yahweh relished. Genital mutilation in the name of the Lord.

Interestingly, there's nothing similar for women. They weren't included in the covenant.

Abram went home and circumcised every male in his household, including himself. He was 99 and Ishmael was 13. We don't know the ages of the others, but I have a hunch that a lot of them didn't go willingly.

Pregnant at Age 90
Yahweh soon promised Abram a legitimate son by Sarai. Abram was dubious, since he was almost 100 years old and his wife was 90. Yahweh said, "To show you I mean it, I'm changing your name to Abraham and your wife's name to Sarah." Then, despite all the regular laws of biology, Abraham went in unto his long-post-menopausal wife and managed to get her with child and she produced a son named Isaac. But that comes later.

....

The Bible, Chapter Four

The Book of Genesis, part 4

Sodom and Gomorrah
Yahweh told Abraham that the town of Sodom, where nephew Lot lived, and nearby Gomorrah, were full of wicked sexual practices and he, Yahweh, was fixing to blast them with fire. Abraham got him to agree not to destroy the innocent with the guilty...*or thought he had.*

That night a couple of angels came to visit Lot and his family. While they were at dinner, a bunch of town rowdies surrounded the house and hollered,"Send out your two visitors. We're going to gang-rape them up the bum!" Which pretty much confirmed Sodom's reputation. Lot said no, and offered them his two hot young virgin daughters instead, but they'd have none of that: they were out for buggery. When they started to break down the doors, the angels struck them blind, which broke up the party.

The angels told Lot, "Take your family and get out of town; these cities are about to be destroyed. Run and don't look back!" So he gathered his family and ran, but his wife looked back and was turned into a pillar of salt, which pretty much ruined her for wifing purposes.

Lot's wife then...   *...Lot's wife now*

After Lot's family was safely away, Yahweh blasted the two cities with fire and brimstone, destroying them and all of their inhabitants: men, women, invalids, old folks, little bitty babies, many of whom had almost certainly not participated in anal sex. *So much for his agreement with Abraham not to kill the innocent with the guilty*

Lot's Randy Daughters
Lot and his two randy daughters had settled into a cave in the hills. One daughter said to the other, "We're not getting any younger, and there aren't any men around to marry us and give us babies. Let's get daddy drunk and have him go in unto us, so we can produce sons for him." Which they proceeded to do. When Lot sobered up and realized that his daughters were pregnant, there's no record of his response. Unlike Noah, he didn't curse them for seeing him with his clothes off. Maybe he didn't mind. Anyhow, this is the last we hear of Lot.

....

Abraham, Isaac, and Yahweh's Infamous Directive
Ninety-year old Sarah gave birth to a baby boy and named his Isaac. When he was 8 days old, Abraham mutilated his penis, per

his agreement with Yahweh.

Later, when Isaac was a little older, Yahweh told Abraham, "Take your beloved only son up onto the mountain, and slaughter him as a sacrifice to me." *Which says something about Yahweh's benevolence.* But anyhow, Abraham led Isaac and a donkey laden with materials for a sacrifice up the mountain.

At one point Isaac asked, "Daddy, we have the firewood and stuff, but where's the lamb for the sacrifice?" Abraham told him never mind, one will show up. When they got to the top, Abraham built an altar and piled the firewood on it. Then he grabbed Isaac and tied him up and laid him on the firewood.

He had the knife out, and was about to slit Isaac's throat, when Yahweh hollered down from heaven, "Stop! I just wanted to find out if you'd really do it when I told you to." So Abraham went and found a wild sheep and sacrificed it instead, and everything was supposedly hunky-dory. *I don't think so. It was a rotten trick to play on Abraham, and giving it a happy ending doesn't make it less so. I find the whole episode despicable.*
....

Jacob and Esau
Isaac grew up and got married and had two sons, Esau and Jacob, twin brothers in a wholly dysfunctional family. Though twins, they were dissimilar. Esau was hairy and burly and an outdoor type who hunted to bring home game. Jacob was a skinny, stay-at-home momma's boy. Esau had been born first, and was entitled to the patrimony due firstborn sons. Plus that, his daddy liked him best because he brought home the venison. Their momma liked Jacob best, setting the stage for serious sibling rivalry. Esau had been out hunting for several days with nothing to eat, and dragged himself home famished. Jacob was cooking up a mess of lentil stew, or pottage. Esau says, "Brother, give me some food." Jacob says, "I will not!" This to his own twin brother! Esau:"I must have some food; I'm starving." Jacob: "Not

unless you sign over your birthright to me." Esau, in raging hunger, agrees to Jacob's blackmail, signs it over, and gets some pottage in exchange.

That's not the end of it. Later on, their daddy was old and blind and his time was drawing near. He told his wife, "Bring me Esau, so I can give him my blessing before I die." But momma had other ideas. Esau was off hunting, so she told Jacob "Go in and pretend to be Esau and get the blessing before he does. The

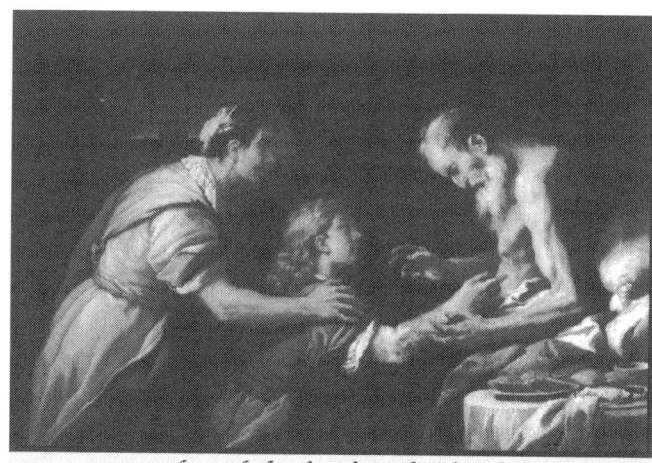
Jacob steals his brother's birthright

old man is blind and can't see the difference." Jacob says, "But if he touches me, he'll know I'm not Esau, because I'm hairless as an apple." Momma says, "We'll fix that," and wraps one of his arms in animal skin. He goes in, pretends to be Esau, the old man feels his hairy arm and gives him the blessing. Esau comes home, learns what happened, and begs his daddy "Give me a blessing too." Daddy says: Can't do it. I had one blessing to give, and Jacob got it. From now on, he's your superior and you have to serve him.

That's how the Bible people, descendants of Abraham, behaved in those days. Blackmail and treachery and lying and fraud. Just the examples to follow, if you pattern your life on the Bible. And by the way, Jacob got nothing by way of divine punishment from Yahweh. He got away with his treachery scot-free, so far as the Lord was concerned.

I'm not done with Jacob (grandson of Abraham) and goings-on he was involved in. Although these Old Testament people are supposed to know the difference between right and wrong (ever since Eve bit the apple), they clearly have a stunted moral sense.

After the episode where he ripped off his brother Esau, Jacob went off and went to work for his uncle Laban, who had a daughter Rachel that Jacob was hot for. He told the uncle, "I'll work for you if you'll let me marry Rachel." Uncle said it was a deal, and Jacob went to work. (For seven years. By then Rachel, who had probably been 13 or 14 when he met her, was about 20 or 21.)

When it came time for the wedding, Uncle decided that it wasn't right for a younger daughter to marry first, so he put a veil on his older daughter Leah and substituted her for Rachel. That night, none the wiser Jacob went in unto Leah. Next morning he saw whom he was with and raised hell. Uncle said, no problem: you can marry Rachel too, if you promise another 7 years work.

So now Jacob had two wives: Rachel and her big sister. But he kept going in unto Rachel more, which pissed off Leah. Rachel produced no offspring, so Yahweh arranged it that Leah, with whom Jacob was also going in unto a lot, got pregnant, and produced a son named Reuben.. Then she did it again. And again. And again. (Meanwhile, Rachel, whom he was still going in unto, remained without child.)

Rachel, naturally, was jealous that her Sister-Wife was giving Jacob all the sons, and complained "You gotta give me children too!" Jacob said, "You're the one that's barren, not me." Rachel said, "Then give me a child by proxy. I have this hot young servant girl Bilhah. Go in unto her and knock her up, and I'll have her give birth with her back to me sitting on my knees, and we'll pretend it's coming out of me." So Jacob, the randy so-and-so, went into Bilbah and knocked her up, and it happened as planned. And he did it again a bit later.

Meanwhile, the other Sister-Wife Leah whom he continued

going in unto (along with Rachel and Bilhah), decided she probably wasn't going to give him any more offspring, so she followed Rachel's lead and pimped off her own servant Zilpah, whom Jacob promptly impregnated. And a few months later did it again. Jacob was now scoring with at least four women: his two wives and their two lovely servants.

While this was going on, Leah managed (despite her doubts) to give Jacob several more sons and a daughter. But finally, Yahweh felt sorry for Rachel. So far, she had been Gone In Unto countless times with nary a child to show for it . So the Lord let her get pregnant and she finally managed to give her co-husband Jacob a son named Joseph. He'll be important later I the story.

The moral of this story seems to be: *If you wish to follow the Bible, marry a pair of beautiful sisters with hot young servant girls, and Go In Unto all of them as often as possible.*
=========
Eventually, Jacob took his womenfolk and the livestock he had earned from Laban, and headed off toward Canaan. Laban suspected he'd been cheated, and took off after Jacob but eventually they made nice and Laban went home. Jacob skipped out on a meeting with his brother Esau –the one whose birthright he had stolen –and continued toward Canaan. At nightfall they arrived at a river, so Jacob sent his retinue on across, but he stayed behind.

From somewhere, a guy showed up and started a wrestling match with Jacob. The guy was either a man, or an angel, or Yahweh himself. It's never made clear. After they'd wrestled all night, Jacob threw his hip out of socket. Then the guy said, "It's daybreak; let me go." (Perhaps he was unable to tolerate the light of the sun.) Jacob said, "Not until you give me a blessing." The guy said, 'From now on, your name won't be Jacob, but Israel, because you have wrestled with me and have won."

A Slightly Erotic Wrestling Match

===========================

The Violation of Dinah
Then there's the dismal tale of Jacob's daughter Dinah, and its attendant treachery and deceit.

One day Dinah was out walking, and was spotted by a young prince named Shechem who thought she was a hottie. So he grabbed her and went in unto her. But after he had raped her, he decided that he loved her and wanted to marry her. He asked his daddy Hamor to get her for him.

When Dinah's brothers heard about the rape they were enraged. Didn't matter that Shechem was trying his best to make an honest woman of her. The rape needed to be avenged and punished.

When Hamor met with Jacob to see if a marriage could be arranged, Jacob told him: Only on one condition. Accept Yahweh as your god, and have all your men cut off their foreskins. Otherwise, we and Dinah are out of here.

Hamor thought it was a good deal, and explained to his people: These are nice peaceable people, well to do with lots of livestock, and it would be beneficial to join our people with theirs through marriage. All you need to do is mutilate your dick, and it will only hurt for a little while. So all of the men in the city were circumcised at the same time.

And while these peaceful men were laid up and hurting from the circumcisions, two of Dinah's brothers roared into town with swords and massacred all of the men, including Hamor and Shechem, and dragged Dinah back to their own camp. They looted the city of everything worth looting, and spoiled the rest, and took the women captive.

Jacob told his sons, "You idiots! You've turned this whole country against us, and they outnumber us. They'll probably come and kill us all." The sons whined, "But daddy, we couldn't let them get away with treating our sister like a whore!"

Instead, what they did was kill a slew of innocent, well-meaning men who had nothing to do with the rape, and what they got was a defiled sister, no longer a virgin and with dim prospects of finding a husband; and the one man who was eager to marry her dead, along with the rest of the town. Smart thinking, lads. I doubt that Dinah was pleased.

I'm not sure what lesson we are to take from this lovely Bible

story. But I'll bet it's not a pleasant one.
....

After the Dinah affair, Jacob packed up his tribe and moved to a place called Bethel, where he built an altar and settled down for a while. Yahweh came along and reminded Jacob that his name was now Israel...a matter of some importance later on. Meanwhile, he's still called Jacob.

Jacob had been getting it on with his wife's handmaid Bilha for some time. *In the Bible, married men typically had girlfriends on the side and nobody thought anything about it.* Anyhow, Jacob's eldest son Reuben availed himself of Bilha's favors as well. This didn't sit well with Jacob, but he didn't make a big deal of it right then.

....

Joseph Sold to Egypt
Among Jacob's sons was the one by Rachel, an enterprising lad named Joseph who was Jacob's favorite, and who wore a multicolored tunic given him by his daddy. He had a bunch of brothers who hated him because they thought their daddy Jacob loved him more than them. They discussed killing him, but Reuben talked them out of it, so instead they tossed him into a dry cistern to let him starve to death. Meanwhile, a group of merchants heading for Egypt came by, so they hauled Joseph out of the cistern and sold him to them as a slave. Then they dunked his fancy robe in goat's blood and showed it to their dad so he'd believe that Joseph had been eaten by animals and wouldn't go looking for him. We'll hear more of Joseph later.

Joseph with the slave traders

Onan's Transgression

One of the brothers, named Judah, had a pair of sons: one named Er, the other named Onan. Er married a lady named Tamar, but before they had any children Er did something to annoy Yahweh, so Yahweh killed him.

In those days, if a man died without any sons to carry on his name, one of his brothers was obligated to impregnate the widow in the name of her dead husband and allow his family line to continue

Onan was appointed to that duty, so he went in unto Tamar; but at the last minute he decided, "I don't want to impregnate her with a child that won't be mine." So he jerked it out and ejaculated on the ground. When Yahweh saw that Onan wouldn't carry out his filial duty to beget a son for his brother, he killed Onan as well. Note that the offense was not the spilling of semen, as is sometimes said. *That probably went on a lot,*

37

without consequences. If he had pulled out without ejaculating at all, the offense would have been the same.

Tamar Plays Harlot

Judah had one more son, Shelah, who was still too young to do the filial duty, so Judah sent Tamar back to her people until Shelah could grow up. Judah's wife died. After a while, Shelah grew up but Judah still hadn't sent him to do the thing with Tamar.

Eventually, Tamar got tired of waiting, so she disguised herself as a whorelady with a veil over her face, and went and sat by the road where Judah would pass by, figuring he would be eager to get laid. When Judah saw her, he asked "How much?" She said, "What'll you give?" He said "I'll give you a goat."

Tamar seduces Judah. Camel seems amused

She said, "OK, but you have to give me something to hold for security until I get the goat." So he gave her his walking stick, and went in unto her, and having got his ashes hauled, he went on his way. Tamar went back home and took off the whorelady suit and put back on her widow's weeds.

A few months later, somebody told Judah, "Your daughter-in-law Tamar has been fooling around, and now she's pregnant." Judah said, "Take the slut out and burn her to death." But as she was being taken out, she sent word to Judah, "I'm pregnant by the man who owns this walking stick." Judah said, "Oh-oh!" and let her go. And never went in unto her again. I imagine that Shelah was disappointed at not having a chance to get into the sack with his sister-in-law.
....

Joseph's Adventures in Egypt
Meanwhile, over in Egypt, Joseph was doing quite well for himself. He was sold to a guy named Potiphar, captain of the palace guard, who thought highly of him and helped him rise through the ranks. Eventually, he was in charge of all affairs of the household. But Joseph was a hunk, and Potiphar had a randy wife who kept pestering Joseph to jump her bones. Joseph wasn't about to jeopardize his position, so he kept rejecting her advances.

One day when the house was empty, the randy wife grabbed Joseph by the robe and said, "Quick. While nobody's here, let's do it!" Joseph didn't succumb; he took off running, leaving his robe in wifey's hands.

Hell hath no fury like a woman scorned. When wifey saw Joseph heading for the hills, she started screeching and hollering "That horrid Hebrew of my husband's just tried to rape me! But when I started screaming, he ran off and left his robe behind."

When Potiphar got home and heard about it, he grabbed Joseph and stuck him in prison. But just as Joseph had charmed Potiphar, he charmed the head jailer and once again rose through the ranks of prisoners until he was in charge of all of the affairs of the prison.

Then a bunch of other stuff happened, and Joseph gained a reputation as a dream-interpreter. When the king heard of it, he had Joseph interpret one of his. As always, Joseph quickly ingratiated himself with the king, and before long Joseph was made governor over all of Egypt.

Punishment by Proxy?
Several of Joseph's brothers came to Egypt to buy grain to relieve their famine in Canaan. They didn't recognize Joseph but he recognized them. Joseph's youngest brother Benjamin wasn't among them. Then a bunch of stuff happened, and Joseph sent the brothers back home with the grain, leaving one behind as hostage, until they brought Benjamin back to Egypt. Their daddy Jacob didn't like the idea at all."What if I never get Benjamin back?" And his son Reuben told him, "If I don't bring Benjamin back, you can kill my two sons."

Let us stop and ponder. When somebody transgresses, you punish HIM by killing somebody else who doesn't deserve it. The knowledge of right and wrong, fairness and unfairness, justice and injustice that Adam and Eve had gained from the fruit of the tree does not seem to have been inherited down through the generations.

Anyhow, Benjamin was taken back to Egypt. Then Joseph jerked them around with a fabricated business about a stolen cup, just to scare them. Joseph finally revealed his identity to his brothers, and they all hugged and made nice.

The End of Jacob

After everybody knew who Joseph was, Jacob packed up his family and moved to Egypt to be with all his sons.

Then there was a famine, and governor Joseph used it as a way to extort land and property from the people in exchange for food from the king's storehouse, until the king owned everything and all the people had sold themselves into slavery. The people were grateful.

Eventually, Jacob was 147 years old, and nearing his time to die. He gathered his family around him and blessed Joseph's two sons who had been born in Egypt. Then he gave a prophecy about each of his sons, pointing out that the eldest Reuben couldn't be the most important because of his dalliance with his father's girlfriend Bilha way back when. Each of them would become the progenitor of one of what would come to be called the Twelve Tribes of Israel, since they were all sons of Israel, aka. Jacob.

The Egyptian Captivity.

Jacob's entire progeny —the "Children of Israel/Jacob"— were now settled in Egypt, under the protection of Joseph, who had become the governor. But still, they were Hebrews, not Egyptians, and in time Joseph passed from the scene, and they became second-class persons — little more than serfs, under the humiliating rule of the Pharaoh.

Thus ends Genesis.

The Bible, Chapter Five

The Book of Exodus
Part 1.

The Book of Exodus takes up long after the end of Genesis. With the passage of time, the Children of Israel had lost Joseph's protection, and were treated as little more than slaves.

At this point in time there were no "Jews", as such. Jews as a category lay thousands of years down the road. What there were, were Hebrews, various tribes and kingdoms inhabiting Palestine and surroundings, united by a common language, and to a certain extent, a common culture.

What set the Hebrews in Egyptian captivity apart from other groups was their common heritage: they were all descended from Jacob, aka Israel: they were Children of Israel, or Israelites. And they were Yahweh-ists.

Hebrews were known to be aggressive and warlike, so to keep the Israelites in line and prevent uprisings, the Egyptians set up a cadre of slave masters too manage them. But that didn't stop the Israelites from reproducing like rabbits, and over the course of 430 years they developed a formidable population.

To stem the tide, Pharaoh told the midwives who tended the Israelites to kill every male baby they delivered. But the midwives weren't about to let somebody tell them how to do their business, so they ignored the directive. When they were asked, "How come so many male Hebrew babies?" the midwives said, "These Hebrew women birth so easily they don't need our services." So next the Pharaoh, no longer relying on midwives, told his soldiers to find and drown all the male Hebrew babies in the Nile. Presumably, they went about doing it. Meanwhile, the

Israelites kept on having babies.

MOSES

An Israelite couple from the tribe of Levi had a son that they kept secret. They figured the soldiers would come for him before long, so they decided to trust Yahweh's providence. They built a basket of reeds, and waterproofed it with pitch, and put the kid in it, and put the basket in the bulrushes at the edge of the river, and hoped for the best.

Sure enough, the Pharaoh's daughter spotted the basket, pulled it in, and adopted the infant. She named him Moses...

Nothing special happened between then and when Moses was grown up.

One day he saw an Egyptian beating on a Hebrew, so he killed the Egyptian and stashed the corpse somewhere. Pharaoh heard of it and put out a contract on Moses. Moses hightailed it out of the country, Then he had some adventures and acquired a wife named Zipporah, who bore him a son named Gershom. It turns out that Moses had a brother named Aaron who had also managed to avoid getting drowned by the soldiers. Aaron became Moses' right-hand man.

Eventually Yahweh appeared to Moses, in the guise of a burning bush, in the outlands where he was living. He gave Moses certain magical powers and told him to lead his people to a rich and fertile land occupied by people who were not descended from Jacob, and therefore didn't count. He, Yahweh, assured Moses that he would put the screws to Pharaoh, to make him let it happen. As we will see, this assurance had conditions.

Moses was afraid that the people wouldn't take him seriously as Yahweh's appointed leader, so Yahweh turned Moses' staff into a snake and then back into a staff to prove that Moses was what he claimed to be, except he didn't do it so the people could see it happen.

Moses was still skeptical so Yahweh chewed him out, and sent him back to Egypt. Moses was a poor public speaker, or maybe had a stutter, so Aaron was appointed to be his spokesman. When they got there, they petitioned Pharaoh to release the Israelites from bondage so Moses could lead them to a better life.

Pharaoh said Hell no; they were needed to carry out the menial work they'd been drafted into. (Pre-echoes of the ante-bellum South: them Negras was needed to fetch in the cotton.)

Then Pharaoh went into a snit and decided to punish the Israelites, saying they weren't working hard enough. A bunch of them had the job of making adobe bricks out of mud and straw. Pharaoh stopped providing the straw, and made them gather their own, but still maintain the same quota of bricks as before. When the foremen complained, Pharaoh told the workers to get their lazy asses back to work and told the foremen to stop making trouble.

When they told Moses about it, he got in touch with Yahweh and told him, "All I've done is bring misery to my people...you haven't rescued them at all." But Yahweh wouldn't let him off the hook. Yahweh preached a long sermon, repeating the promises he had yet to keep, and told Moses to go try the same thing again. Moses was pretty sure it wouldn't do any good.
....

So Moses and Aaron went back and again told the Pharaoh that their god had commanded them to ask Pharaoh to release the Israelites, or suffer bad stuff. Pharaoh said, Do me a miracle, so Aaron flung his staff down and it turned into a snake. Pharaoh said, Pfft! anybody can do that. He fetched in a bunch of his own sorcerers and had them all turn their walking sticks into snakes, just like Aaron.

See? said Pharaoh, but at the same time Aaron's snake crawled over and et up all the other snakes. This is probably significant, but it didn't matter to Pharaoh. He still wouldn't listen.

The Bible, Chapter Six

The Book of Exodus
Part 2.

In reading the Bible so far, I've learned a number of things. One thing I've learned is that someone who actually patterns his life after the Old Testament people is going to be a very unpleasant person to be around.

Another thing I've learned is that Yahweh is not actually an admirable god. He has character traits that, in a human, we generally find deplorable. Yahweh rules not because of his virtues, but because of his power to punish. His people are supposed to obey his wishes, not because they admire and respect him, but because he will put serious hurt on them if they don't.

This comes out clearly in the story of Moses' attempts to lead his people (well, Yahweh's people) out of Egyptian slavery. Pharaoh doesn't want to let them go. Yahweh says to Moses, "Tell him if he doesn't let you go, I'll turn the Nile into blood and it will stink and all the fish will die." Moses tells him; Pharaoh says, "Ha ha. No." Yahweh turns the river to blood and it stinks and all the fish die. Moses says, "How about now?" Pharaoh is about ready to say yes, when, get this, Yahweh HARDEN'S PHARAOHS HEART and he says no. Yahweh says to Moses, 'Tell him if he doesn't let you go, I'll send a plague of frogs." Moses tells him, and he promises to let them go if there's really a plague of frogs. The plague of frogs happens, and gets Pharaoh's attention. He's seen two disasters about to keep his promise when, once again, Yahweh HARDEN'S PHARAOHS HEART and he breaks his promise.

Frogs

It takes a series of ELEVEN plagues, each worse than the last, before Yahweh finally lets Pharaoh let Moses' people go. Not because Pharaoh was a slow learner, but because Yahweh kept hardening his heart so he'd say no.

Why did Yahweh do this? Not because his primary concern was to get his people out of Egypt. He did it to show off to everybody —the Egyptians and his own people— how mighty he is. "Hah! You think boils and hail were something? Check out these locusts. I'll show you what I can do when I want to!" Only when he had satisfied his ego by plunging the land into darkness and finally killing all of the first-born children and animals did he refrain from hardening Pharaoh's heart and allow Moses to lead his people out of Egypt.

The last straw was the Slaughter of the Firstborn Sons. Yahweh announced that he would one night kill every firstborn son, in Egypt. But he would spare the homes of Israelites if they marked their door with the blood of a sacrificial lamb. So they all marked their doors, and Yahweh passed them over but snuffed the firstborn, both adults and little bitty babies, of all the Egyptians. That's what finally got Pharaoh's attention. The firstborn babies hadn't done anything to the Israelites. They were just pawns in

Yahweh's game with Pharaoh. That's how it goes in the Bible: You punish somebody by bashing somebody else. To celebrate the event, Moses initiated the Festival of the Passover.

The Journey Begins

Pharaoh had had enough, so he told Moses, "Get your people together and get the hell out of my kingdom." Which Moses and Aaron proceeded to do. It was some undertaking: there were over a million Hebrews, counting women and children.

And it wasn't a band of peaceful pilgrims. It was an army of 600,000 men armed for conquest, along with their womenfolk and kids. They were fixing to take their Promised Land by force. So they got together and headed eastward.

When the Pharaoh saw them leaving, a realization struck him: With the Israelites gone, there would be no more servants or menial workers to keep the economy going. So he set out with his army to try to drag them back.

Moses' bunch were bivouacked on the shore of the Red Sea. When they saw the Egyptian army approaching, they hollered "Lordy lordy, we'll never withstand them. They'll push us all into the sea and we'll drown." But Yahweh told Moses, "Smite the water with your staff," so Moses did it and a channel of dry land opened across the sea, with a wall of water standing on either side of the path. This probably should have caused a tsunami of some magnitude, but there's no mention of one.

With an escape route open, the people broke camp and headed down the dry path to the Sinai Peninsula on the other side. We aren't told how wide the path was, but it needed to accommodate a million people traveling on foot the 20 miles or so across the Gulf of Suez, fast enough to avoid the Egyptian army. The army must have been a long ways off. It's not clear how the Hebrews saw them coming.

By and by the Israelites all got to Sinai. Meanwhile, the

Pharaoh's army followed them into the dry route between the walls of water. When they were well into it, the water walls collapsed, drowning the whole Egyptian army.

Eventually, Moses' horde made their way to Mount Sinai, where they camped to allow Moses to get instructions from Yahweh.

The Bible, Chapter Seven

The Book of Exodus
Part 3.

One thing I'm learning over and over is that reading the Bible isn't as easy as you might think, if you intend to pay attention to all of the details, since the details can be overwhelming and most of them are of dubious importance.

The Numerous Commandments
The bulk of the book of Exodus after the part about escaping from Egypt is taken up with rules and regulations —laws, and commandments, and instructions. The Ten Commandments are only a starting place.

Moses didn't go up Mt. Sinai just one time, and come down with the Commandments on stone tablets, as you might have gathered from the movie. He went up several times, and the tablets were later on. He first carried the Commandments down by word of mouth on an earlier trip.

The main 10 Commandments come in two flavors. The first four are religious commandments, having to do with Yahweh. The remaining six are principles necessary to maintaining a coherent and stable civilization. Yahweh didn't make **these** rules up out of whole cloth; they don't need his impramatur. They are obvious rules for civilized behavior, to anybody who understands the difference between right and wrong. He just added his authority to them

The first four are:
1. You are forbidden to have any gods before Yahweh. (He is supreme, and you'd better accept it.)
2. You are forbidden to worship idols, statues, or images. (Even

if you don't regard them as superior gods to Yahweh, you still can't worship them. If you want to worship inferior gods, they can't be statues.)

3. You are forbidden to blaspheme the name of Yahweh. (You can only use it in respectful, religious contexts.)

4. Remember the Sabbath Day, to keep it holy. In remembrance of Genesis: The seventh day is the Lord's day, because that's the day he rested. Exactly what this means is spelled out. It carries more baggage than you think. It means you aren't to do any work of any kind, and neither are your domestic help —slaves and servants— and neither are your domestic animals. Violation carries a mandatory death penalty. No cooking, no cleaning, no picking up around the house, no patching the roof if it rains, no rescuing a lamb if it falls in the well, no lighting a candle to help you see, no nothing that might be construed as a productive activity. You must rest, whether you feel like it or not.

The remaining six are:

5. Be respectful to your parents.

6. Don't commit murder. (Some killing —for example, massacreing indigenous people occupying the Promised Land or executing people for capital offenses— is OK; murder isn't.)

7. Don't commit adultery. (Don't violate the bonds and commitments involved between a married couple. This can get complicated when a man has several wives as well as concubines.)

8. Don't steal.

9. Don't tell lies that will harm others. ("Don't bear false witness AGAINST thy neighbor.")

10. Don't hanker after things you have no right to.

But those aren't the end of, or even the basis of, the truckload of additional commandments and instructions that Moses brought with him.

There is a large body of commandments concerning the treatment of slaves (slightly anomalous, since the Hebrews had themselves only escaped from slavery a short time before), and marriage with slaves, and so on. We're told that if a man beats one of his slaves to death, that's murder. But if he only beats the slave up, and he dies a while later, that's okay.

Apparently, in those days, being a slave had an expiration date rather than being a permanent condition. There were rules about the expiration dates, which differed for men and women (women had longer sentences).

Then there are commandments concerning crimes of violence and their punishments, including the eye-for-an-eye principle. And further rules about what to do when an ox gores somebody and whether to punish the ox and how much.

Then there is a catalog of capital crimes for which the death penalty is REQUIRED: For any of these, the miscreant must be killed, by stoning (people throwing rocks at him until he dies), or otherwise.. (These are amplified in the book of Leviticus.)
1. Murder (suitably defined) DEATH
2. Physically abusing a parent. DEATH
3. Verbally abusing a parent DEATH
4. Witchcraft or sorcery DEATH
5. kidnapping DEATH
6. sacrificing to another god DEATH
7. sex with an animal DEATH (The animal must also be killed)
8. sex between a man and a man DEATH
9. sex with a woman and her daughter (a woman and her mother) DEATH
10. blasphemy DEATH
11. failure to observe the Sabbath DEATH

(If you wonder where the Muslims who invented Sharia Law came up with their ideas, this might be a place to start looking.)

All of these are more or less commandments about the conduct of ordinary life. And after them, come a ton of commandments having to do with the conduct of religion.

If you thought simplicity and sincerity were paramount in the worship of your god, you were wrong. It's got be done

RIGHT. Complexity and letter-of-the-law matter most.

The first of many religious commandment prescribed the construction of an altar. It had to consist of of unhewn, natural stone. And it couldn't have any steps leading up to it, lest somebody peek up the priest's skirts and see his unmentionable parts.

Then more commandments are concerned with building a place for Yahweh to live in. Commandments dictated the kind of wood to be used in constructing Yahweh's house, and its dimensions and shape, and the kind of decorations, and the color of the drapes, and pretty much everything else. Yahweh was careful to tell Moses exactly what he wanted, and it wasn't cheap. And he made sure by telling most of it all over again, here and in Leviticus.

Here's the list of things that Yahweh wanted for his house: gold, silver, bronze, brightly colored cloth of many colors, fine linen, dyed sheepskins, goat skins, olive oil (for lamps), spices (for ointments), precious stones, etc. I won't bore you with the construction details. They are long and tedious, and don't carry much of a message for the conduct of life, except that if you're going to build a tent for god to live it, it had better be extra-extra fancy or he won't move in.

And as if that weren't enough, the commandments are followed by an equally lengthy set of rules for the conduct of religious ceremonies and sacrifices and holy days and what to do with the innards of sacrificed animals, and where to smear its blood and what to do with the fat and who gets to eat what parts of it and so on. (The animals sacrificed to Yahweh weren't always wasted -- they were sometimes cooked and eaten by the Levite priests.)

So I am just about fed up with the book of Exodus, but there's one important episode I forgot to mention. It's about the Golden Calf, and I'll get to that next.

The Bible, Chapter Eight

The Book of Exodus
Part 4: The Golden Calf

The children of Israel had been camped at the foot of Mt.Sinai for a whole long time, while Moses made his various trips to the top, to commune with Yahweh and fetch down more commandments.

On his last trip up (as it turned out), Moses had been gone a great long while, and the people got restless about not having a supreme leader. They told the second in command, Aaron, "Look, your brother Moses dragged us out here away from Egypt, and now he's been gone a whole long time and he may have run off and abandoned us for all we know. And now we don't even have a god to worship, so please make us one."

Recall, they had been warned after Moses' very first trip up, that they weren't supposed to worship any gods but Yahweh, and especially not any idols or images. But they probably thought that since Moses had run off, his commandments were no longer operative.

So Aaron collected all the bits of gold and jewelry in the camp, and melted it down, and cast it into a statue of a calf, or maybe a young bull, and set it upon an altar, and told them "I've made you a god; now come worship it."

And so they did. And apparently believing, a la Nietsche, that "since Yahweh was dead, everything was permissible," they took to riotous living and misbehaving, and running around naked, and partying, and I don't know what-all, which shows what can happen when people lose their fear of the wrath of Yahweh.

It's Party Time!

Well, Yahweh and Moses were communing up at the top of the mountain, and Yahweh looked down and saw what was going on, and waxed wroth. He said, "That does it. I've had it with these people of yours. Look what they're up to, after all I've done for them. I'm going to blast the whole lot of them out of existence, and give you what I promised them." But Moses argued against that, pointing out that he, Yahweh, had PROMISED the Hebrews a Promised Land; and did he, Yahweh, want the Egyptians going around saying that he, Yahweh, was a faithless promise-breaker? So to save his reputation among the Egyptians, Yahweh changed his mind and decided not to kill all of the Children of Israel. At least not directly.

Instead, Yahweh carved the 10 Commandments on a couple of stone tablets and gave them to Moses to take back down the mountain.

When Moses got back down and saw what was going on, he pitched a hissy-fit and smashed the tablets that Yahweh had carved for him. And he jumped all over Aaron, who said it wasn't his fault: the people made him build a new god for them when they thought Moses had run off, which suggests a certain deficiency in Aaron's leadership abilities.

So Moses asked the crowd, "Which of you are on the side of Yahweh?" and a bunch of Levites raised their hands. Moses commanded them, "You take your swords and kill everybody who didn't raise his hand; kill your brothers, your sons, your neighbors." So they went and killed everybody including their brothers and sons; but it doesn't say anything about killing their fathers, which would have been a problem because of Commandment #5. And when they had killed everybody, Moses praised them for good work, and told them they were now Consecrated to the Lord because they had massacred their sons and brothers and neighbors. So Yahweh hadn't destroyed them himself as he had at first threatened. Instead, he let Moses do the dirty work.

But then, just to make sure everybody suffered, he visited a plague upon them. And that's how that chapter ends.

I'm not sure what lesson it teaches, except maybe: **if you catch anybody, including your kinfolks and children, worshiping the wrong god, take a sword and kill them.** It will make Yahweh happy.

The Bible, Chapter Nine

The Book of Exodus,
Part 5: The Promised Land

I don't want to get too far away from the beginnings of Exodus just yet.

One thing that's emphasized is that, following their exodus from Egypt, Yahweh had promised his people —Moses' people— the Israelites— a land of their own where they can settle and be free of tyranny and subjugation by foreigners.

But when you look into this Promised Land —the land Yahweh had promised to the Israelites as a final settling place after their escape from Egypt —you learn some unexpected things.

The Promised Land of the Israelites was their goal to be arrived at at the end of their sojourn through the Sinai desert, where they could settle down in peace.

But the Promised Land of the Israelites wasn't unknown or largely unclaimed territory for them to settle in and cultivate and civilize as you might have thought — like the New World for Columbus, or the Mormons' Utah. It was territory already owned and thoroughly occupied by gentile tribes: Canaanites and Hittites and Amorites and Perizzites and Hivites and Jebusites. And Yahweh didn't intend for the Israelites to settle in peaceably among those tribes and join their civilization. He meant his people to claim the Promised Land from the inhabitants by driving them out and killing all the men and boys and taking the women and girls as booty, and taking the property the inhabitants had left behind.

Yahweh had promised that land to them...all the land between the Red Sea and the Mediterranean. All they had to do was clear out the indigenous population, take it over, and it would be theirs. Just as Yahweh had promised.

Yahweh's rules of engagement were strict: the Israelites were to do no intermingling with the natives, nor have any negotiations with them, nor make any compromises or peace treaties with them. They were to drive them out or kill them, as interlopers in the Rightful Promised Land of the Israelites.

Which, if you think about it, is the sort of promise very easily made, and kept, because it's so conditional.

First, **you pick something that already belongs to somebody else.**

Then, **you promise it to your chosen people**. All they have to do is go and take it away from the current owners by driving them out and killing them.

Heck, I could make that sort of promise. I promise you the Empire State Building. I promise you the Fiji Islands. All you gotta do is go and take it away from the current owners.

And if you succeed, it's because I was on your side. And if you don't succeed, it's because you didn't read the fine print about how much you had to worship me in order to keep me on your side. Either way, I win.

That's exactly how it happened, a few books down the road. The Israelites drove out and killed and conquered the Canaanites and other foreigners, and took over their territory. Moses' people had finally reached their Promised Land, thanks to the promise of Yahweh.

Those who use the Bible as their guide may find this instructive: **if you think you are entitled to something, go take it, no matter who currently has it.**

(If you see similarities to modern day Israel, your aren't alone. And it's not coincidence. A number of modern-day descendants of those Israelites still regard Yahweh's promise, and rules of engagement, as determining their attitude and actions toward the indigenous residents of the former Palestine. But I digress.)

The Bible, Chapter 10

The Book of Leviticus

The third book of the Old Testament is Leviticus, which is the book that lays out the laws for the Children of Israel. There is an overwhelming wealth of them, and a lot of them seem to have no underlying justification except that they were put forth by the Levites, who were the tribe chosen to be the priestly caste (along with the Aaronites) because they had pleased Yahweh by slaughtering their sons and brothers after the Golden Calf incident. Having read Leviticus, I'm pretty sure that anybody who claims to run his life according to the Bible has not read Leviticus.

The first part of the book tells in grim detail how sacrifices are to be conducted, and which animals are suitable, and how they are to be butchered, and how their various parts are to be treated, and so on. (There is an unhealthy preoccupation with blood, leading one to wonder what Freud or Krafft-Ebing might have had to say about it.) And there are a half-dozen different kinds of sacrifices, each with its own rules.

But there is one rule in common: an animal to be sacrificed has to be brought to the altar at the entrance to the dwelling of Yahweh, and killed there, preferably on the north side and presumably by slitting its throat while somebody holds a bucket to catch all the blood. Then the blood has to be splashed on the four sides of the altar, and sometimes sprinkled on the onlookers, with the rest poured out at the foot of the altar.

Sacrificing a bull the right way

Sacrifices to Yahweh can only be made at that one specific altar. If a bull is sacrificed, all of his blood has to be splashed and poured on the altar. If a goat is sacrificed, all of his blood has to be splashed and poured on the altar. Same for a sheep. You can't help but think that with all that blood, day after day, lying there rotting, the entrance to Yahweh's tent would have stunk like an abattoir.

Yahweh likes the smell of burning flesh. Not cooking...burning. It says so in the Bible. You kill the animal and then burn it up, to create the smell that Yahweh finds pleasant. Especially the fat.

I'm struck by the fact that the only religious observances mentioned are these sacrifices. There's nothing about worship, as we would understand it. The people's relationship to Yahweh is to bring him sacrifices in hopes of keeping him pacified, so he'll not punish them for their sins by giving them diseases or disasters. Keep the Lord happy, or he'll give you serious trouble. Yahweh is always on the lookout for anyone who fails to obey any of his multitude of commands, so he can bash them with hideous diseases and blindness and drought and famine and wild animals to eat them and foreign armies to conquer and enslave them, and so on.

Consequently, if any of these things happens you can be pretty sure that SOMEBODY did something to annoy Yahweh, and you'd better do a bunch of sacrifices to put him in a better mood, and punish the miscreant if possible.

After the laws about sacrifices, the giving of laws is interrupted by the story of the consecration of Aaron (Moses' brother and second in command) and his sons. It involved a lot of pomp and circumstance, and one curious detail involving blood.

As part of the ceremony a ram was sacrificed, and the person officiating took some of its blood and put it on Aaron's right earlobe, and some more on his right thumb, and some more on his right big toe. Then the same was done to the sons. We are left to wonder why those particular locations were chosen. Maybe the Levites just liked them.

After a bunch more sacrifices and the ceremony was winding down, a couple of Aaron's sons decided to make their own gift to Yahweh, so they put some burning embers in a pan and put some incense on it and offered it to Yahweh. But Yahweh went into a snit because he hadn't told them to do that, so he blasted them with fire and burned them up. Perhaps the smell of their burning flesh was pleasing to him.

The Wages of Incense

After that, the listing of more laws resumed.

The Bible, Chapter 11

The Book of Leviticus
Part 2

The remainder of Leviticus after the business of Aaron's consecration is a disconnected mishmash of commandments and laws on various subjects. But one thing shows up here that I haven't noticed earlier in the Bible: the notion of metaphysical Uncleanliness, or Defilement, or Pollution, which has nothing whatever to do with physical dirt. The number of things and events and practices that are Unclean is well-nigh endless. I haven't been able to figure out any underlying criterion or feature common to Unclean things. Maybe it's just that the Levites believe that Yahweh thinks they're disgusting.

We begin with a list of animals that are not to be eaten, because they are Unclean. After those are eliminated, about all that's left are domestic ruminants: cattle and goats and sheep. *Permissible* edibles would have been a shorter list. The only mammals you are permitted to eat are those with cloven hooves that chew the cud.

If it has no hooves, or it has them but they aren't cloven, or they are cloven but it doesn't chew cud, forget it. No rabbit stew for you. No roast donkey. That also rules out any wild game that might have been around except maybe deer if there were any and if they chew the cud. No reason is given for this: it's just Yahweh's policy.

Similarly for fowl. You can't eat any raptors, or waterfowl, or ostriches, or bats. They seem not to have had chickens in those days, so you were pretty much limited to doves and pigeons and quails, and maybe songbirds if you could catch them.

Only finny scaly fishes are OK. No shrimp, crabs, clams, oysters, catfish or sharks. But there probably weren't many of those around Mt. Sinai anyway, so no hardship there.

Not only are you forbidden to eat the unclean animals...you're forbidden to TOUCH them, especially if they are dead. The corpse of an unclean animal contaminates everything it touches, which needs to be destroyed. Don't try to get rid of that dead mouse. And later on, we learn that if a clean animal dies naturally, its corpse becomes unclean and untouchable.

But enough about animals. Another thing that's unclean is a woman who has just given birth, and she stays that way for a week if it was a son or two weeks if it was a daughter. Also a menstruating woman. (That blood fetish again.)

Then there's a ton of stuff about leprosy —which seems to include just about any skin ailment— and how to recognize it, and what to do about it and how a priest should treat it, and if the patient can't be cured you dress him in rags and shave his head and kick him out of the camp and make him holler "Unclean! Unclean!".

A man with the clap is unclean, because of the unnatural discharge from his male organ, which may be history's earliest mention of gonorrhea or at least its symptoms. And of course any thing or any person he touches becomes unclean.

But even a natural ejaculation will render a man unclean, and a couple who engage in sex are unclean until sundown. And did I mention menstruating women?

We're told that blood is sacred (well, duh! given the earlier stuff) and shouldn't be eaten. And there's a whole raft of regulations on forbidden sexual practices, which seem to rule out anything but an occasional missionary-position coupling between man & wife, which of course renders them unclean until sundown.

At this point, one might be pardoned for getting bored with

Leviticus, but let us soldier on a bit longer.

I learn that you mustn't crossbreed animals, nor plant two different kinds of grain in the same field, nor weave two different kinds of yarn together. And you're not supposed to cut your hair or beard or get tattooed or turn your daughter into a temple prostitute. Nor consult with spirit mediums.

And more stuff about sex, mainly the mandatory death penalty for adultery or incest (very broadly defined), or bestiality. Or blasphemy.

And elaborate instructions for celebrating a bunch of festivals that nobody has ever heard of except Passover.

And dreadful threats of what Yahweh will do to you if you are a Hebrew and fail to obey his commandments.

And that's enough.

The Blasphemer Stoned

The Bible, Chapter 12

The Book of Numbers

The Book of Numbers is #4 in the Five Books Of Moses. It's a chronicle of the Children of Israel as they follow Moses in their 40 year passage from Sinai to the edge of their promised land.

If you are thinking of them as a band of weary pilgrims trudging along behind Moses toward their final place of refuge, you are thinking wrong. It was basically an army of over half a million men —not counting women and youngsters, who weren't included in the census— just men fit to serve in battle. And their journey wasn't anything like a pilgrimage. It was an army of conquest, surging up the Sinai Peninsula, and (with Yahweh's help) trampling over any who got in their way. They made no alliances and gave no quarter. They just kicked butt, and killed the men of the tribes they encountered, and took their women and property as booty, and surged onward. But back to the narrative.

****

They are encamped at the foot of Mt. Sinai. The first thing to do is take a census of the people. There are 603,550 of them, not counting women and children. Later down the Bible we'll see that Yahweh has a dislike for censuses. But that will be then, and this is now. Next, organize the setting up of camp—at this stage of the campaign, the Children of Israel are like nomads, living in tents as they move from place to place.

Early on, the tribe of Levites were given special status. Yahweh has a special tent, so the Levites are put in charge of it. Anybody else who messes with it gets killed.

Yahweh tells Moses, "All of Israel's first-born are my property. But I'm going to substitute the Levites for them." Then the duties of the Levites are laid out in lavish detail.

Lepers (i.e., anybody with a skin disease) and men with a bodily discharge (i.e., the clap) are unclean, and need to be driven out of the camp so they don't make others unclean by touching them.

Lepers

****

Suppose a man suspects his wife of being unfaithful. To settle the matter she's taken before the priests and handed a mug of muddy water to drink. Then she's made to swear that if the water makes her sick, it will show she's guilty. (Actually, they said that if guilty, her belly would swell up and her private parts would rot...but I imagine that just about any sickness would yield the same verdict.) If she's found guilty, she'll be ostracized. (In Leviticus, she'd be stoned to death.) Nothing was said about what happens if a woman suspects her husband of being unfaithful. Apparently, "adultery" was gender-specific: If a woman fools around, it's adultery; if a man fools around, it's just boys being boys.

****

There's a lot of stuff about those who become unclean by touching a corpse. They're prohibited from various things until they get clean again. *But I'm curious about this prohibition against touching a corpse. How do they bury their dead? They surely don't leave them out for the crows and buzzards to take care of.*

****

After a year and two months in Sinai, they break camp and head off on their campaign.

Their goal, you may recall, was the land Yahweh had promised them, even though it was already thoroughly populated by Canaanites and other non-Israelites. And the method of claiming their Promised Land was by killing and driving out the indigenous population, so that only Children of Israel would remain. One nation, one people, one blood, one land.

There are episodes where Yahweh, petulant and capricious as ever, gets pissed off about something and deals with (some of) them severely, But it never really interrupts their forward progress. The Children of Israel are basically a juggernaut headed toward their goal.

****

For a long while, the people had been living on nothing but manna, which was a substance sort of like boiled grain or cream of wheat. They complained to Moses that they were tired of living on mush, and would really like some meat for a change, which promptly sent Yahweh into another of his snits. "They want meat? I'll give them meat until it's coming out of their ears, until they're sick of it." And he sent them flocks and hordes of quails, coming from the sea —seagoing quails itself a minor miracle—, until they were piled up several feet deep. So the people cooked and ate them, and THAT made Yahweh mad all over again, so he laid a plague on the people to show his displeasure.

It's not nice to mess with Yahweh, even if you're never sure what's going to set him off next.

Somewhere along the way, Moses had managed to marry a Cushite woman named Zippora. The land of Cush is today known as Ethiopia: the wife was a black African.

Moses' sister Miriam and brother Aaron didn't like that, and told him so. Then they started pouting: "Moses thinks he's the only one Yahweh speaks through. What about us? Can't he also speak through us?"

Moses and Zippora

This put Yahweh into a snit. He chewed them out for being uppity, and ended up by inflicting Miriam with leprosy, which "turned her white as snow." I think I've mentioned before that that's not a symptom of leprosy; for the Bible people, almost any skin condition was dreaded as leprosy. However, I find some interesting symbolism here. Miriam complained about her brother marrying a black woman, so Yahweh turned Miriam snow white. "How do you like that, Whitey?"

Later, in Deuteronomy, Yahweh will forbid intermarriage with non-Israelites, but apparently Moses was given a pass. We learned in Exodus that Zippora had given him a son named Gershom, so Moses had at least one mulatto child.

****

Some members of a Levite clan rebelled against Moses, deciding not to follow him any more. Yahweh took care of that by sending an earthquake, which opened a chasm and swallowed up the rebels along with their wives and kids.

****

Another episode: At one point some poor mope was found gathering firewood on the sabbath. To teach him a lesson, they dragged him outside the camp and bashed him to death with stones. Remember the sabbath, to keep it holy.

****

Yahweh made them burn up a red cow –the whole thing—and save the ashes for making holy water.

****

The Israelite juggernaut continued onward. Eventually they pitched camp in Moabite and Midianite territory, just across the Jordan river from Jericho. This scared the crap out of the Moabite and Midianite kings, who had heard how the Israelites did business, so they sent for a diviner named Balaam, who had the power to give blessings and lay curses on people. The Moabite king, Balak, wanted to hire Balaam to lay a curse on the Israelite horde, hoping to weaken them enough that the Moabites might be able to drive them off.

Balaam said, wait until tomorrow. I need to check with Yahweh and see what he says. Yahweh said: No curse; the Israelites have my blessing. Don't go with them Moabites.

Balaam told the king to go on home; he couldn't help them.

The king next sent a group of bigwigs to beg Balaam to change his mind, offering him a ton of money. Balaam said nope, he wasn't going to disobey his Lord. But the told them, "Hang around until tomorrow. He might have different instructions." That night Yahweh told him: if they ask you to go with them, go; but don't do anything except what I tell you. So the next morning, Balaam saddled his donkey and went with the Moabite retinue.

True to form, this somehow made Yahweh angry. No telling with Yahweh what's going to set him off.

Anyhow, Balaam on his donkey, and a couple of servants set off down the road. Meanwhile, Yahweh had stationed an angel with a sword, invisible to Balaam, to block the path. When the donkey saw the angel, he veered off the path out into the grass. This pissed Balaam off. He beat on the donkey, and dragged him back to the path. The path led through a narrow defile between stone walls. When the donkey saw the angel on the other side, he scrunched to one side and mashed Balaam's foot against the wall. This made Balaam angrier yet, so he beat the donkey some more and forged on ahead. Around the next bend there was an even narrower defile, with no place to go on either side.

This time, when the donkey saw the angel, he simply lay down in the middle of the road.

Balaam was furious. He began whailing on the donkey, when suddenly the donkey spoke. He said, "Why did you beat me so hard three times?" Balaam said, "Because you've made me look like a fool. You're lucky I didn't have a sword, or I'd have killed you." (Apparently, Balaam was able to take a talking donkey in stride.) The donkey said, "You've been riding me most of your life. Have I ever done this to you before?" Balaam said, "Well, no."

72

Then Yahweh made the angel with the sword visible to Balaam, who flopped down on his face. The angel said, "Why did you beat your donkey these three times? I was stationed here to keep you from your journey. But your donkey saw me, and saved your bacon. If he hadn't turned aside before you got to me, I'd have killed you…but I would have spared the donkey."

Balaam said, "I didn't know you were there. But I do now. Since you were sent to block my way, I suppose I'll turn around and go home."

But the angel said, "No, go along with the Moabites. But only say what I tell you to say." So Balaam continued on with the Moabites as before

I find this story incomprehensible. The whole thing makes no sense. First Yahweh tells Balaam "Don't go with them." Then he says "Go with them." Then he gets mad when Balaam goes with them, and sends an angel to stop him. Then there's the ridiculous business with the donkey. Then the angel, having stopped Balaam, tells him to go on with them after all. Go figure.

The Moabite king takes Balaam to three different places, where he can observe the Israelite troops and lay a curse on them. Instead, each time he laid a blessing on them. The king says, "Dammit, I was trying to hire you to curse them, and instead you've done the opposite." Balaam said, "I told you Yahweh told me not to curse them." Then he turned round and went home.

There's something about this that tends to go unnoticed. **Balaam was a Yahweh-ist**. *He respected the same god as the Israelites, though he wasn't one. This means that when Jacob and his crew packed up and migrated to Egypt, they didn't take Yahweh with them The Children of Israel had no monopoly on Yahweh. Many of the Canaanites left behind worshiped him also. Evidently then, the people that Joshua was slaughtering in the name of Yahweh included other Yahweh-ists: co-religionists of the children of Israel. But not all Yahweh-ists were equal in the eyes of Yahweh. The Children of Israel were his favored people. No doubt because Jacob had wrestled with Yahweh, and won.*

****

Next there was the business with the Midianite women. The Children of Israel were camped near Midianite territory, and some of the young bucks took to consorting with Midianite women, going in unto them and participating in their ceremonies. That upset Yahweh terribly, so he instructed Moses to kill all of the transgressing males. While that was happening, a randy young Israelite showed up in camp with a Midianite woman, and took her into his tent for a little private time. A lad named Phineas took umbrage, grabbed a spear, barged into the tent, and skewered both of them as they were Doing It. Which made Yahweh very happy, and earned Phineas a reward. In the meantime, Yahweh had laid a plague on His Chosen People, as punishment for their sins. Because of Phineas, he lifated the plague

Eventually, the Israelites decided it was time to conquer the Midianites, so they overran the territory, killed all the men and boys including Balaam, and took the women and girls as booty,

This outraged Moses, who said the women were to blame for getting those Jewish boys in trouble earlier. He said they were part of a plot. Moses believed that Balaam had explained how Midian could get the Israelites to curse themselves, by recruiting Midianite women to act as whoreladies in order to debauch the Israelites and get them to defile themselves and eat non-kosher food and the like. I've seen no evidence that Balaam did this, but that's what Moses believed.

So Moses had all the non-virgin Midianite women killed too.

Virgins and girls were kept as spoils for the conquering Israelite men, presumably for their non-adulterous pleasure.

Too bad for the Midianites...

****

Moses appointed Joshua to be his successor. Then there's a lot of directions for conducting religious observances that I won't bother to relate. Then there's directions for how loot is to be divided.

****

A couple of tribes who had a lot of livestock liked the land east of the Jordan River, and asked Moses if they couldn't just settle down there and raise their cattle, without going across the river to the Promised Land. Moses had a fit, and said Yahweh would come down on them if they didn't join in the fighting to take over Canaan. So there was a compromise. They would establish a settlement where they were, to leave their livestock and families, and then join in the invasion of Canaan. But after the conquest, they wouldn't ask for any property in Canaan; they'd just go back to their settlement on the other side of the river. Moses said that would do.

****

Then there was a lot of talk about how things would go in postwar Israel. The book ends with a discussion worth a cadre of lawyers about different kinds of homicide, and their various punishments, and a rule that in order to preserve inheritance rights, women were required to marry men from their own (their father's) tribe.

And that was that.

The Bible, Chapter 13

The Book of Deuteronomy

Deuteronomy is the last of the Five Books of Moses, concerning the children of Israel and their journey to the promised land;, and in some ways is the most distressing of the lot. The Deuteronomist writers wanted to make sure everybody got the message laid down in the previous Books, so they repeat most of the details once again, but with embellishments grim enough to frighten the liver out of you. ("Deuteronomy" means something like "second telling of the laws".)

Yahweh is still framed as the stern despot who rules through the power to inflict suffering on those who don't do as he wants.

We are told that Yahweh assists the Israelites in the battles against their enemies. But the "enemies" in question aren't the aggressors: they are the people being aggressed. No doubt, the quickest way to make an enemy of someone is to attack him.

Here's how it worked. The armies of Moses arrive at the territory of King Sihon and ask him to allow them to pass through peacefully on their way to the Jordan. Sihon has two options: he can say "Sure, come ahead," and hope for the best. Or he can look at that half a million armed men at his gates, and decide it's not a good idea.

So what happens is that Yahweh hardens Sihon's heart and makes him stubborn —just like with the Pharaoh a few years earlier— which causes him to reject the request. Giving a perfect excuse for the children of Israel to conquer the territory by force, which they do, killing EVERYBODY in it: men, women, children, little bitty babies, leaving no survivors. That's how the children of Israel operate in war —except sometimes, when they just kill all the men and take the women & kids as spoils.

Then they pull the same tactic with King Og, and end up slaughtering everybody in his kingdom too.

They do it that way, because that's the way Yahweh has directed them to do it. There are to be no negotiations with the "enemy": when you invade a country, just kill them all. The reason for this eventually becomes clear, as we shall see.

Back in Exodus, we seemed to detect a vein of tolerance in Yahweh: at that time he seemed willing to let the Baal people go ahead and worship Baal, so long as none of HIS people did it.

None of that here in Deuteronomy. Yahweh actively hates anybody who doesn't worship him, and especially anybody who worships some other god. They are on his shit list, and the only thing to do with them is kill them. Because...and here's the nub of it...if you start negotiating and socializing with them, they're liable to start converting some of *Your* people to *Their* ideas, And that is the wickedest thing that could possibly happen. Yahweh can't allow his people even to entertain the thought that there might also be other gods worth worshipping, or that Yahweh's commandments might not be all that good. So before the Enemy gets a chance to generate doubt, they need to be eliminated.

Not only are his OWN people forbidden to listen to any other views, they are forbidden to listen to their own conscience. If something that was commanded seems somehow wrong to them (like slaughtering women and children), they are commanded not to put themselves before the Lord, but to ignore that, and to obey Yahweh's commands no matter how wrong they seem.

When the children of Israel conquer another kingdom, they are commanded not only to kill all the people —and usually the livestock along with them—, but especially to tear down and destroy all of the things those people held sacred...building, temples, writing, images, everything. Leave nothing that might start a child of Israel to start thinking and wondering...

Internal government is equally draconian. Judgments of the priests and judges are to be obeyed to the letter, under pain of death. And the only accepted method of execution is to have the people fling rocks at the victim until he (or she) finally dies. Stoning is how it must be done. The executee is dragged outside the camp to a place where there are lots of rocks, whereupon a mob bashes him or her to death with them. This is one of the lessons from Deuteronomy. There are others.

We learn that if a son is disobedient, he is to be taken before the judges who will condemn him to be stoned to death.

We learn that sexuality is strictly regulated.

If a woman is suspected of not being a virgin on her wedding night, she's in trouble. Should her husband accuse her, her parents are required to take the bloodstained nuptial sheet before the judges to prove her virginity. If they can't produce the blood evidence, the wretched girl gets stoned to death.

If a young woman is betrothed, and some other man is found going in unto her in town, both are to be stoned to death: the man because he stole the virginity promised to the betrothed, the woman because she didn't holler loud enough for people to come and interfere.

But if it happens outside of town, only the man gets killed, because even if the girl hollered there was no one around to hear.

However, if she's not yet betrothed when she gets gone in unto, there's no death penalty: just a shotgun wedding.

If two guys are fighting, and the wife of one of them grabs the other guy by the balls to help her husband, she's to have her hand chopped off.

A man can't be one of Yahweh's people if he has damaged genitals. That's disgusting in the sight of the Lord. Likewise a person born out of wedlock can't be one of Yahweh's people, nor his descendants for ten generations. Drive the bastards out of camp and keep them there. Of course, wedlock is very loosely defined; but that's a different matter.

There's more, including Yahweh's promise that if his people are scattered to the ends of the earth, they will all eventually come back to reclaim the Promised Land they have taken from the former inhabitants. *Which has an eerie sense of prescience.*

The Bible, Chapter 14

The Book of Joshua

Joshua is a narrative, or chronicle, of the second half of the invasion and conquest by the Israelites of the lands Yahweh had promised to them. It is, by and large, an endless tale of slaughter and cruelty. Those who call this "The Good Book" probably never bothered to read this part of it.

Moses had led the army of the children of Israel as far as the land to the east of the Jordan River, killing and pillaging as they went. Then Moses died, and the mantle fell upon his second in command Joshua, to complete the task. The Jordan, for some reason, was an important boundary.

An early goal was to destroy the city of Jericho, an important city just west of the Jordan. You have probably heard that Joshua fit de battle of Jericho, and de walls came a-tumblin' down. But you may not have heard that it might not have happened without the assistance of a whorelady named Rahab who lived in Jericho.

Before rashly invading, Joshua sent a couple of lads across the river to spy out Jericho and report back what they found. When they got there, the first thing they did was to take up lodging in Rahab the whorelady's house...no doubt for purely innocent reasons as travelers, though why we are informed of her profession remains uncertain if it wasn't material to the story.

Rahab hides the spies

The Jericho officials learned there were spies in town, and told Rahab to turn them over. Had she done so, it would have put a serious crimp in Joshua's plans. But she lied to the officials and told them the spies had run off, even though she had hidden them in the attic. The officials went off to hunt for them, and Rahab told the spies she'd help them escape if they'd promise, when Joshua came to sack and pillage the city, he'd leave Rahab and her family be. So they promised, and the spies made it back to Joshua's camp.

Remember, Joshua's army consisted of over a half-million fighting men, plus their families and old folks, so getting them across the river to invade Jericho was no small undertaking. On the day for the advance, Yahweh made sure they didn't get their feet wet by replicating his trick with the Red Sea, and parted the waters of the Jordan River. The waters below the barrier flowed on down to the Dead Sea, presumably leaving a lot of fish to die high & dry, while the waters upstream simply piled up behind the barrier. Normally one would worry that the piled up waters would flood the surrounding countryside, but that was no problem because the lands were already flooded, it being harvest time. This leads one to wonder about the agricultural practices of the locals, who had their harvests in the spring during flood season rather than in the autumn which would be more normal.

With the river blocked off, Joshua led his army across. We aren't told how long it took for them all to get across, but we can imagine it was several days...a million or so people on foot along with their provisions and livestock. The amount of flooding during that time would have been notable, though we aren't told much about it.

Jericho

Jericho was a well-fortified city that had no quarrel with Joshua, but it was on land that Yahweh had promised the children of Israel, so Jericho had to go. Joshua's troops weren't equipped to breach its walls and conquer it, so Yahweh was enlisted to help. If they would perform a certain ritual, blowing horns and hollering at the right time, he would knock the walls down for them.

So they did, and he did, and they swarmed into the city and killed everyone in it. Everyone —men women, children, old people, little bitty babies— because that's what Yahweh demanded them to do. (Well, everyone except the whorelady's

...And de walls came a-tumblin' down

family, because they had promised they wouldn't.) It had been

Moses' divinely prescribed modus operandi, and Joshua continued to follow it: When you conquer a city, don't just take it over: sack and pillage and massacre every blessed inhabitant in the process and take all their stuff.

Except in this case, Yahweh told them not to take any stuff but to burn all of it up along with the rest of the city. However, one guy ignored that and kept some stuff. So they got him to confess, and then stoned him and all of his family to death (or burned them at the stake...not clear which).

Do what Yahweh say, or face the consequences.

Then Joshua took his men up to the city of Ai, and captured it, and slaughtered the entire population of twelve thousand. But this time they looted it and took all the stuff before they burned the city, because Yahweh had told them to.

When word got out that the children of Israel were overrunning the territory and massacreing whole populations and burning down cities, a bunch of the local kingdoms —Hittites, Amorites, Canaanites, Perizzites and so forth— banded together in a defensive alliance. It wasn't to do them much good.

One bunch, the Gibeonites, didn't join the alliance. They used subterfuge to trick the Israelites into not killing them, so they were just taken as slaves instead. Five Amorite kings didn't like it that Gibeon had made peace with Joshua, so they decided to invade Gibeon. Big mistake. The Gibeonites called on Joshua to protect them, So Joshua took his horde and decimated the Amorites and the ones that weren't killed were chased off. Yahweh took care of those by raining huge hailstones down from heaven, killing more that way than had been slain in battle.

Then to celebrate their big victory, Joshua commanded the sun to stand still...and by golly it did it! It stood still in the middle of the sky and didn't go down for a whole day. That's what it says, but clocks hadn't been invented by then; so it's not clear how they

84

determined the length of time the sun stood still.

Then he executed the Amorite kings, and took his army off to the town of Makkeda, where they slaughtered everybody and took their stuff. Then they proceeded to the town of Libnah, where they slaughtered everybody and took their stuff. Then to Lachish, where they slaughtered everybody and took their stuff. Did the same to Gezer. Then to Eglon. Then to Hebron. "He left none remaining, but utterly destroyed all that breathed, as the Lord God of Israel commanded."

Now you may not be wondering, but I am, about these tens of thousands of corpses that the children of Israel were leaving behind them. There was nobody left to bury them. Were they just left on the killing fields to rot for the buzzards and crows? We'll never know, but that seems downright uncivilized.

As you can see, this chronicle of endless slaughters, one after another, becomes repetitious. Some more kings formed an alliance to repel the Israelites, and were destroyed along with their cities. The Israelites also crippled the enemy's horses by severing their hamstrings and leaving the creatures to die screaming in misery, because Yahweh said to. Then they moved on to Hazor and smote it and took their stuff. Then they moved on to Goshen and smote it and took their stuff. Then they moved on to a bunch more places and smote them and took their stuff.

In all, the children of Israel under Joshua overran thirty-one cities and kingdoms and territories, and destroyed them and killed all the people and took their stuff. It was not only their right, but their obligation to do that, because Yahweh had commanded them to...and we've seen what happens when somebody disobeys one of Yahweh's commands.

There was a lot more territory left to conquer, but Joshua decided to take a break from conquering, and parcel out the lands taken so far. The remainder of the book of Joshua is a catalog of real estate transactions, as various parts of the country were given to various tribes among the Israelites. I found no lessons for the conduct of life in those chapters.

Then Joshua got old, and addressed his people and commanded them to faithfully observe all the laws of Yahweh.

And then he died, and I'm glad to be finished with this appalling tale.

The Bible, Chapter 15.

The Book of Judges
Part 1

Perhaps you are tired of these unremitting tales of bloodshed and slaughter and attacks on unthreatening people. But there's no getting away from them because they are in the Bible.

Here in Judges, before we're past the 12th verse of Chapter 1, the Israelites have chased down the king of one of the places they invaded, and chopped off his thumbs and big toes. Then they captured Jerusalem and slaughtered all of its people and burned it to the ground. In just 12 verses.

There's a recapitulation of parts of Joshua's campaign, except sometimes they deviate from the Joshuan principle: "kill everybody". Instead, once in a while they just capture the people and make slaves of them.

After Joshua dies, no one person takes over as leader of all the Hebrews. Instead, there's a lot of jockeying for position. During this time of no central leadership, the Israelites revert to being slow learners. Time after time they stop worshiping Yahweh and quit following his laws and start worshiping some other gods. So Yahweh punishes them, until they realize their error and come back to the fold. Then before long they do the same thing again. And again.

****

There's the charming tale of King Eglon of Moab. To punish the Israelites for another episode of apostasy, Yahweh makes Eglon stronger than Israel, so they defeat the Israelites and retake

Jericho, and rule the Children of Israel for a bunch of years.

Eventually the Israelites hatch a plot to assassinate King Eglon. They assign a left-handed guy for the job, for a reason soon apparent. The southpaw Ehud makes him a short double-edged sword, and straps it onto his righthand side (because he's left handed) and covers it with his cloak so it can't be seen.

Then he heads up to Eglon's place with a gift for the king. Eglon, who was an enormously fat individual, gladly accepted Ehud's gift (it was probably something to eat). The guardians could see that Ehud wasn't armed (they thought) so they weren't worried about him.

Ehud says to the king, Let's step back into your private chambers so I can tell you a secret. When they were away from the guardians, Ehud whipped out his left-handed sword and jammed it into the fat king's belly, so hard that "the haft went in after the blade. And the fat closed upon the blade so that he could not draw the dagger out of his belly; and the dirt came out." It's right there in the Bible.

Then Ehud locked the door so nobody could get in, and escaped out the window, and took over as leader of the children of Israel, and they all went down to Moab and slaughtered ten thousand people and took over the country.

Eventually a guy named Barak replaced Ehud as leader, and took off to wage war on King Sisnera. The Israelites managed to kill

88

all of Sisnera's army, but Sisnera himself escaped and ran off.

By and by, he arrived at the tent of a woman named Jael, and asked her to shelter him from his pursuers. She welcomed him in, and gave him a drink of water, and fed him some milk, and told him to go lie down and take a nap. He did. Then Jael snuck in with a hammer and a tent stake, and drove the stake through Sisnera's head, nailing him to the ground. When the pursuers showed up and asked if she had seen Sisnera, she said "You bet!", and showed them his body, nailed to the ground.

The next leader was a man named Gideon, who had his army of thirty thousand prepared to go attack the Midianite camp. And do you know what Yahweh said to him? He said: Don't take that many men! If you do and they whip the Midianites, they might think they did it by themselves, and I wouldn't get any credit for helping! *Yahweh is afraid of not getting credit for an Israelite victory if they simply go down and kick ass by force of numbers!* Yahweh is as publicity-hungry as any modern-day politician, making sure everybody knows what He did for Them.

Gideon says Okay, i'll reduce the invading force by 2/3. Yahweh says No No, still too many. Take just 300 men, so when you whip them everybody will give me the credit for your victory.

So Gideon sent his 300 troops and, to make a long story short, they whipped the Midianites and chopped off the heads of their leaders, and brought them back to Gideon for souvenirs. And you-know-who took credit.

Then there was more invading and killing and falling away from Yahweh and so on. Besides Gideon's bevy of wives, and a ton of legitimate children by them, he had a concubine who bore him an illegitimate son named Abimilech. Gideon died, and Abimilech decided he's like to take over command.

So he went down and convinced the gullible crowd that he would make a better leader than any of Gideon's other sons. They made him leader, and he put together a posse, and rounded up all 70 of

Gideon's other sons, and had them executed, which took care of that.

Then Abimilech waged war on a bunch of places and killed all the people and finally attacked a city that had a strong tower where the people took refuge. When he got up next to the tower, a woman dropped a millstone on him, which cracked his skull. He hollered to his arms-bearer "Quick! Run me through with a sword so nobody can say a woman killed me!" So he did it, and Abimilech died with his pride intact but not much else. And when the men saw that he was dead, they turned around and went home. "Thus Yahweh rendered the wickedness of Abimelech, which he did in slaying his 70 brothers." Yahweh took his time.

DEATH OF ABIMELECH.

After more warmongering and sinning against Yahweh and that sort of thing, we come to the tale of Samson.

■■■

Samson has always intrigued me. His mother had been barren until an angel informed her that she would finally have a son, who would be dedicated as a Nazirite from his birth. As Moses described it several books back, the Nazirites were those who chose to devote their lives to Yahweh by vowing never to use strong drink or cut their hair or touch dead bodies, etc. Normally, people chose to be Nazirites. Samson had it foisted on him.

As Samson grew up, he turned out to be a great hulking lout and a bully and a permanent spoiled brat who got mad and broke stuff when he didn't get his way.

One day, visiting the Philistine town of Timnath, he took a shine to a young Philistine girl, and told his parents "Go get her for me so I can marry her." They would have preferred he marry within his own tribe, but he bullied them so the three set off to Timnath.

On their way, they heard a young lion making noises, so Samson went and found it and killed it with his bare hands, "as easily as he could have killed a lamb". Just to show that he could.

They met the girl and Samson said 'Yep, I want her." What she said isn't recorded. A few days later, headed back down the same road to Timnath, he came across the young lion he had killed, and found that a swarm of bees had settled in it, and made a bunch of honey. [I personally find this part of the story dubious; bees would never hive up in a rotting corpse, and if they did, it requires more than a few days to construct a comb and fill it with honey. But that's what it says, and it's in the Bible.] Samson ate some of the honey and took the rest home to his folks.

At the time of the wedding feast, a bunch of young Philistine men came to hang out with Samson. He made them a bet: said "I'll tell you a riddle, and I'll bet each of you a suit of clothes that you can't tell me what it means before the end of the week." They took the bet, and he said "Out of the eater came something to eat; out of the strong came something sweet." After a few days they hadn't figured it out, so they went to his new wife and said "Wangle the answer out of him for us. Otherwise, we'll burn your house down with you in it." So she nagged the answer out of Samson and gave it to them.

At the end of the week, Samson went to the guys and said, "Well?" They said "What could be sweeter than honey? What could be stronger than a lion?" That of course was the right answer, and they had satisfied the terms of the wager. But it pissed Samson off, who said "You wouldn't have known the answer if you hadn't somehow gotten it out of my wife!" In a blazing fury, he went off to another town, killed 30 men, stripped them of their clothes, and gave them to the young Philistines in satisfaction of the wager. Then he stomped off home in a huff, leaving his new wife-to-be behind. So she was given to a man who had been his friend.

A few months later, he went back to see her and told her father, "I have come to go in unto my wife." Her father said, "Sorry, you can't do that. When you abandoned her, we gave her to somebody else. She's now his wife. But she has a hot young sister you can have instead."

That enraged Samson again, so he decided to get revenge on the whole Philistine tribe. He went out, and caught 300 foxes. [Here again I must say that I find that part dubious. Unless foxes were as bunched as mice in a granary, his chances of finding that many clustered in one place are zero. In fact, foxes are solitary; they don't travel in packs. And they can run faster than you can, and they are very good at hiding. If Samson had managed, implausibly, to catch 10 foxes a day, it would have taken him a month to collect 300 of them. And if he didn't keep them fed, the ones he caught first would die of starvation and he'd have to keep replacing them. So, no, Samson didn't catch any 300 foxes. Except it says he did, right there in the Bible.]

He took a pair of these foxes and tied their tails together along with a torch, and did the same with the rest of them. Then he set the burning foxes all loose in the Philistine's grain fields. The upshot was that their entire grain crop, what was in the field and what was harvested, got burned up along with their olive orchards. [Again, I have questions. Somehow, Samson took a pair of panicked, angry, wild foxes and managed to grip their tails, and grab a torch, and tie the three things together with string while the foxes were writhing and jumping and and snapping and biting and doing everything to get away. And Samson did this 150 times and never got bit, or burned, or let any of them get away. Or so it says. I must say: give me a break.]

The Philistines asked who did it and why. They were told it was Samson, and he did it because he was pissed off at the father of his abandoned wife, because the erstwhile wife had been given to somebody else. So instead of going after Samson, they went and burned down the father's house and the woman along with it. Go figure.

And THAT set Samson off into another tantrum. So he went on a rampage and killed a bunch of Philistines. Then he went off and hid in a cave to sulk.

Meanwhile, the Philistine army set out to capture Samson and take him prisoner. When they attacked the town where he lived, the people said, "HEY! What are you attacking us for?" They said, "We've come to get Samson and punish him for what he did to us."

So the people went up to Samson's cave and convinced him to let them tie him up and turn him over to the Philistines. But when they got close to the Philistine army, Samson burst the ropes, grabbed up the jawbone from a donkey carcass nearby, and proceeded to beat a thousand armed Philistine soldiers to death with it. Some jawbone. You'd have thought it would break after the first hundred or so.

Samson then became the latest ruler of the Israelites, which lasted for 20 years. His downfall began with a visit to a whorelady in the city of Gaza. A bunch of people waited in ambush to catch him in the morning when he left her crib, but instead he left the whorelady early, and took off, and tore down the city gates as he was leaving.

Eventually he fell in love with a Philistine lady of uncertain provenance named Delilah. During the time they were getting it on, Philistine elders approached her to find out the source of Samson's great strength. She worked on it over and over, but he kept giving her answers which proved wrong. Eventually he gave in —apparently not remembering the perfidy of his first wife— and told her it was because of his Nazirite hair. First chance she got, she lulled him to sleep, cut off his hair, and turned him over to the authorities, who put out his eyes and set him to work doing the work of an ox pushing a grinding mill. Eventually he managed to pull down the pillars of an auditorium, killing himself and all the people inside.

That's the Samson story. But there's yet more in Judges that we need to get to.

So far, however, I haven't gleaned any pointers from the book of Judges on how to conduct my life.

The Bible, Chapter 16
The Book of Judges
Part 2

The last four chapters of Judges (after the Samson tale) are among the strangest in the book.

It begins with a gentleman named Micah. Somebody had stolen a bunch of his mother's silver, and she had laid a curse on the unknown miscreant. Well, Micah confessed that he had stolen it, and gave the silver back. But that didn't get rid of the curse. So to remove the curse, Micah's mother dedicated the silver to Yahweh. It was to be used to make a carven idol and a molten idol. She took it to a metalworker and he made the idols for her. She then gave them to Micah to keep.

Now if you have been keeping up with things at all, you would probably suppose that dedicating an idol to Yahweh would be the surest way to get blasted with fire and brimstone, given what Moses had to say on the matter (remember that golden calf). But that's not what happened. In fact, nothing happened to either Micah or his mother. Micah, it seems had a whole bunch of idols in his worship room. Apparently the idols that Moses had forbidden back in his day were OK now, during the time when the Israelites had no central king. At least, Yahweh doesn't seem to have minded.

Micah also made an ephod and teraphim (which I'll leave it to you to look up) and consecrated one of his sons to be his priest. But that didn't last long because a genuine Levite soon showed up, and took over the priesting duties.

****

The Danites were a rapacious tribe that somehow hadn't managed to get any territory when land that had been liberated from its inhabitants had been parceled out to the tribes by Joshua. So they set out to liberate some land on their own. First they sent out some spies to see who was vulnerable. The spies stayed overnight at Micah's place, and took note of what he had. They then found that the town of Laish was a pigeon waiting for the plucking. It's people were peaceful, and lived far away from others so they had no troublesome allies. It was Yahweh's gift to the Danites.

When the Danite armies passed by Micah's place, they stopped in and liberated all of his idols and his ephod and hired away his Levite priest. And there wasn't much that Micah could do about it given how badly outnumbered he was.

Then the Danites went ahead and attacked Laish and slaughtered everybody and burned the town and claimed the territory for their own. And used the liberated idols for their gods. Thus ended that episode. No mention anywhere of divine intervention. *The ways of Yahweh are inscrutable.*

****

The Levite and his Concubine.
There was this Levite, never named, who claimed a young lady to be his concubine or mistress, which in those days was a common arrangement. She didn't like it, and ran off back home so the Levite went to get her. He and his retinue stayed with her family for several days, then her dad let the Levite have her back, so Levite set out for home with his mistress.

At night they found themselves in a strange town in Benjaminite territory called Gibeah, where they knew no-one, and had nobody to put them up. They were hunkered down in the town square, when an old man came along and offered them lodging at his place.

While they were there enjoying his hospitality, a bunch of perverted "sons of Belial" surrounded the house and pounded on the door, hollering "Send the Levite man out. We all want to Go In Unto him." The old man refused, saying that would be a terrible thing because the man was his guest. Instead, he sent the Levite's mistress out and said "Have your way with her instead."

Dead concubine, in transit

So they did. After a night of jolly and repeated gang-rape and abuse, the mistress managed to crawl back to the door of the old man's house, where she died. When the Levite saw that she was dead on the doorstep, he put her body on his donkey and headed toward home.

When he got there, he took a knife and cut the concubine's body into twelve pieces and sent a piece to each of the 12 tribes of Israel.

Dead concubine in pieces

Receiving a piece of a dead concubine upset them, but not for the reason it would upset you or me. Rather, it led them to decide the Levite needed vengeance on the perverts that had raped his mistress to death.

They formed up an army and headed up to Gibeah, where they said "Turn over your perverts to us, so we can kill them." Which didn't happen. Instead, the entire Benjaminite nation sent out their own army, which soundly kicked the Israelites' collective butt, inflicting 22,000 casualties..

The Israelite's went off and thought it over, and asked Yahweh, "Should we try to attack them again?" Yahweh told them to go for it. So they did, and got their butt soundly kicked a second time, suffering eighteen thousand more casualties. Victims of faulty advice So they went and thought it over again, and did some sacrifices and stuff and asked Yahweh, "Should we give it a third try, or quit 40,000 down, and go home." Yahweh said "Attack them again. This time I'll let you win."

So they attacked the Benjaminites a third time, using a smarter tactic than a simple frontal assault. This time, they kicked the Benjaminites' butt, and killed all of their soldiers — over 25,000— except a few hundred who escaped to the hills. Then, since there was no one left to defend the town, they swarmed in and killed everybody: women, children, and animals. And burned the town. And did the same to every town in the area. Which served to teach those perverts a lesson.

But that left the Israelites with a moral problem. At the start of the campaign, they had collectively sworn never to give any of their daughters to a Benjaminite for a wife. And without wives to produce children, the tribe of Benjamin would eventually become extinct.

So even though the Israelites had exterminated all of the female Benjaminites and most of the males, they couldn't bear the thought of having one of the twelve tribes cease to exist. The Benjaminites needed wives, but the the Israelites had sworn not to provide any of their daughters.

The solution they came up with was typical Old Testament stuff, reminiscent of how Samson got the clothes to pay off his lost bet. They found that the people of Jabesh hadn't provided any soldiers to the army, meaning they could be scapegoats. So they sent troops to Jabesh to kidnap all the virgins and kill everybody else. Then the Jabesh girls were given to the Benjaminite survivors as wives. But there weren't enough to go around; they were still a couple of hundred brides short.

That was taken care of by invoking a technicality. They sent a secret messenger to the Benjaminites, who told them, "Look. In a few days there's going to be a big celebration in Shiloh, and all the young girls will be out dancing. You needing wives go hide in the bushes, and when a girl comes near, grab her and cart her off to be your wife."

And that's what happened. So every Benjaminite got a wife. But no Israelite girl had been GIVEN to them as wives. Rather, the girls had been snatched by the Benjaminites. So the Israelite vow had therefore not been broken...at least, not technically. And that's the end of the book.

What I've learned from this part of the Bible is that it's okay sometimes to worship idols, even if they're stolen, and if you need something, go kill the people that have it and take it, and that you can always find a way around a vow without actually breaking it. And given a choice between having a guest gang-buggered and a girl raped to death, the girl loses. And if your girlfriend gets raped to death, you should cut up her corpse and send the pieces to your friends so they will become your allies.

The Bible, Chapter 17

The Book of Ruth

The book of Ruth is a nice little story, completely devoid of the mayhem and slaughter we have come to expect. Makes one wonder whether it belongs in the Bible.

In the time when the Israelites were ruled by tribal chieftains ("Judges") rather than by a king, there was a famine going on. So a Judean moved his family from Bethlehem to Moabite country, where things might be better. The Moabites weren't children of Israel, but there seems to have been no animosity at the time.

The man had a wife named Naomi, and two sons. Soon, the man up and died, leaving Naomi to rely on her sons for support. The sons married a couple of Moabite girls, one named Orpah and the other named Ruth.

Somewhere along the line, both sons died too, leaving the three women without any means of support. Naomi decided to move back to Judea where her people lived, and told her two widowed daughters-in-law to go back to their own families in Moab. Orpah took her advice; Ruth would not. She was adamant that she was going to stick with Naomi no matter what, and would accompany her back to Israelite territory and become an Israelite and adopt their religion.

When they got to Bethlehem, the harvest was beginning, so Ruth went out to the fields to glean behind the harvesters, to get something for her and Naomi to eat. "Gleaning" meant collecting the dropped heads of grain left from the harvest. The field happened to belong to a well-to-do local gentleman named Boaz, who, by coincidence, was a kinsman of Naomi's late husband.

While Ruth was busy gleaning, Boaz arrived on the scene and asked about the young hottie out there in the field. They told him she was Naomi's daughter-in-law, who had accompanied her back from Moab. That made her sort of a part of Boaz's extended family, so he took her under his wing.

First, he warned her not to glean in anybody's field but his, since the unruly harvesters over there would tend to make unwanted advances and one thing and another on her; and told her when she was thirsty she could drink from the water jars brought for the harvesters. She asked why the kindness to a foreign woman, and he told her it was because he had heard her story and knew of her devotion to Naomi.

He invited her to lunch; and later told the harvesters to let this young woman glean wherever she liked...and to be sure to drop some extra grain so she would have plenty to collect.

When Ruth got home that day with a big sack of grain, she told Naomi about her encounter with this guy Boaz. Naomi was tickled pink, and told her that Boaz was a relative, and had some responsibility to take care of them. And she started thinking...

As soon as the harvest was over and Ruth was done gleaning, Naomi told her "You need to get a husband so you can have your own home, and Boaz would be an excellent catch. Pretty yourself up and go up to his place while he's sleeping, and curl up at his feet, and see what happens." I can think of other modes of curling up that might have had more immediate results, but that's what Naomi told her.

So Ruth did it, and when Boaz woke up in the middle of the night and said Who Are You?, she told him "I'm Ruth, Naomi's daughter-in law and you're a relative and I need a husband so how's about marrying me?"

Boaz said, quote, "It's true that I'm your near kinsman; but there's an even nearer kinsman that should have the first chance at you."

[I pause to worry about the notion of "near kinship" at work here. Boaz in the first instance is a "near relative", not of Naomi, but of Naomi's late husband Elimelech. Ruth's connection to Elimelech was that she had been married to one of his sons. So if Boaz and Elimelech were, say, first cousins, then Ruth was something like Boaz's second-cousin-in-law. Familial closeness was calculated differently back then. Especially if the "near kinship" between Boaz and Elimelech turned out to be something like third or fourth cousins.]

Says Boaz, "He's entitled to the first option to marry you; but if he refuses, then I will." But Boaz was fixing to make sure that the other guy would NOT go for the deal. Here's what he told the near relative:

"Naomi wants to sell the land that belonged to her late husband, our kinsman. The right to buy it belongs first to you and then to me. Do you want to buy it?" Near relative says Yes Indeedy. Boaz then says, "Remember, if you buy it from Naomi you're getting Ruth in the bargain, so the land will stay in Elimelech's family." Near relative says, "In that case forget it. If I bought the land under those terms, my children would be unable to inherit it."

So Boaz immediately bought Elimelech's entire estate from Naomi, including Ruth, with whom he quickly married up. Naomi also became part of the household, so she was taken care of. Eventually, Ruth had a baby boy and named him Obed. Naomi became his doting grandma.

And Obed would become the grandfather of David, about whom much will be learned as the Bible continues.

The Bible, Chapter 18

The First Book of Samuel,
Part 1

1 Samuel is an account of the events leading from tribal governance of the Israelites in the period of Judges, to the emergence of the first kings, and the beginning of the Israelite monarchy. It's long, tedious in places, and riddled with details of dubious importance. We don't get to killing and bloodshed until a while further on

The main characters in the first part are:
- An Ephraimite woman who desperately wants a son;
- Eli, the head priest at Shiloh;
- Eli's two wicked sons, also priests;
- Samuel, a future prophet; and
- Saul, a future king.

The woman prays, and promises that if Yahweh will give her a son (though not in the New Testament way), she will dedicate his life to the service of Yahweh and never cut his hair. *(Co-opting the child's future, leaving him no choice in his career — remember Samson).*
Yahweh hears her prayers, and she has a son and names him Samuel.

As soon as he's old enough to get along without his momma, she ships him off to Shiloh to study for the priesthood under Eli. Except he can't ever REALLY be a priest, because he's not a Levite.

Then we don't hear much about Samuel for a long time.

Eli has two rascally sons, both priests, and about as corrupt as anything you might find during the Borgia papacy a few thousand years later. They would rip off the best part of the meat brought for sacrifices, and were continually Going In Unto the holy women who were supposed to be guarding the door to Yahweh's tent, and doing other sacrilegious stuff, and generally being bad. This did not sit well with Yahweh. But instead of punishing the culprits, he jumped on Eli for not making them behave —even though Eli had chewed them out for their wicked deeds— and laid a curse on Eli and all his descendants forever. (*"Hey Lord, I didn't DO anything." "Tough luck. Your great-great-great-etc. grandfather Eli's sons did, so you're paying for it."*)

Samuel was doing well under Eli's tutelage, and one night he heard voices which he eventually figured out was Yahweh talking to him, telling him that he, Yahweh, was fixing to wreak serious harm on the House of Eli for his sin of omission in failing to curb his sons.

Samuel told Eli about it.

When word of his conversation with Yahweh got around, Samuel was recognized as a prophet.

****

The Israelites went to war (again) with the Philistines. And in this campaign got their butts seriously kicked, with thousands of casualties. The Philistines killed both of Eli's rascally sons, and made off with the Ark of the Covenant. When Eli received word about his sons and the Ark, he fell over backwards and died.

The "prize" of the Ark of the Covenant brought the Philistines nothing but trouble. Wherever they took it, Yahweh hit the population with a plague of mice and emerods, which apparently were not hemorrhoids as first thought, but tumors of some kind. They decided, after consulting their priests, that the only way to get rid of the bad luck was to return the Ark to the Israelites along with a tribute of 5 gold mice and 5 gold emerods. Which they did. *I'm trying to imagine what a gold emerod might have looked like.*

105

In the course of the return, a couple of unfortunates peeked inside the Ark, so Yahweh smote them and 50,068 of their fellow citizens for daring to peek. Naughty, naughty, mustn't look. Mustn't be a tribesman of anybody who looks. Guilt by association is the name of the game.

****

The Philistines, still pissed off about the plagues, re-started the fight with the Israelites. But this time, they got their own asses kicked, and decided to leave the Israelites alone for now. This was only a temporary armistice.

Samuel continued to rule the Israelites for a long time.

The Request for a King

This part of the story is hard to make complete sense of. Samuel was getting along in years, and the question of succession came up. The people didn't want either of his ne'er-do-well sons to be the next Judge, so they asked Samuel instead to appoint a king to rule over them. Apparently, they were tired of being ruled by tribal chieftains ("Judges") and wanted someone who could rule all of Israel.

This completely pissed off Samuel, and Yahweh as well (according to Samuel, who was Yahweh's spokesman). Samuel saw it as a repudiation of his leadership. Yahweh saw it as a repudiation of HIS leadership. "Oh, I'm not good enough for them; now they want a king."

I can understand Samuel's jealousy: a king would limit Samuel's political power. But Yahweh? He says, "I am the one they have rejected as their king." Then he starts carrying on about the various times they have temporarily strayed from his fold, before being brought back by threats and disasters…like a petulant old woman with a grudge, "Remember the time you…?" "And after all I've done for you…"

Trouble is, Yahweh had never acted as a king, and never pretended to be one, until now. Yahweh sat in his fancy tent and enjoyed sacrifices, and handed down edicts and occasionally influenced natural events (plagues, earthquakes) and the outcomes of battles (by infusing power into this or that army).

But he never pretended to do any of the stuff that a king does, which is handling the business of a kingdom: settling disputes and planning military strategies and leading troops and appointing officials and keeping order among the tribes and whatnot. So it's unfathomable where Yahweh gets off as treating the request for a king as a rejection of HIS authority. To me, it smacks of pouting. We've seen how he likes to get all the credit for everything.

Anyhow, Yahweh says "Go ahead and give them a king, and see how they like it." So Samuel explains to the people that if they get a king he will be a tyrant who will make the people his servants, and arrogate their best stuff to himself and impose taxes. And when they get tired of that, they'll have no one to blame but themselves.

But the people said, "Nope. We want a king, like the other nations have." So Samuel gave up in disgust, and started keeping an eye out for a candidate.

Saul

Saul was a good-looking Benjaminite lad, a head taller than the rest of the people, who lived in the town of Gibea. (You may recall it as the town where the Levite's concubine got raped to death, and laer was cut into pieces for distribution.). A likely candidate. One day Saul was out looking for a herd of lost donkeys, and showed up in Samuel's territory. Yahweh had told Samuel, "A Benjaminite is going to show up. Anoint him as ruler of my people."

When Samuel spotted Saul, Yahweh told him "That's the one,"

so Samuel went ahead and anointed Saul as the ruler of his people. Then he made some predictions, and ended by saying "Do what the Lord tells you. You are to go ahead of me to Gilgal. But you must wait there seven days, until I come and tell you what to do."

Then Samuel assembled the people to formally regcognize Saul as their king. They shouted "Long live the King!" And everybody went home.

****

Eventually, Saul went off to resume the endless war with the Philistines. He assembled an army, and had them join him at Gilgal. They soon found themselves outnumbered and surrounded by about forty thousand Philistine troops. This scared he crap out of Saul's troops, who snuck off and hid out in the bushes and in caves. Saul waited out the seven days for Samuel to show up. When he didn't, Saul decided he's better appeal to Yahweh on his own. He was just finishing a burnt sacrifice, when Samuel arrived and started hollering "What are you doing?" Saul said, "My men were deserting, and you didn't show up to offer sacrifices like you said you would, so I did it myself."

Did Samuel say, ,"Sorry I was late."? He did not. Instead, he tore into Saul for being stupid and "disobeying the command of the Lord", and ended by revoking Saul's charter as king, saying "Yahweh wants somebody else who will obey him."

Apparently Saul didn't believe it. He kept on acting like he as king.

. Samuel says that Saul "disobeyed a command of the Lord. There's no record of Yahweh directly addressing a command to Saul. Any "commands of the Lord" would have come from Samuel. And the only directive that's relevant is when he said, "Go to Gilgal, but don't do anything until I get there and tell you what to do. I'll be there in seven days." So Saul went to Gilgal.

108

And he waited seven days. And when Samuel didn't show up on time, he took some action on his own. THAT must be the sin that lost him his crown. **He acted on his own.**

He had followed Samuel's terms to the letter. Samuel hadn't followed his own terms. That should have freed Saul to do whatever seemed best. But Samuel was itching to depose Saul, and he settled on the first lame excuse that came along."I told you to do nothing until I was here to tell you what to do." "You told me you'd be here in seven days. You weren't. I couldn't wait forever to take some action to try and help my troops." "That doesn't matter. I told you to do nothing until I was here to tell you what to do. That was a command from Yahweh. So you're busted." Sometimes, these Bible people are unbelievable.

The people continued to regard Saul as their leader. So he continued to make war with the Philistines, and the people followed him. (He turned out to be a martinet, demanding absolute obedience. Remember Samuel's warning?)

One day during the war, Saul's son Jonathan and his arms-bearer chanced upon a group of several dozen Philistines. After some foreplay, Jonathan jumped in and attacked them single-handed, killing 20 of them before the others ran off terrified.

When word got back to the Philistine camp, the troops panicked. And while they were in disarray, Saul swooped down with his troops and was victorious.

****

After another battle, Saul's men were weak from hunger because Saul had stupidly forbidden his men to eat anything until he was satisfied that he had taken revenge on his enemies. Saul's son Jonathan hadn't heard about it. They were passing through a woods full of honey trees, so Jonathan poked the end of his stick into one of the honeycombs, came out with a gob of honey, and ate it. At once it gave him new energy.

The men told him about his daddy's edict against eating, and Jonathan blew up. "That's just dumb, if he's trying to win a war. See how the honey renewed my energy? An army travels on its stomach. Feed them and they'd be in better shape for battle!"

That day, the half-starved Israelites managed to kick the Philistines' butt and capture a bunch of sheep and livestock, which they promptly butchered and ate without bothering to drain the blood. When Saul got wind of it, he had a fit. "Eating meat with the blood? You're a bunch of sinners and traitors!" Then he built an altar, and had them butcher a bunch more animals the right way.

Next day, Saul asked Yahweh if he would be successful in the next battle, and when he didn't get an answer he decided somebody had sinned. He vowed that if Yahweh granted him victory in the next battle, he would track down the sinner and kill him, no matter who he was.

The Israelites won the battle, and at the inquest it was determined that Jonathan was the sinner because of eating the honey, so Saul was all set to execute his son. But the people said, "No you won't. He's the one who won this victory for us." So Saul gave up the idea, and left off fighting the Philistines for the time being and they went home.

****

Saul went to war with every tribe and nation he could think of, and he always won. One day Samuel told him, "Yahweh wants you to go exterminate the Amalekite people, because their long-ago ancestors opposed the Israelites coming out of Egypt." (*More guilt by association...Yahweh needs no connection between "guilt" and "being personally responsible". Who did it doesn't matter. What happened centuries ago falls directly on the descendants who had nothing to do with it.*) Yahweh's instructions were in the Joshuan mode: Kill everybody, men, women, children, old people, little bitty babies. And kill all the domestic animals too.

So Saul's army went and killed all the people except the king, whom they took captive. And they kept the best livestock, but killed the rest.

When Yahweh got wind of it, he told Samuel, "Saul has disobeyed my wishes, and is no longer fit to be king." Next day, Samuel caught up with Saul, who rushed out and said, "I've carried out the Lord's instruction. Samuel said, "I don't think so; look at all this livestock you didn't kill." Saul said, "Look, I only saved them to make sacrifices to Yahweh." Samuel told him, "The Lord values obedience more than a lousy sacrifice." And he thereupon revoked Saul's charter as king.

(*Moral: When God tells you to kill everybody, kill EVERYBODY. Otherwise God will get mad and punish you.*)

Despite the revoked charter, Saul continued to be in charge. But he was king in name only and needed to be replaced.

Yahweh told Samuel, "There's a guy named Jesse over in Bethlehem who has several sons. Go interview them and see if any is fit to replace Saul as king." Samuel checked them out and decided that the youngest of them, David fit the bill. David was a comely lad in charge of the family sheep, and had also learned how to play the harp. Yahweh said "Anoint him," so Samuel poured the anointing oil on him, and David was certified to be the next king. But they didn't tell anybody about it just yet There was still Saul to deal with, who continued acting like a king.

The tale of David and Saul is one of the most interesting in this book.

The Bible, Chapter 19

The First Book of Samuel
Part 2

SAUL AND DAVID
This saga makes fascinating reading as historical literature. It's amazing that no one has used it as the basis for a play or a movie..

Saul has been decommissioned as king by Samuel (and Yahweh), and David has been quietly anointed to be Saul's eventual successor as king of Israel.

As Saul aged, he began losing his mind ("evil spirits"), with periods of irrational behavior and off-and-on acute paranoia. Young David was recruited to play the harp for Saul during his spells, to help calm him. It seemed to work most of the time. Saul soon took a liking to David, and got Jesse's permission for David to stay with Saul full time. David would play the harp, the evil spirits would depart.

****

The Philistines got to feeling their oats, and decided it was time to make war again. They amassed their troops, and stationed them on a hill overlooking a valley. The Israelites stationed theirs on the hill on the other side of the valley. Then the two sides sat there and looked at one another.

Eventually the Philistines sent out their champion, to dare the Israelites to do something. His name was Goliath of Gath. He was nine feet tall, and wore scale armor that weighed a hundred and twenty-five pounds. His spear shaft was as big as a two by four, and the spear point alone weighed 15 pounds. We're talking big.

Goliath would go out in the valley and dare Saul's army to send a champion against him. "If he kills me, we're your subjects. But If I kill him, you're our meat."

The Israelites dithered around, trying to think of who could stand against him. They decided to appeal to Jesse (David's dad) who has seven other strapping sons, three of whom were seasoned in battle. They were up on the hill with the rest of the army, and young David was sent with a donkey-load of supplies for them. While he was chatting with his brothers, Goliath came out again and roared out his challenge.

The Israelites said, "Look at him! King Saul has promised a ton of money and the hand of his daughter in marriage to anyone who can take him down." David said, "Say that again?" and they told him again. David's brothers started ragging on him for getting into the conversation. "He's only a boy." David blew them off and said, "Never mind. I'll go out and fight him." Saul said "Go ahead, and Yahweh be with you."

They tried to outfit him with armor and a sword, but he wasn't comfortable in them and stuck with his familiar weapon: the sling he used to ward off varmints from his sheep.

Goliath came stomping toward him, hollering his usual threats. David taunted him right back. Then he loaded his sling with a smooth stone and slung it. It hit Goliath between the eyes, and buried itself in his skull. He fell like he was pole-axed. David went over, took Goliath's sword, and cut off his head with it. And that was that.

****

The people sang David's praises, which made Saul jealous, leading to a paranoid delusion that David was out to get him, and that David needs to be killed. Saul's son Jonathan became

David's beloved friend, and saved him from his father's mania on numerous occasions.

At one point, while David is playing his harp, Saul chucks a spear at him trying to kill him. When that fails, Saul sends David off on dangerous military missions, hoping he will be killed in battle. Instead, David is victorious, which makes Saul even more fearful of him.

Saul's daughter Michal had taken a shine to David. When Saul heard of it, he offered her in marriage to David. The price was to be "a hundred Philistine foreskins." David goes out, kills a bunch of Philistines and harvests their foreskins. Then he brings them back to Saul, and marries Michal. (*This conjures an unsettling mental image of David exploring the piles of corpses, pulling out their dicks and nipping off their foreskins. Is that creepy, or what?*)

By the way, since one foreskin is much like the other, we can wonder how David proved to Saul that these were all genuine Philistine foreskins, rather than from some other unfortunate easier-to-kill lads, or maybe just leftovers from local circumcisions.

****

Saul's paranoia continues to grow. He sends assassins off in the night to take care of David; but David, with his wife's help, manages to elude them and hide out. Saul sets out in pursuit, and finds himself at a town in the grip of an epidemic of mass hysteria, one of the earliest reports of such an event, in which the people dance and shout and preach endlessly and uncontrollably. Saul's men, and Saul himself are caught up in it. Eventually, Saul tears off his clothes and collapses naked in the street, where he lies until morning.

Later, Jonathan convinces his father that there's no need to kill David, and Saul, in a period of lucidity, agrees. David returns and all is quiet for a spell. Saul's madness returns and he once again attacks David with a spear. David runs away, and Saul sets out with troops to track him down and kill him.

Various sightings are reported to Saul, who follows them up. However, David manages to stay ahead of him. At one stopping place, David is assisted and given supplies by the local priests. When Saul gets there and hears about it, he flies into a rage and has all of the priests executed.

The pursuit continues for many days, David always managing, with Jonathan's help, to avoid capture. During all this time, David's loyalty to his king never wavers. Saul, in his dementia, sees David as an enemy, whereas the opposite was the case.

Saul interrupts his pursuit of David to go fight the Philistines for a while. When he gets done with that he resumes the hunt. One day he passed the mouth of a cave. He went in to relieve himself then sat down in its entrance to rest in the shade. Unknown to him, David and his servants were hiding further back in the cave.

When David's men saw Saul dozing at the front of the cave, they saw that their luck had turned, and urged David to sneak out and dispatch Saul while he had the chance. David started to do that, but when he got to Saul, he was unwilling to kill his king, and instead of stabbing him he sliced off a piece of Saul's robe and went back into the cave.

Later, when Saul got up and started off, David ran after him and paid him obeisance. He said: you've been claiming that I'm your enemy and that I'm out to get you. But just now I could have killed you if I had wanted to. I was close enough to stab you, but I just cut off this piece of your robe.

When Saul heard and saw this, his reason returned. He agreed that he had acted wrongly, and that David was a loyal subject and had never been his enemy. Then he took his men and turned around and went home. But David didn't accompany him.

That's how this part of the story ends.

The Bible, Chapter 20

The First Book of Samuel
Part 3

*The remainder of **1 Samuel** is no less strange than the earlier parts. Anybody who takes these people as role models has problems.*

...Saul had made peace with David at the cave, but it wasn't going to last. And if you were thinking of David as a nice harp-playing boy, think again. He's grown into a man, and is as ruthless as the rest of them.

David wasn't about to go back to Gibeah where Saul was, so he and his crew of a few hundred men continued to wander the country, getting handouts wherever they could.

****

There was a rich sheep farmer with a lot of land, named Nabal. He had a hot wife named Abigail, but Nabal himself was a foul-tempered scrooge.

David and his crew had been hanging out in Nabal's territory and had made friends with the people that tended the sheep. Because they were low on supplies, David sent his emissaries to visit Nabal, with a polite and obsequious request for any help Nabal might provide for David and his men.

Nabal's reply to David was to Stuff It. He had no idea who David was, and he wasn't about to share any of his goodies with a bunch of vagabond strangers who, for all he knew, might be runaway slaves.

That pissed off David. His polite request had been met with insults, and he wasn't about to take it lying down. In the way of these Bible people, he decided to revenge himself by slaughtering not only Nabal but also his family, servants, and farm hands.

Meanwhile, a servant informed the lovely Abigail that trouble was brewing. He told her David —the one who slew Goliath— had sent messengers with greetings for Nabal but they had been chased away with insults...and the servant feared what the result was going to be.

Abigail, not only beautiful but smart, quickly put together a huge load of supplies, packed it on donkeys, and set out to meet David halfway.

David was fuming about the insult and about killing everybody, when he came upon Abigail's party coming toward him. Abigail said: Please don't take it out on the rest of us for what my stupid husband did. He's a rude old fool, but the rest of us are all good people, not your enemies at all. If you come roaring in and kill everybody, it will simply be murder. You're the future king; don't do evil.

David said: If you hadn't come along and met me, all of your people would be dead, and I would have done an evil thing. But that won't happen now. I'll accept the supplies you've offered, and let Yahweh take care of punishing Nabal. He went on his way.

When Abigail got home, her husband was roaring drunk and had no clue that his wife had just saved his life. In the morning, when he sobered up, she told him everything, which gave him a stroke that left him paralyzed. He died a few days later. *Yahweh had taught HIM a thing or two.*

When David heard Nabal was dead, he promptly claimed the hot widow as a new wife. It's not recorded who was left to run the sheep ranch.

****

Meanwhile, back at Gibeah, we are about to see a re-run of previous events. One of Saul's scouts had found out where David was, so Saul gathered his army and set out to hunt David down and kill him, just as if the business at the cave had never happened.

When he got near David's territory, Saul bivouacked for the night. David learned where they were camped, and with a companion sneaked into Saul's camp late at night when everyone was asleep. They spotted Saul, and the companion says, Let me kill him for you. David said Nope, he still wouldn't kill the king that Yahweh had appointed. Instead, they grabbed Saul's spear and water jug, and beat it back to a safe distance.

David hollered back, You guys aren't very good sentries. I could have killed Saul just now. Saul woke up and said Is that you, David? David said Yes it's me, and why are you still trying to kill me when I'm not your enemy. I could have killed you just now But I didn't, and here's your spear and water jug to prove it.

Hearing this, Saul gave David his blessing, turned his armies around, and went back home. *We have heard this song before. Saul was not a trustworthy person.*

David didn't think so either, so he decided to take his crew and settle in Philisitia, where Saul wouldn't follow him.

Let's get clear about some things. In these stories there are two kinds of people: Israelites, and Everybody Else. The Israelites worshipped Yahweh, the non-Israelites didn't. The two were pretty much at each other's throats all the time. Special enemies of the Israelites were the Philistines and the Amalekites. The enmity with the Amalekites was because of what their ancestors had done to the Israelites' ancestors back in Moses' time.

Going to war with somebody was the main industry of the times, it seemed. But the most common motive had nothing to do with politics or religion. It was pure rapaciousness. The object of the game was to find somebody you thought you could whip, and invade them and kill everybody and take their stuff and burn their cities down.

The Philistines did it to the Israelites; the Israelites did it to the Philistines. Both side believed it was okay to slaughter the other side, because they worshipped the wrong god. Sometimes Israelites did it to other Israelites. Then their justification was simply: They got stuff; we want it.

Genocide isn't a 20th century invention. The *required* procedure, especially among the Children of Israel, when they invaded somebody was to kill everybody: men, women, old folks, little bitty babies, to prevent those people from ever propagating again. The goal was to wipe them from the face of the earth. Because Joshua had said that *Yahweh required it*. It was a practice also followed by Tamerlane, Gengis Khan, and similar historical charmers, as well as you-know-who in modern times.

****

The Philistines were a powerful force, and Saul had the good sense not to invade their territory to get at David. David let on to the Philistines that he was a turncoat who had come over to their side. But that was pretense. David and his men would go on raids into non-Israelite territory, where they would kill everybody and take their stuff. But he told the Philistines he was raiding the Israelites, so they accepted him.

Meanwhile, back at headquarters, Samuel had died and was buried. The Philistines gathered their armies, and prepared to assault Saul's territory, which terrified him. He wasn't sure he was capable of holding them off, so he asked Yahweh what he should do. Yahweh laid low and said nuffin', which frightened Saul even more. He told his people: Go find me a medium that can summon spirits; I'll consult her about what I should do.

They said: Did you forget you chased all the spirit mediums out of the country? But I think there's witch down in Endor that might do. So Saul disguised himself and went to the witch, and she conjured up Samuel's spirit. Saul asked Samuel's spirit what he should do about the Philistines. The spirit told him: It doesn't matter; you're screwed anyway because you disobeyed Yahweh back then, in the matter failing to kill ALL of the Amalekites and their cattle.

This laid Saul prostrate and ineffectual, in no shape to conduct a defense against the Philistines.

Meanwhile, back with the Philistines, they asked David if he would join them in their attack on Saul. He said: You bet! but the other kings said Wait a minute: We don't want no turncoat Israelite in our attack. He might be a spy. So they sent David home. When he got there, he found that his town had been raided by a band of Amalekites, who had taken all the people captive and grabbed all the stuff and burned the town.

Here, I need to depart from the narrative and comment. Earlier in this book, Saul had exterminated all of the Amalekites except for their king (whom he later sliced & diced) and their best cattle. So there shouldn't have been any Amalekites around later, to raid David's town. Either they arose, like the phoenix, from their own ashes, or the narrator goofed somewhere along the line. I'm betting on the latter.

Anyhow, David went out and found the raiders and killed them all and took back his stuff, along with other stuff they had, and shared it among his men.

Back at the battle lines, the Philistines were trouncing Saul's army and killing everybody. Saul got wounded, and his sons were killed. Saul told his attendant: Take your sword and kill me, so these damned Philistines can't have the satisfaction of doing it. But the kid was too terrified to do it, so Saul took his own sword, pointed it at his breast, and fell on it. The attendant did the same.

When the Philistines found Saul's corpse, they chopped off its head and nailed the rest of it to the city wall. Eventually, some people on the Israelite side rescued the body, and gave it a decent cremation. Later, they dug the bones out of the ashes and buried them.

That brings us, finally, to the end of the First Book of Samuel (who is now dead, along with Saul, Nabal, and a lot of unnamed citizens).

The Bible, Chapter 21

The Second Book of Samuel
Part 1

We are now up to the second book of Samuel (who already died in the first book). In it, we continue to learn what an unpleasant person David is. We also encounter a certain anomaly in the tale.

Among David's other flaws is his cluelessness. Especially in his continuing respect for the guy who's trying to kill him. On two occasions he's had the opportunity to take out Saul, who was trying to kill David, because he wouldn't kill "a king who had been anointed by Yahweh." But Saul's charter as king had been revoked and annulled by Samuel, before David got the anointing oil poured on him. Which is how David came to be the potential king. And if he didn't know that, it was willful ignorance.

The book starts with David's getting word of Saul's death in the battle with the Philistines. A young man, who turns out to be an Amalekite, shows up at David's camp with word that Saul and his sons have died. David asks if he's sure Saul is dead. The kid says, Saul was mortally wounded, and didn't want to have been killed by the Philistines; so he asked me to kill him, and I did. Then I took his royal jewelry and brought it to you. David promptly has the kid executed, for killing "the one Yahweh had chosen to be king", even though Saul had begged him to do it. *The ways of David are inscrutable.*

Let us remember that in **1Samuel**, Saul had died by his own hand by falling on his sword, after his aide refused to do it for him. Now we have him dying after an Amalekite kid agrees to do it for him. Those who proclaim that every word in the Bible is true must therefore agree that Saul was killed twice. His revival between killings is not recorded.

David then asked Yahweh where he ought to settle and was told to go to Hebron, a city in Judah. David went there, and before long was made king of Judah.

****

And now we have to pause for a bit of back story, which I just HAD to go look up in order to try to make sense of things.

The first thing to know is that the territory of the Israelites consisted of two parts, united by a common worship of Yahweh, but separated by certain political and sectarian differences. The northern, larger portion, was the territory of Israel. The smaller, southern portion, was the territory of Judah. In the days before there were kings, when ruling was managed by tribal chieftains or "Judges", neither side had a central government. They were simply loose confederations of tribes. When Saul came along and took over as king, he brought central governance to the northern territory of Israel, which became the Kingdom of Israel under his rule.

Judah still had no king to unify it, and remained a loose tribal confederation...until David came along. As he rose to power, the people of Judah came to accept him as their king, and Judah became the Kingdom of Judah. There were then two Israelite kingdoms, each with aspirations to become the kingdom of all the Israelites, not just of their half. That's where we're at, at the beginning of **2 Samuel.**

The second thing to know, and the most striking, is the incredible smallness of the territory we are talking about. All of these adventures, wars, kingdoms, etc. take place in an area

ISRAEL and...

California

Maps drawn to same scale. Israel shown in blue.

Information Regarding Israel's Security
http://www.iris.org.il

smaller than one of California's larger counties.

The promised land of the Children of Israel, the scene of almost all of the early Old Testament action, was the narrow strip of land between the River Jordan and the Mediterranean Sea...a rough trapezoid about 200 miles long, 80 miles wide at its widest southern end tapering to 20 miles wide at its narrowest northern end. A few surrounding non-Israelite kingdoms that figure in the narrative —Moab, Edom, Ammon— add to the total area. But the actual land of the Israelites was just that narrow strip. It was smaller than modern-day Israel by a third, since today's Israel includes a large chunk of what was then Egypt. Modern Israel is about 8000 square miles in area. The biblical land would have been a fraction of that ...about 6000 square miles, roughly equivalent to a rectangle 100 miles long and 60 miles wide. Some of the minor "kingdoms" were no more than a few square miles. And the distances between the places were correspondingly small, measured in terms of a few hours' or a few days' journey on foot. This is the area that these Books are about.

============

The King of Israel, Saul, was now dead, so his son Ishbosheth became Israel's new king. A conference was called between the two kings, which didn't turn out well. A duel between champions from the two sides ended in a draw, so the two armies engaged in battle and the armies of Judah kicked the Israelite butt. Israel's top general was Abner, who retreated in the face of defeat, but was pursued until he found some allies to protect him. He hollered over at David, Do we have to keep fighting each other like this? We're all a common people, and nothing is to be gained by fighting. David pretended to agree, and turned his troops around. But the wars continued on, with David taking the upper hand.

One day Ishbosheth accused his general Abner of getting it on with one of the king's concubines. Abner was outraged at the accusation, and promptly defected to David's side. He told David, Make me a deal and I'll help you defeat the Israelite side.

126

David said, "Here's the deal: Bring me back my wife, Saul's daughter Michel. I paid a hundred Philistine foreskins for her, and she's mine."

Remember now, David had abandoned Michel from the get-go. It's not clear their marriage was ever consummated. When David deserted her, she had become another man's wife and had been his wife for years. David's demand was pure spite. Michel had done nothing to harm David, and neither had her husband. He was just being nasty. And he already had several wives. Michel was heartbroken at leaving her husband, but that mattered not to ol' Dave. He got his way.

Abner joined David's forces and was guaranteed safe passage by David. But some of David's men, not knowing of it, killed Abner. When David heard of it, he went into a funk that lasted days. He had the killers' hands and feet cut off, to show his displeasure.

When the Israelite king Ishbosheth heard of Abner's assassination, he went into hiding. But some of David's men found him, cut off his head, and carried it back to David to show him that the opposing king was dead. Did that please David? It did not. It pissed him off, because Ishbosheth was the "son of Saul, who was the anointed etc. etc." *The ways of David are inscrutable.*

But anyhow, with the Israelite kingship vacant, David grabbed it and was now king of Judah **and** Israel.

David decided to move the Ark of the Covenant from Hebron north to Jerusalem, because it was more centrally located. So they loaded it on a cart and started off. On the way, the cart hit a bump and the Ark started to tumble off. A poor mope named Uzzah kept it from falling, and was promptly struck dead by Yahweh for daring to touch the sacred box. One may wonder whom Yahweh would have smitten if the box had fallen off and smashed.

Never try to figure out what's going to annoy Yahweh. There is no pattern.

Then a bunch of stuff happened that I'm not going to try to relate.

****

David went to war with the Philistines again, and whupped them. Then he went to war with the Moabites and whupped them. He made them all prisoners, made them lie on the ground, and killed two out of every three, just because he could.

Then he went to war with some Syrians, and defeated them, capturing 1,700 horsemen and 20,000 foot soldiers. He kept a hundred of the horses, and hamstrung the rest, leaving them to die in screaming agony. Just because he could, I suppose.

When some reinforcements showed up to help the Syrians, David's men killed 22,000 of them, leaving the land littered with rotting corpses.

With all the thousands being killed in all these battles, the population density of this tiny territory must have been way up there, to keep supplying victims.

David then invaded the territory of Edom, killed 18,000 of them, and set up occupation outposts to show who was boss.

Then there's some stuff about the late Ishbosheth's club-footed son Maphibosheth that I won't go into.

Then there's a long detailed account of David's campaign against the Ammonites and the Syrians, which ended with David's men killing 40,000 horsemen, plus others.

And that's enough bloodletting, for now. So far, David has killed 102,760 men, plus 2/3 of the Moabites. And we're only though **2 Samuel:10.** David's own casualties are not recorded.

128

The Bible, Chapter 22

The Second Book of Samuel,
Part 2

Bathsheba

We resume here with what may be the most sordid episode in King David's unlovely career.

David was looking down from the rooftop, and spotted a young hottie taking a bath. "Who's that?" he asked, and was told it was Bathsheba, the wife of Uriah the Hittite. "Wife, schmife," said David. "I want her. Go bring her here." So they brought her, and he spent the night going in unto her and sent her home in the morning pregnant, though they didn't know that for a while. She had just finished her period the day before David got into her, so she wouldn't have suspected pregnancy until she missed her next one a month later. One imagines that David went in unto her frequently during that time.

The discovery of her condition presented a problem: husband Uriah had been away in the wars for a long time, and hadn't gone in unto his wife for a long time, so you can see the difficulty. If it became known that Bathsheba was an adulteress, she would have been stoned to death, and David didn't want that. So he quickly sent word to the front for Uriah to be sent home (so he would go in unto his wifey, and never suspect the child wasn't his). But when Uriah got back, he wouldn't go to his home as David urged him to do. He thought it would be unseemly for him to be enjoying the comforts of home and the marital bed while his comrades were still out there fighting and dying in the wars. So instead he stayed and slept by the city gates.

David then decided on a strategem tried unsuccessfully on him by Saul a few years back: send Uriah off to be killed in battle. Uriah was sent back to the front, and a message was sent to general Joab to make sure that Uriah didn't survive the next battle. And he didn't. This time it worked.

When word got back of Uriah's death, David waited until Bathsheba was done mourning, then added her to his harem.

All of this didn't sit well with Yahweh, who decided that David had to be punished for his misdeeds.

You may remember that some poor dude had been stoned to death just for gathering firewood on that sabbath, and that Yahweh had smote another guy dead just for keeping the Ark of the Covenant from falling over and smashing, so we can imagine that David's punishment for prolonged adultery (a capital offense according to Leviticus, though it's not clear that applied to men), and murder-by-proxy would be something pretty severe.

So here's how Yahweh punished David: he sent all of David's wives out into the street, and had a local dude come and copulate with all of them, in public, where everybody could watch, whether the wives were willing to be copulated with by him or not.

Take that! David!

To strengthen the punishment, Yahweh made David's son (by Bathsheba) get sick, and then sicker, and sicker. After many days of suffering, the child died. David's response wasn't grief, but "Well, that's that." He went home and took a bath and had dinner.

Take that! David!

Yahweh had now punished David by making his son suffer in a fever and die, and by turning his wives into a porn sideshow for the amusement of passers by. Somehow, it looks like the instruments of Yahweh's punishment ended up worse off than the one who was being punished. *The ways of Yahweh are unfathomable.*

****

By and by Bathsheba bore David another son, which he named Solomon but which Yahweh named Jedediah, just to confuse things.

Meanwhile, David had sired a ton of other sons and daughters by various different wives. And thereby hangs another sordid tale.

Absalom and Amnon were half-brothers, and Tamar was Absalom's sister, all part of David's progeny. Amnon developed a raging desire to Go In Unto his half-sister Tamar, but figured there was no chance to get into her pants, since virgins were kept away from male company. However, he and a sneaky friend came up with a plan to get him alone with her, so's he could ravish her.

Amnon then pretended to be sick in bed, and asked his father David to make Tamar come over and bake him some cookies. When the cookies were done, he sent everybody away and asked Tamar to come into the bedroom and feed them to him herself.

Once she was in the bedroom, he said "Hey sister; climb into this bed and Let's Do It." Tamar was having none of that and protested mightily; so Amnon just slapped her down on the bed and went in unto her by force. Once he had gotten his rocks off, he became disgusted with her, and told the servants to throw this woman out of the house and lock the door. Amnon was a man of low character.

Tamar, no longer a virgin, went over and moved in to live with her brother Absalom. When David learned of the matter, he was angry. But Absalom was more than angry...

Two years later, Absalom threw a sheep-shearing party and

invited all of his brothers and half-brothers (including Amnon) to attend. "Revenge is a dish best served cold," somebody once said, and it was about to be served here. Absalom told his men, "When Amnon gets good and drunk, I'll give the signal and you kill him. Nobody will blame you, because it's at my orders." So Amnon got good and drunk, and Absalon gave the signal, and his men killed Amnon for raping Absalom's sister, and that was that.

Absalom headed for the hills. Everybody else climbed on their mules and headed home. Meanwhile, David received a garbled message that Absalom had killed ALL of his brothers and half-brothers, which put David into a funk. But his nephew soon set him straight: nobody had been killed except Amnon, and that was revenge for the violation of Tamar. David mourned for Amnon, but soon got over it and started wishing he could see his son Absalom, who was in hiding in another country.

The Bible, Chapter 23

The Second Book of Samuel,
Part 3

We continue the history of David's tortured career and his shifting motivations and priorities, reflecting a lack of any clear guiding principles on his part. David is coming off as a clueless vacillating twit. One begins to suspect Yahweh's judgment in selecting kings for his Chosen People. First, the dysfunctional Saul. Next, ol' David.

Earlier on, David had been the valiant warrior and leader of his men into battle. At this point in his career, his job is to sit back and watch while his faithful Joab commands the troops and conducts the battles.

To reprise: Absalom killed his half-brother Amnon in revenge for raping his (Absalom's) sister. Then Absalom headed for the hills, fearing the wrath of his father, King David. David might not care for the avenging of the rape of one of his daughters by one of his sons.

****

The catalog of lying, mood-shifts,, and betrayals continues.

After David got over being concerned about his son Amnon's death, he started longing to see his dear son Absalom again. Whether he wanted him back to kiss him or to kill him is not made clear.

David's faithful go-to guy (and commander of the armies) Joab works a stratagem to get David to promise not to kill Absalom if he comes back. David finally promises, but he says, "I never want to see him again."

134

After a couple of years back in Jerusalem, Absalom wangles an audience with David. Absalom bows, David kisses him, and you'd suppose that all is well again between them. Think again. Absalom has it in mind to get rid of David, and replace him as king.

Absalom is put in charge of the troops guarding the city gates. As soon as he has some soldiers under his command, and the power as gatekeeper, he starts to curry favor and gain supporters among those who pass through. After several years biding his time, Absalom sets off with his men on a trip to Hebron, further down in Judah, where he has arranged for the people there to proclaim him king. Meanwhile, he'd sent messengers to all of the tribes up in Israel, announcing that Absalom had been made king down in Hebron. This put most of the land of Israel on Absalom's side.

When David got word of the insurrection, and realized the strength of Absalom's support, he got nervous and headed for the hills, in fear that Absalom would soon be coming after him. He left ten of his girlfriends to watch over Jerusalem.

Since Absalom was down south in Judah, David headed north into Israelite territory, where he had a mixed reception. A guy named Ziba befriended him, and provided supplies for David and his men. Another guy named Shimei threw rocks at him, and cursed him for stealing Saul's kingdom. One of David's men wanted to kill him, but David said: Leave him alone: Yahweh told him to do it. *Remember that for later.*

While David was getting his act together up in Israelite territory, putting together an army of Judeans, Absalom down in Judah marched on Jerusalem and took over the city. His advisers told him, "To convince the people that you really are David's enemy, why don't you have a public show and Go In Unto these girlfriends of his that he left in charge?" Absalom thought that was a wonderful idea, so they set up a tent on the palace roof and the people came to watch Absalom do it with David's women.

135

This supposedly greatly encouraged Absalom's followers.

Absalom then continued up into Israelite territory, to do battle with David's forces. As the battle became imminent, David, in another lapse of judgment, told his warriors "Be sure not to harm Absalom. After all, he IS my son." David never was very good at distinguishing between his enemies and his allies.

The two sides met in battle, and David's army of Judeans whupped Absalom's army of Israelites. Absalom took off riding on a mule. As he rode under an oak tree, his head caught in the crotch of a low-hanging branch, and left him dangling while the mule departed.
One of David's soldiers ran and told general Joab, "Absalom's hanging in a tree over there, and we don't know what to do." Joab said, "For crying out loud, why didn't you kill him?" The guy said, "Because David said he wasn't to be harmed."

Joab, who always had David's best interests at heart, even if it occasionally meant disobeying him, said "Bah!" and speared Absalom through the chest, then had his men finish him off in case that hadn't killed him.

When David learned of Absalom's death, he flew into a paroxysm of grief, screeching "Oh Absalom! My son Absalom!?" Joab came up to him and said, "You idiot! Do you have a clue about what's going on? Absalom was your ENEMY! He was out to kill you and take over your kingdom. Your soldiers have been fighting and dying to protect you from him, and you mourn over their success! Do you have any idea how demoralizing and humiliating that is? You turn against those who support you, and support those who hate you. Go make amends and reassure your troops, or by tomorrow you won't have a soldier left!"

For once, David took some good advice, and did it.

The people of Israel started saying: We accepted Absalom for our king, but David kicked his butt. Now we'd like to have

David for our king again.

This, oddly, put David into a snit. Instead of being pleased, he complained "Why are these Israelites the first to reclaim me as their king, instead of my own people of Judah?" So he sent emissaries to Judah to correct the matter. To cement the deal, he demoted his longtime supporter Joab and put one Amasa, a Judean, in charge of his armies. *Showing once again his insensitivity to what was what.*

Joab, after his long service to David, didn't take that lightly.

During all these shenanigans there is very little mention of Yahweh. We assume he was willing to sit back and watch, and let things take their course, rather than jumping in as in the past, and determining outcomes and punishing transgressions.

The Bible, Chapter 24

The Second Book of Samuel
Part 4

The Judean faction and the Israelite faction took to quarreling over which of them had the strongest claim to King David. The Judeans managed to shout down the Israelites, which pissed them off. Then a scumbag Benjaminite named Sheba blew his horn to get everybody's attention, and hollered "To hell with David. We aren't going to follow him any more. Let's all go home." The Israelite faction thought that was a good idea, so they took off, leaving the Judeans as David's army to accompany him to Jerusalem.

As soon as he got home he rounded up the ten girls he had left in charge, the ones that Absalom had publicly gone in unto, and sequestered them in a nunnery for the rest of their lives. HE wasn't going to go in unto anyone that Absalom had gone in unto, and by golly neither could anybody else.

Then he decided something needed to be done about Sheba, so he sent Amasa, his newly appointed general in charge, to go assemble the Judean troops and "be back here with them by day after tomorrow." But Amasa failed to show up at the specified time, so David put together another plan.

He got together the soldiers that were there, along with his personal bodyguards, and sent them out under Joab's leadership to try to hunt down Sheba. Before long, they ran into Amasa, coming with the rest of the troops. Joab said to Amasa, "Come over here old friend, and let me greet you." Amasa came over, Joab seized him by the beard as if to kiss him, then disemboweled him with a dagger in his left hand. That took care of that. Joab was back in command of the army. It is not recorded what David thought of this change of leadership. Or whether he cared.

They tracked Sheba to a walled city, and laid siege to it, battering its walls. A lady hollered down, "Hey! Why are you trying to destroy our city? We've done nothing to you." Joab replied, "We're not after your city; we're after a guy named Sheba who's taken refuge here." The lady said, "Just a minute." They rounded up Sheba, removed his head, and tossed it over the wall to Joab. With that settled, Joab took his armies home.

By and by, Yahweh decided his chosen people needed a famine, so he sent them one that lasted three years. David finally asked Yahweh, "What has anybody done to deserve this?" and was told, "Blame it on Saul. He had his people kill the Gibeonites, even though they had been promised amnesty. That made it murder; so I'm punishing all of Saul's descendants for it, plus everybody currently living in what was once his kingdom, with this here famine."

David convened the people of Gibeon and told them, "Yahweh is punishing everybody for what Saul did to your ancestors. What can we do to make amends, and get him off our backs?" They said, "Send us seven of Saul's male descendants. We'll kill them, and call it good." So they rounded up seven sons and grandsons of Saul and turned them over to the Gibeonites, who hanged them on the hillside and called it good. *This, in the Bible, is what passes for justice: People who have done nothing wrong need to be punished for what one of their relatives did a long time ago.* It satisfied Yahweh, who lifted the famine and was no doubt praised for his goodness.

****

The final chapter of this book is one that makes absolutely no sense.

At some later time, for unspecified reasons (*the ways of Yahweh are inscrutable*), Yahweh again got mad at Israel for something or other, so he directed David to teach them a lesson by conducting a census of all the people of Israel and Judah. This was supposed to be a hardship on the people, as punishment for whatever it was that annoyed Yahweh about them.

Unless the census takers used some draconian procedures we aren't told of, it's a mystery to me how "being counted" constitutes a hardship. But that's what it says.

When David told Joab to round up a posse and go count all the tribes of Israel and Judah, Joab protested "What in the world for? What's put this bee in your bonnet to find out how many people there are in your territory?" David told him, Never mind, just do it. So Joab went off and did it.

Nine months and twenty days later, he got back to Jerusalem and gave his report: There were 800,000 men capable of military service in Israel, and 500,000 in Judah. Note, as before, that the census makes no mention of women, children, or old people. Joab apparently didn't consider them as relevant to his job. They only come into consideration when it's time to kill everybody and take their stuff.

No sooner had he received the report than David's conscience smote him, and he said unto Yahweh,"Oh Lord I have sinned greatly in that I have done; and now I beseech thee, take away the iniquity of thy servant; for I have done very foolishly."

If you are like me, you will at this point say What!? *Taking a census is a great sin? In the first place, Yahweh had* TOLD *him to go take the census. He only did it because Yahweh was peeved at Israel and made David "punish" them by counting them. So doing Yahweh's bidding was a very great sin? To the best of my memory, there's nothing in Leviticus or anywhere else forbidding census-taking. When Yahweh commanded Moses to take a census of his people, back in the book of Numbers, Moses pulled it off with nary a recrimination. What's suddenly so bad about counting people when David does it? Trace it, perhaps, to Yahweh's moods. He can make up new sins whenever he feels like it.*

Yahweh agreed that David needed to pay for his grievous sin, and offered him three different punishments to choose from.
1. Seven years of famine for Israel.
2. Three months of running from his enemies.
3. Three days of pestilence in the land.

Two of these consist of "punishing David" by killing a lot of other people. Only number 2 would directly affect David...he'd have to do a lot of fleeing, with the certainty that at the end of 3 months he would not have gotten caught. Which one, in David's wisdom, would he choose?

David chose number 3. "Let the Lord himself be the one to punish us, for he is merciful." Note "punish US", even though David was the only transgressor. So Yahweh sent a lethal epidemic, overseen by an Angel, that lasted just three days but killed seventy thousand Israelites. Thus reflecting Yahweh's mercy.

There would have been more casualties, but just as the Angel was about to blight Jerusalem, Yahweh suddenly felt remorseful for what he had done, and told the Angel, "Stop. You've killed enough." So the Angel went away, and Jerusalem was saved. Yahweh's feeling remorse is quite out of character with everything we've seen of him so far. Still, apparently the remorse wasn't strong enough for him to bring the pestilence to an end just yet.

David hurried and bought the land where the Angel had last been seen, and built an altar there, and held burnt sacrifices and offerings to Yahweh. "So the lord was intreated for the land, and the plague was [finally] stayed from Israel." The burnt offerings did the trick.

Thus ends the strangely named **Second Book of Samuel**, who had died before the book even started.

And we end up with 70,000 Israelites dead of the plague as punishment because David followed Yahweh's orders to conduct a census

And with Amasa's entrails spilled on the ground through treachery, so that Joab could get his old job back.

And with a nation starved by famine, and seven people hanged, for something somebody else did.

And with ten of Absalom's rape victims banished from society for what was done to them.

These are the lessons learned from this book of the Bible.

The Bible, Chapter 25

The First Book of Kings

In this book we find out how Solomon managed to become king, and what **"the wisest man in creation"** did to deserve his title.

I must say, as a preface, that these bible people seem to have no moral sensibilities, and no moral principles, at all. They just do stuff.

We begin with David in his extreme old age. His servants couldn't keep him warm with blankets, so they decided to find a young virgin to snuggle up to him and keep him warm. Who they found was a young hottie named Abishag. She became his caretaker nurse and bedmate-warmer, but he never went in unto her. One might suppose his age had something to do with that.

Since David was fixing to die before long, the question of succession loomed large. His eldest surviving son was named Adonijah, and since he was eldest, he decided he had a right to be the next king.

He had a couple of supporters: Joab, the long-time commander of the armies, and Abiathar, an important priest. However, most of David's cabinet were against the idea. These included Zadok (a priest), Nathan (a prophet), Beniah (a hit-man), plus others along with David's personal guard. *Remember these names.*

Adonijah decided to seal the deal by getting himself anointed by Abiathar as king-to-be, so he threw a big anointing party and invited most of his brothers and half-brothers, and most of the officials of the realm. But he didn't invite any of David's cabinet, and he didn't invite his half-brother Solomon. *To the best of my memory, this is the first mention we've had of Solomon since his birth was announced, shortly after David had scragged Uriah in order to marry his wife.*

When Bathsheba heard about Adonijah, she went to David and said, "Hey! Do you remember you promised that my son Solomon would be your successor?" David agreed. Then she told him what Adonijah was up to. David summoned his cabinet and told them to mount Solomon on David's own mule, hustle him down to a special place and anoint him king of Israel. So they did, and then blew horns and made loud noises on their way back, proclaiming the anointing of the next king.

When word got to Adonijah, the party broke up in a hurry and Adonijah headed for safety. He ended up at the altar of Yahweh which had a horn projecting from each of its four corners, and anyone was safe from being killed so long as he held onto the horns. *Or so everybody thought.*

They dragged Adonijah away from the altar and put him before the king. David told him to go on home, and that seemed to be the end of it. It wasn't.

Later, on his deathbed, David called in Solomon and told him there were a couple of pieces of unfinished business he wanted Solomon to take care of after he, David, was gone. **Number 1**: Have Joab assassinated. **Number 2**: See to it that Shimei (the guy who had cursed him and then repented) was executed.

Let's take these one at a time. Joab had served David faithfully as commander of his armies throughout the thirty years David reigned over Israel. He had always acted in what he felt was David's best interest, even if it sometimes meant disobeying one of David's stupider orders. Nobody had served David better during his lifetime. So why did David want him punished with death?

To understand his **excuse**, we need to go back to an incident many years before. Go back to when David was battling the armies of Saul's successor under their commanding general Abner. Saul's army had been defeated, and Joab with two of his brothers were chasing after Abner to kill him. Abner kept hollering back, "Stop chasing me so I don't have to kill you." When they kept on, Abner flung his spear over his shoulder and skewered the lead brother, killing him dead.

Some time later, Abner defected from the Saul side and came over to join David. David accepted him and gave him a guarantee of safety. Joab didn't like that, and first chance he got, he murdered Abner, avenging the death of his brother.

This 30-year old event was the reason David gave for the delayed death sentence against Joab: Joab had "killed innocent men" and needed to pay for it.

That's what David said, but I don't buy it for a minute. If David felt that justice required Joab be punished for the murder of Abner, why didn't he administer it at the time? Instead, he continued to rely on Joab to lead his armies for the rest of his life. Only when he was dying did he dust off this old offense and claim that, now, Joab had to die for it.

But that doesn't hold water. The only real reason had to be that *Joab had favored another of David's sons to succeed him as king*, and it pissed David off. David felt no sense of obligation, or even gratitude, for Joab's long service to him: "Solomon, once you're king, get rid of him. He favored your brother. But it'll look better if you pretend it's punishment for a decades-old crime." *That's how these Bible people operate.*

Next, there's Shimei, and a testimony to the worthlessness of David's promises. Back during the Absalom rebellion, David took refuge up in Israelite territory, where Shimei cursed him and threw rocks at him "for stealing Saul's kingdom". At the time, David's guards wanted to whack Shimei, but David pardoned him, saying Yahweh probably told him to do it.

Some time later, at a Jordan crossing, Shimei met David,

apologized for what he had done, and begged forgiveness. David granted it, giving his word that Shimei wouldn't be put to death.

Now, on his deathbed, David says, "I know I gave him my word. But after all, he can't be allowed to get a way with what he did, so after I'm gone, make sure he's gets executed." *That's how these Bible people operate.*

What we learn from these passages is that promises, and years of faithful service, don't mean diddly.

■■

{The Bible is the best of all books, for it is the word of God and teaches us the way to be happy in this world and in the next. Continue therefore to read it and to regulate your life by its precepts. ——John Jay, first Chief Justice of the U.S. Supreme Court.}

The Bible, Chapter 26

The First Book of Kings
part 2

David died, and Solomon became king. First thing, he set about exterminating all possible opposition. The principals were his half-brother Adonijah, who had failed at gaining the throne, and Adonijah's two supporters, Joab the military leader and Abiathar the priest.

Adonijah needed to be gotten rid of first, and any excuse would do. It arrived when the crestfallen Adonijah came to Bathsheba with a simple request: ask her son's permission for Adonijah to marry the lovely Abishag, who had been David's nursemaid and companion.

When Solomon heard the request, he pitched a hissy-fit and screeched "Marry Abishag? Why doesn't he ask for the throne as well? Where does he get off making a request like that? He shall be punished." He then sent Beniah the hit man to snuff Adonijah, which took care of one of the three.

Next was Abiathar. Solomon told him, "Get out of here and go back to your country home. I ought to kill you; but I won't because you served my father well." Abiathar quickly got out of there. That took care of the second one.

When Joab heard about Abiathar, he figured he would be next so he ran to Yahweh's compound and took hold of the horns of the altar, as protection against being killed. Solomon heard that Joab was holed up at the altar, and sent a messenger demanding to know why he had gone there. Which was a stupid and pointless question, because the answer was obvious: to protect himself from Solomon.

Solomon already had his excuse to kill Joab: the deathbed promise made to David. So he sent Beniah the hit man over to the altar where Joab was holding out, to tell him "Solomon wants you to come out." Joab replied, "Not a chance," so Beniah said "Altar, schmaltar," and killed him right there gripping the horns, showing that divine sanctuary doesn't always work. That took care of the third one.

The one remaining bit of leftover business was Shimei, the curser and rock-thrower. David had promised he would never be killed, so Solomon figured a way to get around it. He told Shimei that as long as he stayed inside the Jerusalem city limits, nobody would kill him; but if he wandered outside, he was toast. Solomon then bided his time.

A few years down the road, Shimei unwisely went over to the neighboring township to retrieve a couple of runaway slaves. When he got back, Solomon told him —no doubt "more in sorrow than in anger" — "You knew the rules and broke them, so this is your own fault." He then had Beniah go do the dirty work, and that was that. Another biblical hero had cleared the way for further biblical heroism.

Meanwhile, Solomon was vigorously practicing his religion, offering hundreds of sacrifices at the main altar. In response, Yahweh came to him in a dream and asked, "What can I do for you?"

Solomon: "Give me the wisdom to rule with justice and to know the difference between good and evil," clearly confirming that, at that point he didn't understand the concepts.

Yahweh: "Because you asked for wisdom instead of riches, I'll give you more wisdom than anybody ever had or ever will. And because you asked nicely, I'll give you the riches as a bonus." It's worth observing that "knowledge of good and evil" was what got Adam and Eve busted out of the garden of Eden; yet here Yahweh was handing it out for free. *The ways of Yahweh are inscrutable.*

Thus Solomon became the wisest man the world would ever see...and also one of the wealthiest. We would soon see his wisdom at work. It is illustrated in the case of cutting the baby in two.

Two women were disputing over ownership of a baby. Woman #1 said, "Woman #2's own baby died, so she stole mine and I want him back." Woman #2 said, "She lies. Her baby died and now she wants mine. This baby is mine and I intend to keep him."

Solomon grabbed a sword and said, "No problem. We'll cut the baby in two and each of you can have half." Woman #2 said, "When you split it, I get to pick my half." Woman #1 said, "No! Don't harm the baby. Give him to Woman #2!" Solomon then said, "Woman #1 has shown that she is the real mother of the baby; give him to her." And the people of Israel marveled at Solomon's wisdom in deciding the case.

The Bible, Chapter 27

The First Book of Kings
part 3

King Solomon, continued

Besides baby-splitting, Solomon had a better head on his shoulders for organization and governing than his daddy ever did. David had trouble keeping the kingdoms of Israel and Judah from making war with each other. Solomon achieved a union of the two by sending out regional governors to keep the various tribes away from each others' throats, so the kingdom as a whole could prosper in peace.

He also set up a regular system of tithing, so the various tribes could each do their part to keep the royal court supplied and fed...which was not cheap. The DAILY requirement was several hundred bushels of grain plus 150 or so head of cattle & sheep, which over the year added up to over 50,000 meat animals and a gazillion tons of grain. The royal court was well fed.

Another difference between the two kings is that David apparently had little desire for finery and riches and goodies, while Solomon had an unquenchable thirst for them. By squeezing tribute out of his own tribes, and the surrounding kingdoms, he quickly made himself filthy rich.

Solomon was said to be the wisest man in the world, more or less. His reported wisdom was massive, and widely recognized. As evidence of his wisdom, he composed several thousand proverbs and songs, and was an authority in the fields of botany and zoology. Mention of these accomplishments seem to be equating talent and knowledge with wisdom, but in those days they apparently didn't know the difference. Solomon was the Goethe of his day.

During David's time, the tent housing Yahweh and the Ark of the

Covenant was constantly being moved around because of the wars going on . Now that Solomon had a stable and peaceful kingdom, he decided that Yahweh ought to have a fancier permanent dwelling than a tent, namely a temple. So he set about building it, with a level of opulence and magnificence pleasing to any god with the same lavish tastes as Solomon. Yahweh wasn't consulted in the matter, but in the end he seemed to be pleased. An interesting theological revision takes place about this time, which we'll get to in a little while.

The Yahweh tent setup had two main chambers: a large outer tent defining a holy space, and within it a smaller tent defining an even holier space, where Yahweh dwelt with the Ark of the Covenant: the chest containing the stone tablets of Moses.

Likewise, the temple had a main room corresponding to the outer tent, and a smaller room within it corresponding to the inner tent. Except these were bigger than the tent, and built out of imported materials, and gussied up with all kinds of valuable metals and trinkets. There are detailed descriptions of the building and furnishing of the temple, but they are boring and if you want to know about them, read for yourself.

It took Solomon seven years to complete this majestic dwelling for Yahweh, who would no longer be stuck in a nomadic tent existence. (About this time, Solomon was building a palace for himself which was even bigger and fancier than the temple. It took thirteen years to build that one.)

When the temple was finished, Solomon assembled the leaders of the various tribes to participate in the ceremony of moving the Ark of the Covenant from the tent in David's city of Zion to the temple in Jerusalem. The tent and its equipment were also moved to the temple, presumably to serve as a backup, in case of emergency.

The place of the Ark in the inner sanctum was guarded by a couple of golden cherubim or "cherubs", which weren't the chubby little cupids you're probably thinking of. These were more like big winged lions or sphinxes, with wings that extended above the Ark to protect it.

After the Ark was positioned properly and the priests were leaving, Yahweh put in a personal appearance. The place was suddenly filled with clouds, "so that the priests could not stand to minister...for the glory of the Lord had filled the house of the Lord."

Solomon then gave a speech, to the effect that Yahweh had chosen to live in darkness, so he, Solomon, had constructed a permanent location for his, Yahweh's abode, and for the tablets of Moses.

When the speech was over, Solomon took to praying, and prayed a mighty prayer which includes the aforementioned theological revision:

As Solomon describes Yahweh, he is not the earthly god who walked and talked with Adam and Eve, and who abides in the holy of holies along with the Ark. The god that Solomon describes is more like the transcendent god people talk about nowadays, who is not of the earth but is everywhere and nowhere. Solomon blows off what his people have believed ever since the first tabernacle tent was built: It's holy because it's a dwelling place for the god of Moses.

Says Solomon to Yahweh: "I know you can't really dwell on earth; even heaven and the heaven of heavens can't contain you...but we'll say you live in heaven since you have to be someplace. You certainly don't live here in the room with the Ark. But please look favorably on this temple anyway, and we'll use it as a place of worship from which to direct our prayers to you." The prayer then goes on and on with the usual stuff, begging Yahweh to be good to him and his people.

But this theological shift looks like the first step along the path of apostasy that will eventually lead to Solomon's downfall. It's not clear that Solomon is even talking about the god of Moses. It implies that the "holy" places within the tent, and now within the temple, never were really holy by virtue of the actual presence of Yahweh in them. But if not that, then what? Were they holy at all? Generations of Jews had been deceived on the matter, until the wisdom of Solomon came along to set them straight? If the priests picked up on what Solomon was saying, it couldn't have set well with them.

After the prayer was done, there was a big temple-dedicating party where 22,000 cattle and 120,000 sheep were sacrificed. The party lasted for a week, and everybody went home satisfied.

Shortly thereafter, Yahweh paid another visit to Solomon. He told him that he liked the temple, and that he would watch over it and protect it, so long as Solomon remained faithful to him. But if Solomon ever deviated, the shoe would be on the other foot and Yahweh would reduce the temple to a pile of rubble. Yahweh didn't comment on Solomon's revisionist description of him, so maybe he thought it was OK.

The temple and the palace weren't Solomon's only great public works. He also rebuilt and extended the city walls of Jerusalem, and rebuilt several cities that had fallen victim to Egyptian attacks, not just within his kingdom, but in Jordan and elsewhere. He also created the beginnings of a navy on the Gulf of Aqaba at the northern tip of the Red Sea. The first thing they did was sail to the land of Ophir and bring back sixteen tons of gold for Solomon to ooh and aah over.

All of these works —temple, palace, and everything else— were carried out by forced or slave labor. And the labor force contained not a single Jew, but consisted entirely of "gentiles" from the tribes that Moses' army had conquered when they invaded the Promised Land. Since the conquest, they continued to be slaves to the Israelites, who served as soldiers and construction bosses and foremen over them.

During this time Solomon remained faithful to Yahweh, and held thrice-yearly sessions of sacrifices and burnt offering. And of course, continued to amass more and more wealth.

The Bible, Chapter 28

The First Book of Kings
part 4
(this is an awfully long book)

The Queen of Sheba
The Queen of Sheba had heard about Solomon's great wisdom and came to check it out for herself, with a camel train full of gifts and goodies for him, including 5 tons of gold.

I pause here for a moment. Scholars believe that the kingdom of Sheba was a real place, located near the mouth of the Red Sea, either on the Arab side in what is now Yemen, or on the Africa side in what is now Ethiopia. Ethiopians believe their first emperor was the offspring of the Queen of Sheba and King Solomon, but that's another story.

The Red Sea is 1,200 miles long, and Jerusalem is a couple hundred miles from its northern end, so the queen had a long ways to go. I'm not sure how fast a camel train can travel in desert heat, but I'd suppose 30 miles per day, tops. So it took her at least a month and a half, probably more like two months, to get to Solomon. That woman had a powerful curiosity. And lots of camels. Supposing a pack camel can carry a load of 300 pounds plus driver, it would have taken nearly 40 camels for the gold alone, not to mention the loads of spices and other goodies she brought with her. And traveling through the desert like that, they had to be carrying much of their own supplies and water, for themselves and the livestock. Plus tents and camping gear. So we can conservatively suppose a train of well over a hundred camels traveled two months across the desert to check out the rumors of this person Solomon. As I said: a powerful curiosity. Or perhaps a WEE bit of exaggeration on the part of the chronicler.

Anyhow, when she got there she was impressed with the prosperity of the place, and the opulence of Solomon's living conditions. No matter what topics she grilled him on, he answered all her questions with ease, so she was convinced that Solomon was the wisest man in the world, and that his god Yahweh really liked him. He accepted the hoard of goodies she had brought for him, and loaded her up with gifts to take back with her. Then she turned around and went back home, apparently satisfied that the trip had been worth it.

There's no mention of a dalliance between them, so the Ethiopians are probably mistaken. Besides, Solomon had no need to hanker after the Queen, since he had 700 wives and 300 concubines to take care of.

After the Sheba story, we are given a sort of inventory of just how rich Solomon really was, and how he managed to continue to increase his wealth. At that point he was the richest king in the known universe, not to mention the wisest. But his wisdom had some weak spots when it came to dealing with Yahweh.

The Decline of Solomon

Yahweh had, early on, warned the Children of Israel not to intermarry with foreign tribes, lest it dilute their devotion to him (Yahweh). But Solomon ignored that. He loved women from throughout his kingdom, and his harem included both Israelites and non-Israelites, including Hittites, Moabites, Ammonites, Edomites, and Sidonites. All those cultures worshipped gods other than Yahweh, so these foreign wives tended (as Yahweh had feared) to give Solomon an ecumenical outlook on the matter of worship. His Sidonite wives continued to worship Astarte, so he built places of Astarte-worship for them, and places of Milcom-worship for his Ammonite wives, and places of Chemosh-worship for his Moabite wives, and so on. That kept his wives happy, which is important when you have that many wives to deal with.

As another aside, 700 wives and 300 concubines gave him a thousand women to service, so if he went in unto a different one every night, it took him several years to get all the way through the list and start over. Meanwhile, that meant that these women had to wait years for their one-night stand with the king, which leads one to suppose that most of them managed to Fool Around in between times. It's not recorded whether Solomon realized this, or whether he cared. He probably didn't even know most of their names, and couldn't tell the difference.

Anyhow, Solomon built all of these altars to foreign gods for his wives, and allowed his foreign wives to worship them, to keep the peace. There's no indication that Solomon ever participated in those worships, but that didn't matter to Yahweh. That Solomon permitted the worship of foreign gods was enough get Yahweh, in his usual thin-skinned way, pissed off enough for him to arrange for Solomon to lose his kingdom.

No matter that, for forty years, Solomon had managed to rule a unified, peaceful, and prosperous kingdom. Yahweh didn't give a hoot for good works. It didn't matter whether you stole other men's wives, or slaughtered whole populations, as David had, so long as you continued to make your sacrifices to Yahweh. But give so much as a hint that others might have a right to worship other gods, and you, Solomon, were toast. *Ayatollahs come to mind.*

A disgruntled expatriate named Hadad with a grudge against David had been living the good life in Egypt. A similar one was holed up in Damascus, and became king of Syria. Because they hated David, they hated his son Solomon and plotted to take over his territory.

Another chief conspirator was a guy named Jeroboam, who managed to gain favor, and a good job, from Solomon. One day while he was traveling, a vagabond prophet hit him up and said: "Yahweh says he's going to take Solomon's kingdom away from him, and give YOU ten tribes to rule over. When Solomon dies, his son will get Judah, but that's all. You get all of the tribes of Israel." Apparently Jeroboam believed the tale; and when Solomon heard about it he put out a contract on Jeroboam, who skedaddled to Egypt.

Solomon died, and was succeeded by his son Rehoboam (don't confuse him with Jeroboam), which marked the beginning of the breakup of the unified kingdom of Judah and Israel.

Remember: the kingdom of Israel was the northern half, the kingdom of Judah was the southern half. Jerusalem, Solomon's capital, was in Judah. The capital of Israel was Jezreel. The kingdom of Israel consisted of a number of different tribes. The kingdom of Judah was just the one tribe, plus Benjaminites.

Rehoboam was as stupid as his father had been wise. As soon as Rehoboam took office, Jeroboam came back from Egypt prepared to follow up on Yahweh's promise. He got together with the northern tribes, and they went to confront Rehoboam to find out how he intended to rule his kingdom.

They said: "Your dad was pretty rough on us. If you make life easier for us, we'll be your loyal subjects." Rehoboam had his chance, but he blew it. Based upon unbelievably bad advice from his buddies, he told them: "Not a chance. Dad was a pussy compared to me. I'll be twice as harsh as he was. I'll make your lives thoroughly miserable." He seemed to think this would inspire fealty. I said he was stupid.

Instead, the tribes of Israel revolted, and proclaimed that Rehoboam would not be their king, stoned his emissary to death, and chased him back to Jerusalem, leaving him only the kingdom of Judah. The northern tribes then proclaimed Jeroboam as their king. As the vagabond prophet had predicted.

This left Jeroboam with a problem. The temple, the place where sacrifices were made to Yahweh, was in Jerusalem, which was down in Rehoboam's territory. Jeroboam figured, probably correctly, that if his people traveled to Jerusalem to do their

158

worship, they would likely transfer their loyalty to Rehoboam, who owned the holy temple, meaning he Jeroboam would be toast.

So he proceeded to give them local places to do their worshipping, so they wouldn't have to travel to Judah. He had a couple of golden bulls made, put one in Bethel and one in Dan, and told the people "You don't have to go all the way to Jerusalem for your sacrifices. Here are your gods, who brought you out of Egypt." He also built other places of worship, and consecrated non-Levite priests, and in general set up a competing religious establishment to the one in Judah, with its own festivals and ceremonies at the same time as those in Judah.

It's beyond me how he thought he could get away with this. He didn't, of course

Yahweh arranged for a Judean prophet to sneak into Bethel, and watch Jeroboam doing sacrifices there. The prophet then prophesied a mighty prophecy: the house of David would rise again, to destroy Jeroboam's program and all its participants. Jeroboam tried to shut him up, but couldn't, and his altar disintegrated.

Jeroboam's ass was grass, but he didn't seem to realize it. He kept on pursuing his alternative religion, ignoring Yahweh's serious warning. His son got sick, and he sent his wife to consult a prophet about it, who delivered a Jeremiad against Jeroboam and his family and his descendants (if they died in the city, their bodies would be eaten by dogs), and ended by saying that the kid would die as soon as she got back to the city. Which he did.

Here we fall into a certain dismal pattern of the kings of Israel and Judah.

Rehoboam's people down in Judah had screwed up in the eyes of Yahweh, who dumped on him and sent the King of Egypt to invade him and take his stuff. Also meanwhile, he had been constantly at war with Jeroboam

Jeroboam died and was succeeded by his son Nadab (not the one who died) as king of Israel. It's not said whether Jeroboam was eaten by dogs before he was buried.

Rehoboam lived eighteen more years, died and was succeeded by his son Abijah as king of Judah. Two years later, Abijah died and was succeeded by his son Asa.

Asa stayed on the good side of Yahweh, and ruled Judah for 41 years, while Israel continued to flounder through a succession of kings.

Nadab ruled Israel for two years, and was assassinated. He was succeeded by the assassin Baasha, who proceeded to kill as many of Jeroboam's people as he could find.

Baasha ruled Israel for 24 years before getting in trouble with Yahweh. He died and was succeeded by his son Elah.

Elah got drunk and was assassinated by one of his employees Zimri. Elah was succeeded by Zimri, who proceeded to kill as many of Elah's people as he could find.

He ruled for just one week, before he was overthrown by general Omri who eventually became king of Israel. (Meanwhile, King Asa has managed to hang on down in Judah for 36 years and counting).

Omri ruled for two years, got in trouble with Yahweh, died, and was succeeded by his son Ahab. Ahab was even worse than Solomon when it came to ecumenical behavior. He did more to annoy Yahweh than any of his predecessors, but he was still allowed to hang in there for two decades. *The ways of Yahweh are inscrutable.*

This brings us to a break in the succession of Israel's kings.

The Bible, Chapter 29

The First Book of Kings
part 5
(this is an *awfully* long book)

The remainder of 1 Kings is concerned with events during the reign of Ahab as king of Israel. Ahab lasted a surprisingly long time, given that he did everything he could to piss Yahweh off. For one thing, he married a woman named Jezebel who was a worshipper of Baal, and he converted to her religion and built altars to Baal, and used them.

One thing I learn from reading the Bible is that propheting is not always an honored profession. A king or somebody asks a prophet for advice, and if it's not to his liking he looks for another prophet, and has the first one killed. Prophesying could be a risky business.

A prophet named Elijah prophesied (correctly) to Ahab that a two or three year drought was coming. Ahab didn't like that news, so Elijah headed for the hills where ravens brought him food every day. I don't know whether they were trained ravens, or wild ravens with a streak of human kindness.

Sure enough, the drought happened.

Eventually Yahweh sent him to a nearby town where a widow would take care of him. When he got there, the widow only had a tiny bit of flour and oil —enough to prepare a last meager meal for herself and her son. Elijah fixed her up with a magic bowl that never ran out of flour and a magic bottle that never ran out of oil, so she was able to feed all three of them. Later, her son died of a fever but Elijah raised him from the dead. This greatly impressed her. *It would have impressed me too. I thought only Jesus could do that.*

After 3 years of drought, Yahweh told Elijah, "Go confront Ahab, and I'll end the drought." When Elijah and Ahab met, he immediately started chewing Ahab out for being a scoundrel and a Baal-worshipper, with a wife who insisted on killing Yahweh's prophets.
He then challenged Ahab to a contest to see whether Baal or Yahweh was the greater god.

The people of Israel were summoned, and Elijah had the prophets of Baal slaughter an ox and chop it up, pile firewood on their altar and pile the beef on top of the firewood.

Then Elijah told the Baal prophets, "Now, pray to your god and see if you can get him to light your fire." So the Baal prophets prayed and prophesied and cavorted and carried on and mortified their flesh for the rest of the day, and nothing happened.

Elijah then said, "Now watch this." He went to the remains of an altar to Yahweh and reassembled it. Then he slaughtered another ox, chopped it up, piled firewood on his altar, and put his own beef on top. He had water poured on the beef and the firewood until it ran down and filled a trench he had dug around the altar. Then he prayed, "O Lord set fire to this wood, so people will know who the true god is."

Yahweh blasted down a lightning bolt that didn't merely set fire to the wood: it completely burned up the wood, and the meat and the stones of the altar and the surrounding earth and dried up the water.

That got the Israelites' attention and they immediately proclaimed Yahweh the true god. Then they rounded up all the prophets of Baal and killed them. I said that being a prophet was a hazardous occupation.

Soon clouds came and the rain started and the drought was over and Ahab went back to Jezreel and told his wife Jezebel all about it. She immediately put out a contract on Elijah, so once again he lit out for the boondocks. He was sitting down, depressed and suicidal, when he had a visitation from an angel, followed by a visitation from Yahweh himself.

He was directed to go to Damascus in Syria, and make some appointments. He was to anoint Hazael king for Syria, some guy Jehu to be king of Israel (which would be a surprise to King Ahab), and to appoint a successor for himself: a man named Elisha. The idea was for these new leaders to conduct a bloodbath among the Israelites who had deserted Yahweh, and among the Syrians on general principles.But apparently they didn't take office right then, because the next King of Syria mentioned is named Benhadad, and the King of Israel is still Ahab. I don't recall Hazael or Jehu ever being mentioned again...at least not in this book.

To cut to the chase, Benhadad waged war on Ahab two different times, and got his butt kicked both times, even though the Syrian army vastly outnumbered those of Israel. Yahweh had a hand in the proceedings.

In the second war, the Israelites killed 100,000 Syrians. The remaining Syrians ran to a nearby city, where the walls collapsed on them and crushed another 27,000 to death. This left a hundred and twenty-seven thousand corpses littering the territory, to rot and stink and spread disease, but there's no word that anybody did anything about them.

One of the few who survived was Benhadad, who arranged a meeting with Ahab, and offered to return to Israelite control all lands earlier conquered by Syria. It seems to me that he had little choice, since his army was decimated, but Ahab thought it was a good deal and let Benhadad go; which didn't make Yahweh happy, since his plan had called for Benhadad to be killed. But Yahweh took a roundabout way to make his unhappiness known.

He needed someone who looked like an injured soldier, so he had one of his prophets ask a guy to beat him up. When he

163

declined, the prophet said, "Just for that, a lion is going to eat you up." So the guy left, and sure enough, a lion ate him up.

Eventually, the prophet got somebody to beat him up so he looked injured, Then he disguised himself and when Ahab came by he said,"I was on the battlefield, and they brought me a captive to hold, and said if I let him get away I would be killed. But he managed to get away. What will happen to me?" Ahab said, "You've already said what will happen to you. You will die."

Then the prophet shed his disguise and said, "You've just passed judgment on yourself, because YOU are the one that let the captive get away. Yahweh says:
'Because thou hast let go of the hand of a man whom i appointed to utter destruction, therefore thy life shall go for his life.'"

This did not please Ahab.

The Bible, Chapter 30

The First Book of Kings
concluded

A guy named Naboth had a plot of land with a vinyard on it, and King Ahab decided he wanted it to plant a garden there. Naboth wouldn't sell it because it had been in his family for generations. When Ahab told his wife Jezebel about it, she said "No problem," and had Naboth framed for blasphemy and stoned to death. Then she told her husband, "Naboth's dead; go take his land." So he did.

This ticked Yahweh off, so he sent Elijah to chew Ahab out for it and tell him: Yahweh is going to visit disaster on you and your family, and when any of them dies he will be eaten by dogs or buzzards.

Remember, Ahab was already in hot water for worshipping Baal, so this really scared him. He dressed himself in sackcloth & ashes and moped about until Yahweh said: since he's humbled himself, I won't visit disaster on him while he's alive. Instead, I'll wait until he's dead and visit it on his family.

This is one of the things in the Bible that is constantly annoying. Somebody does something to upset Yahweh, but instead of punishing him, Yahweh busts people who had nothing to do with it...the family of the offender after the offender is dead. That's like somebody punches me in the nose, so I wait until he's dead and then go beat up his sister. That's how divine justice and vengeance and punishment works in the Bible, from which we are supposed to find guidance in the conduct of our lives.

There had been several years' peace between Israel and Syria for a change, but that couldn't be allowed to continue. Jehoshaphat, the king of Judah, came up to Israel and told Ahab "Let's go make war on Syria." Ahab said, "First, let's consult some prophets." This was Yahweh's chance, and he rigged the prophets to lie to Ahab and predict victory. So Ahab and Jehoshaphat went ahead and attacked Syria, and they were doing okay until a stray arrow managed to hit Ahab where his armor wasn't, and killed him and dogs licked his blood as prophesied.

Ahab was succeeded by his son Ahaziah, who continued in the wicked ways of his daddy Ahab and his mommy Jezebel.

And that was the end of the First Book of Kings

The Bible, Chapter 31

The Second Book of Kings

The first half of this book is concerned mainly with the adventures of the prophet Elisha, after he took over from Elijah.

Ahab had died and been succeeded by his son Ahaziah as king of Israel. And let me say here that there seem to have been two different kings named Ahaziah, but we'll get to that complication later on.

This Ahaziah fell off the roof and hurt himself, so he sent emissaries to find a prophet of Beelzebub to tell him whether he would recover. Instead, they encountered Elijah, who said no, he wouldn't recover. When Ahaziah heard this, he sent companies of soldiers to bring Elijah back, but Elijah kept having Yahweh blast them with lightning, killing them all. Ahaziah eventually died, as predicted, and was succeeded as king of Israel by his brother Joram.

Elisha's replacement of Elijah happened this way. Yahweh was wanting to take Elijah to heaven, and Elijah wanted to be by himself when it happened, but Elisha refused to leave him. After wandering about together, along with a retinue of other prophets, they arrived at the Jordan river, where Elijah repeated the Moses trick and parted the waters so they crossed on dry ground.

As we pointed out earlier when Joshua did it, parting the waters of a flowing river would have unpleasant side effects: water on the upstream side would pile up and flood the countryside, while the downstream side would go dry and the fish would all die. Apparently, nobody noticed this while it was happening.

When they got to the other side, Elijah appointed Elisha to be his successor as a miracle-worker prophet. Then a burning chariot pulled by burning horses showed up and collected Elijah, and a tornado came and sucked them up to heaven, and that was the last ever seen of Elijah.

Elisha immediately tested his powers and performed his first miracle by parting the waters again, which greatly impressed the retinue of prophets gathered there, and made Elisha's reputation.

There was a problem at Jericho: the water had gone bad and the crops wouldn't grow. Elisha made the water sweet and good by scattering salt on it, which is a genuine miracle if you think of it, since normally if water is bad enough to kill the crops, adding salt would just make it worse.

As he was leaving, a bunch of rowdy kids started teasing him about his bald head, which pissed him off. He cursed them, and arranged for a couple of bears to come out of the woods and rip the innards out of 42 of the little pests. *Never tease a bald prophet.*

The lesson in conduct of life from this is: If children annoy you, get them killed. Write that down.

****

King Mesha of Moab, the country to the east of Israel, had been paying an annual tribute of several thousand sheep to King Ahab. But when Ahab died, Mesha decided to discontinue the practice, which riled up King Joram, who regarded it as rebellion. So he enlisted Jehoshaphat, the king of Judah, to join him in making war on Moab.

Unfortunately, they chose the worst possible route to carry out the attack, and in a week they found themselves lost in the boondocks and out of food and water for themselves and the troops and livestock. They decided they needed the advice of a prophet, so they went and looked up Elisha, who coincidentally happened to be in the territory.

Elisha didn't want to help Joram the Baal-worshipper, but he DID want to help Jehoshaphat, so he had them bring him a musician. While the harp was played, Elisha had them dig ditches in the dry stream bed. He told them water would appear without any rain falling, and that they would enjoy a scorched-earth victory over Moab.

Sure enough, next morning there was water in the ditches, and the Israelite-Judean army went and attacked Moab and killed everybody and destroyed their cities and chopped down their orchards and poisoned their springs and made their fields untillable by covering them with stones. Teach them to withhold their sheep.

The Moabite king tried to get away to Syria but they stopped him. So he took his eldest son up on the city wall, and killed him, and offered him up as a burnt sacrifice.

This totally grossed out the Israelite army, so they turned around and went home. Go figure. They had just got done slaughtering thousands in a blood-bath, but a human sacrifice was too much for them to handle.

****

Then Elisha did some more miracles. He helped a widow who was in danger of being foreclosed on, by supplying her with a magic oil bottle. She went and borrowed every jar, bucket, and container she could lay her hands on, and filled them all up from her little magic bottle. Then Elisha told her to sell the gallons of oil and pay off the mortgage. She probably did.

There was a woman who dearly wanted a son, but couldn't get one because her husband was an old man. Elisha invited her up to his room and told her, "This time next year you will have a baby boy." *And I have a pretty good idea what happened up in the room to make his prophecy come true, which it did. And I'm not talking about praying. I don't regard this as a miracle in the usual sense.*

A few years later the boy got sick and died, but after he'd been dead for a couple of days and his brain and other internal organs had started to melt, Elisha resurrected him from the dead which greatly pleased the mother.

Some time later one of his servants was directed to cook up a big stew to feed his retinue of prophets. The servant found a bunch of wild gourds and added them to the stew, not knowing they were poisonous.
When they tasted it, they said "Ick! This stuff is poison. If we eat it, it will kill us." Elisha de-poisoned it by scattering some meal on the stew. They went ahead and ate it with no bad effects.

Another time, a guy gave him a few loaves of bread, and with them Elisha managed to feed a multitude of a hundred or so men, and at the end there was bread left over. I think a similar event takes place in the New Testament, but that comes later.

The next miracle is complicated, so I'll save it for the next chapter.

One of the most interesting developments in this book is that Elisha —like Elijah— seems to be doing these miracles on his own. There's no mention that he calls on Yahweh to do them for him: he just does them because he has the power to do miracles. Presumably, he has the power to do miracles because he inherited it from Elijah, who got it from somewhere.
I suspect that if I continue to see holy men with the power to do miracles, it won't seem as remarkable when we get to the Jesus stories. Prophets will have done it for a long time already.

The Bible, Chapter 32

The Second Book of Kings,
part 2

Further Adventures of Elisha

A Syrian general named Naaman had come down with leprosy, and was told about the miracle-working prophet in Samaria who could cure him. So off he went, with a letter from his king to the king of Israel, saying "Naaman is my main man. Please cure him." The Israelite king said "Can't do it.

But Elisha said "Send him to me," and told him to wash himself seven times in the river Jordan —that would get rid of his leprosy. When Naaman heard this, he had a cow. "Did I come all this way just to get some quack advice from this guy? He didn't pray or lay on hands or anything, just told me to go dunk in his river. Hell! we have better rivers that that back home in Syria." His servant got him calmed down and told him, "Go try it. You've got nothing to lose."

So Naaman dunked himself seven times, and came out cured with skin as smooth and pink as a baby's bottom. *Leprosy miracle #1.* He tried to pay Elisha, but Elisha said Nope, I won't take anything. So Naaman headed on home.

Elisha had a servant named Gehazi (remember that name) who decided Naaman shouldn't get cured for nothing, so he ran after Naaman with a made-up story of Elisha's needs and was given a pile of silver and other goodies.

When Gehazi got back home, Elisha (whose powers apparently included clairvoyance) told him "I know where you've been and what you've done, so now you're going to come down with Naaman's disease, you bad boy." Sure enough, Gehazi forthwith came down with leprosy, and his skin turned white as snow. *Leprosy miracle #2.*

I can't help pointing out again that leprosy, or Hansen's Disease, doesn't turn a person "snow white", though it may cause some white blotches. These primitives were probably mistaking vitiligo, or Michael Jackson's Disease, for leprosy. Vitiligo causes a person's normal skin pigment to gradually disappear, leaving him "snow white". It's not communicable and has no other effects except whiteness. A similar tale was told of Moses' sister Miriam, who had "leprosy" laid on her for questioning Moses' authority, which turned her "white as snow". When she repented, her color returned. Back then, apparently every skin ailment got identified as leprosy and scared them.

Elisha's next miracle was more mundane. He caused an axe-head which had fallen into the river, to float so it could be retrieved. 2:6

Next he caused an invading Syrian army to go blind, so he could lead them away from their intended target and into Samaria. When they got there, he restored their sight, fed them dinner instead of killing them, and sent them home. This led Syria to stop making raids into Israel...for a little while. But it wasn't a prudent move on Elisha's part.6-18

Before long Syria was at it again, laying siege to Samaria. This led to a severe food shortage in the city and people were starving. A woman went to the king and complained, "This woman told me, 'Let's eat your baby today, and we'll eat my baby tomorrow.' So we killed my son and boiled him and ate him...but the next day she had hidden her baby so we couldn't eat him."

This totally grossed out the king. But rather than settling the dispute between the women, he blamed Elisha for not killing the Syrian army when he had the chance, and threatened to have Elisha's head.6-30

Then a bunch of stuff happened and Yahweh conjured up noises that made the Syrian army think they were about to be overrun; so they decamped, leaving much of their gear and supplies behind. The people of Samaria went and collected it, and the famine was over. But I don't think Elisha gets credit for this one. I think Yahweh pulled his chestnuts out of the fire for him this time.7:7

Remember the lady whom Elisha had provided with a son, who died and was resurrected? Elisha warned her that Yahweh was about to lay a famine on the land, so she should take the boy and hide out among the Philistines until it was over. So she did. When she finally came back she saw Elisha's servant Gehazi (the one to whom Elisha had given leprosy and was snow white, though that isn't mentioned here) telling the king about Elisha's miracles. When Gehazi saw them, he introduced them to the king as the woman and her resurrected son, so the king restored all the property she had abandoned when she cut out for Philistia.8:6

I still think the kid was more than an acquaintance to Elisha. I think Elisha and the woman had something going.

The king of Syria got sick and sent one of his officials Hazael to ask Elisha whether he would get well. Elisha told him, "Yahweh tells me he's going to die; but I want you to tell him he'll get well." Then Elisha broke down into tears, telling Hazael it was because he, Elisha knew the terrible things Hazael would eventually do to Israel. "How me?" says Hazael; "I got no power." "You will have," says Elisha; "You're going to be the next king of Syria."

So Hazael went home and smothered the ailing king with a water-soaked blanket and became the next king of Syria.8:15

And that's about all of these tales of morality and justice we need for now..

The Second Book of Kings
interrupted

Ten commandments were given to Moses on Mt. Sinai (as well as a whole bushel more in Leviticus). Of these ten, the first four are religious: Yahweh is God, don't worship other gods, don't worship idols, keep the Sabbath holy. The remaining six are social: honor your parents, don't do murder or adultery or theft or lying to harm someone or covet things not yours.

But so far in this tale, Yahweh doesn't seem give a hoot about any but the first four.

If he finds anybody, but particularly his own chosen folks, worshipping any other gods, he smites them ruthlessly and mercilessly, including those who themselves haven't transgressed at all; they just have the misfortune to be related to somebody who did.

Some poor dude gathering firewood on the Sabbath gets stoned to death. Cultures who know no other god than Baal are persecuted for their faith, and slaughtered like sheep. Kings who adorn altars to Yahweh with golden statues are stomped on. Religious transgressions are punished, either directly by Yahweh or under his direction.

But violations of the remaining six of the Ten Commandments, as well as the Several Hundred Commandments in Leviticus, fail to raise his dander at all.

The wholesale murder of conquered peoples has Yahweh's enthusiastic approval. David's adultery and his murder contract on Uriah is laughed off. Joab's murder of Amasa (remember? Pretended to kiss him, then grabbed him by the beard and gutted him with a dagger) passes without notice. Saul's unrighteous persecution of David is okeh with Yahweh.

Absalom's treachery is unnoticed by Yahweh. David's deathbed recantation of promises he had made leads to no famines or plagues of mice or other signs of Yahweh's displeasure.

Solomon's ruthless murder of all other possible pretenders to the throne? So what? His other ruthless actions went unnoted.

But what got Solomon in trouble? Allowing his foreign wives to continue worshipping their own gods. When Yahweh noticed that, Solomon was toast.

In other words, so long as the main religious commandments were observed, Yahweh was unconcerned about the others.

There's no record of any divine retribution for murder, or theft, or adultery, or treachery, or coveting (come to think of it, the Children of Israel clearly coveted the lands they were about to conquer through force.) Nor for homosexuality, nor for marrying your mother-in-law nor for eating shellfish, nor for any other of the myriad things Yahweh had forbidden.

So if one wishes to take the Bible as a guide for proper conduct, it would seem right to adopt Yahweh's own priorities in the matter of such things. Obey the commandments about religion, and you're righteous, no matter what else you do.

In the early 1900's, there was a popular song about rapacious bankers, corrupt politicians, and similar miscreants, with the recurring refrain:

> *But he goes to church on Sunday*
> *And they say he's an honest man*

Which just goes to show that there is very little new under the sun.

175

The Bible, Chapter 30

The Second Book of Kings
continued

I'm tired of inflicting boring details on you, so I'll try to condense the material, to the essence required for you to gain guidance for the conduct of your life.

Jehoram succeeded Jehoshiphat as king of Judah. Azakiah (a different one) succeeded Jehoram as king of Judah. Judah and Israel went to war against Syria.

Elisha had different ideas about the Israelite succession, and rigged it so that Jehoram's brother Jehu got secretly anointed king of Israel. Jehu sealed the matter by shooting King Joram in the back with an arrow, killing him. They flung his body in a field where the buzzards could find it. King Ahaziah of Judah was a witness, so Jehu had his men kill Ahaziah too. Jehu had his men throw Queen Jezebel out the palace window, where she splattered on the pavement and the local dogs ate her.

Jehu had all seventy sons of King Ahab rounded up and beheaded, and piled their heads in the courtyard.
Then he killed all the rest of Ahab's family.
Then he killed most of the relatives of King Ahaziah.
Then he pretended to be a convert to Baal, and had all the worshipers of Baal come to town and gather in the temple of Baal. When they were all there, his soldiers went into their temple and slaughtered them all.

Moral: If people don't worship the way you do, trick them into coming together into a congregation and then kill them in their house of worship.

Jehu died and was buried. His son Jehoahaz became king of Israel.

Meanwhile, down in Judah...

When King Ahaziah's Baal-worshipping mother Athaliah learned of his death, she saw her chance to become Ruling Queen, and ordered that all of his male relatives be killed, eliminating all possible rivals for the throne. But her sister managed to smuggle one of her infant grandsons, Joash, out of the palace and put him in keeping of a priest named Jehoidah.
 When the kid was seven years old, Jehoidah recruited the palace guards to his side, smuggled young Joash into the temple of Yahweh (left over from Ahaziah), and crowned him king of Judah. When Queen Athaliah heard the fuss, she came running out screaming "Treason!", so the guards dragged her down to the horse stables and hacked her to death... and that was that.

During his time in office, King Joash ran a good kingdom and raised money to get the temple fixed up. But he was a pacifist when it came to war. The Syrians up north decided to attack Israel (what a surprise); they conquered Gath and decided to go for Jerusalem (in Judah). When Joash heard of it, he bought them off by giving the king of Syria all of the palace treasures, and all of the temple treasures dedicated to Yahweh. Syria accepted the bribe and went home (for the time being). Joash's people were outraged, and had him assassinated. He was succeeded by his son Amaziah as king of Judah.

Meanwhile, up in Israel...

Elisha was on his death-bed. He gave the Israelite king Jehoash a prophecy that he would fight the Syrians and defeat them. Then Eiisha died and was buried. Some time later, a band of undocumented aliens were holding a funeral for one of their own. When they heard soldiers coming, they chucked the corpse into Elisha's tomb and beat it. As soon as the corpse touched

Elisha's bones, it came back to life and walked out. *Elisha's final miracle.*

Meanwhile, down in Judah...

King Amaziah killed a whole lot of people, picked a fight with Israel, his troops got their butts kicked, and he got taken prisoner by King Jehoash...who then proceeded to assault Jerusalem, and take all its goodies back to Israel. Amaziah's enemies killed him and he was buried on Judean soil.

He was succeeded by his son Huzziah as king of Judah. Jeroboam succeeded Jehoash as king of Israel. Are you keeping track of all this? Huzziah came down with leprosy and was put in isolation. When he died he was succeeded by his son Jotham as king of Judah.

Meanwhile, up in Israel...

Zechariah succeeded Jeroboam as king of Israel.
He was assassinated by Shallum, who took over as king.
Menachem assassinated Shallum, and took over as king.
Menachem killed a bunch of people and ripped open the bellies of a bunch of pregnant women. Eventually he died and was succeeded by his son Pekahiah as king of Israel.
Pekahiah was assassinated by one of his officers, Pekah, who took over as king. Pekah was assassinated by
Hoshea, who took over as king of Israel.

Meanwhile, down in Judah...

King Jotham built the north gate of the temple, eventually died, and was succeeded by his son Ahaz as king of Judah. Then there was a bunch of intrigue and fighting involving Syria and Irael and Edom and Assyria and the bronze appointments of the temple of Yahweh. Ahaz died and was succeeded by his son Hezekiah as king of Judah.

Meanwhile, up in Israel...

King Hoshea had a serious falling out with Emperor Shalmaneser of Assyria, who invaded Israel and took all of the Israelites back to Assyria as prisoners.

And that's about all of these inspiring stories I can stand for now.

The Bible, Chapter 31

The Second Book of Kings
concluded

The last part of Second Kings is a mishmash of political warfare and intrigue, with few noteworthy individual events to break the monotony.

Hoshea was king of Israel. He stopped paying tribute to the emperor of Assyria, so the emperor had him imprisoned, then went ahead and conquered Samaria and took all the Israelites back to Assyria. He could pull this off because Israel had been disobeying Yahweh's religious commandments.

Then the Assyrians colonized Israel, much as the Children of Israel and done when they took over the Promised Land.

Meanwhile Hezekiah became king of Judah and led a righteous life. Isaiah sent a taunting letter to the Assyrian emperor and then an angel killed 185,000 Assyrian soldiers, . The emperor went back to Nineveh, and was promptly assassinated by two of his sons.

While king Hezekiah was ailing, some Babylonian spies came to visit him, and scoped out all his treasures. Isaiah warned Hezekiah that the Babylonians would come take all his stuff.

Then Hezekiah died and was replaced by Manasseh, who took up idolatry and all the other things Yahweh disapproved of, so Yahweh vowed punishment. . Manasseh,also killed a lot of people. Then he died and was replaced by Amon.

Amon disobeyed Yahweh and was assassinated. Then his assassins were killed and Josiah became king of Judah.

While Josiah was being king, somebody turned up a copy of the Laws that had been stuck off in some corner of the Temple. Then Yahweh vowed punishment again. However, Josiah decided to clean house, and got rid of all the signs of pagan worship[that had been bugging Yahweh. Then he died and was replaced by Joahaz.

True to form, Joahaz went back to sinning against Yahweh. Then the king of Egypt captured him and replaced him with Eliakim, who changed his name to Johoiakim, because it was longer. Or maybe it was Johoiachin. Then king Nebuchadnezzar of Babylonia came and conquered Judah and hauled everybody back to Babylon and made Mattaniah king of Judah and changed his name to Zedekiah.

Zedekiah rebelled against Nebuchadnezzar, so Nebuchadnezzar put down the rebellion, and had Zedekiah's sons killed before his eyes, and had Zedekiah's eyes put out and shipped him off to Babylon. Then because he'd had enough of these pesky Judeans, Nebuchadnezzar invaded Jerusalem and destroyed the Temple and laid waste to the city, and made off with all the Temple goodies. He had all the priests and other important people killed and appointed Gedaiah to be governor of Judah.

Then some Judeans kill Gedaiah and his retinue, and took off for Egypt before the Babylonians could catch them.

Then Evilmerodach became king of Babylonia, and released king Jehoachin (or Jehoakim) from prison, and treated him nicely for the rest of his days.

Thus ends the Second Book of Kings.

One thing we notice is that, at this point, Yahweh is mostly bluster and no action. He keeps vowing to wreak divine punishment on various persons and peoples,

But there's no good old plagues or famines or earthquakes. Just threats. Not the best way to keep people in perpetual fear of your wrath.

The Bible, Chapter 36

The First Book of Chronicles

The first 8 chapters of 1 Chronicles contain a genealogy from Adam to Jephunneh and beyond, and is tedious reading with few bright spots. The rest of the book is a re-telling of the tale of the perfidious and clueless David.

The genealogy starts out with Adam, who begat Seth, who begat, Enosh, who begat...

But you may notice a certain person missing here, namely Cain, who was *persona non grata*, but nevertheless was one of the official characters.

Cain, eldest son of Adam and Eve, was noteworthy for two things. (1) He beat his little brother to death as a result of a religious dispute. (2) He participated in a miracle, by going off to the land of Nod, and marrying a wife there, and raising a family. Up to that point, Cain and his parents had been the only three people in the world. Where the people of Nod came from is unstated.

Anyhow, it continues on from Enosh for an appalling number of generations and side branches, listing people never heard of before or since.

We are reminded throughout that it was quite common for these men to have girlfriends along with their wives, and go in unto them and sire children with them, and nobody ever thought anything about it, least of all Yahweh. who apparently thought it was peachy-keen.

Keep this in mind as a talking-point when discussing the advantages of taking the Bible as a guide for righteous living when cheating on your wife.

Jacob, the one who cheated his brother Esau out of his birthright, had a son named Judah, who begat three sons with his wife, and two more with **his daughter-in-law** Tamar!

This bit of news gives one pause. You'd suppose that this would somehow count as incest or adultery or SOMETHING forbidden in Leviticus, but apparently it was acceptable in the eyes of Yahweh. Perhaps Tamar was the widow of Judah's eldest son Er, whom Yahweh had slain because of his wickedness, and Judah's motive was to "raise up seed" to his late son. Or perhaps not. Because then the begotten sons would technically count as Er's offspring, making Judah the biological father of his own grandchildren. Besides, the duty to "raise up seed" for the departed fell on brothers, not fathers. It all gets so complicated. Maybe Judah just had the hots for Tamar, and that was that.

The descendants of one Simeon waxed and multiplied and spread out and needed more land, so they found fertile valley occupied by a peaceful tribe of people, whom they killed and occupied their land and took their stuff. Same old same old.

The tribe of Reuben attacked the Hagrites and killed most of them and took their stuff.

Michael, Obadiah, Joel, and Isshiah had so many wives & children their descendants were able to provide 36,000 men for military duty.

There is a list of the priests who lived in Jerusalem, and a list of the Levites who lived in Jerusalem, and a list of the temple guards who lived in Jerusalem, and another one of some more Levites who were in charge of such things as wine and music.

This brings us up to the re-tellings of the David stories.

The Bible, Chapter 37

The First Book of Chronicles
Concluded

The Story of David, Redux

You may remember the first story of King Saul's death. it was by his own hand: At the end of 1 Samuel, he fell on his sword to avoid being captured and killed by Philistines. The second story at the beginning of 2 Samuel is that he was killed, at his own request, by a young Amalekite, whom David promptly had executed. In **1 Chronicles**, both of those stories are trumped: Saul was slain by Yahweh, because of his many transgressions. That's what it says. Perhaps it meant to say something else. Maybe Saul was killed three times, by different agents for different reasons. Or whatever.

David took over as king of the united kingdom of Israel & Judah, and one of the first things we are given is a list of his favorite soldiers, one of whom killed both a lion and an Egyptian, though not at the same time.

Then we are given inventories of his followers from the tribes of Benjamin, and Gad, and Manasseh. Then we are given an enumeration of the number of troops in his armies and under his control. By more or less actual count it was 460,000 troops, plus a few hundred more from outlying areas, all of whom gathered at Hebron to celebrate his kinghood.

Then there's a re-telling of the moving of the Ark of the Covenant, and Uzzah being killed for saving it from falling over and smashing. And a re-telling of David's numerous battles and victories.

Then we're told again how David took a census, and Yahweh

came down on him like a ton of bricks for doing so. Again, no clue as to what Yahweh's objections were.

Then David started making preparations to build a Temple, but Yahweh told him it would be left to one of his sons to finish. He went ahead anyway, and we are given tedious details of all his preparations.

Then David died and his little boy Solomon became king of Israel & Judah, and thus ended the first book of Chronicles.

The Bible, Chapter 38

The Second Book of Chronicles

The second book of Chronicles is little more than a re-telling of the things related in the First and Second Books of Kings. Rather than simply repeat those reports, I have skimmed the pages of this book, for particular items not noted before, or for things deserving wider treatment.

****

One thing I didn't notice before is that after Solomon started work on the temple, he took a census of all of the foreigners, "similar to the one David had taken". And what did Yahweh do this time?

NOTHING!

David had been raked over the coals by Yahweh for taking a census; Solomon did the same thing with impunity. The only difference I notice is that, while David was counting only the Jews in the united kingdom, Solomon was counting only the non-Jews...the "foreigners". Apparently, Yahweh didn't want David to know how many of Yahweh's Chosen People there were. But because Solomon just wanted a head-count of the documented aliens, that was okay. Go figure.

****

Another thing I didn't notice before: After the episode where

Yahweh came down and filled the temple with a cloud of glory which drove out the priests, Solomon decided to celebrate. He did so by sacrificing 22,000 oxen and 120,000 sheep. All at once. If they did it the right way, per Leviticus, the blood of 142,000 critters got splashed on the altar at more or less the same time, because the only permissible method for slaughtering a sacrificial animal was for a priest to slit its throat and catch the blood in a bucket and splash it on the altar. I can only speculate on how many priests armed with butcher knives took how long to dispatch a quarter of a million animals. And what the area around the altar would have smelled like afterwards.

****

Another thing I didn't notice before is that when Solomon's navy went off to Tarshish to bring back gold, they also brought back apes. And peacocks. We are not told what Solomon did with them.

****

And another thing I learned is that Rehoboam (remember him? the clueless twit who assured people he'd be even more harsh and draconian than his father had been) had a thing for marrying his nieces. First he married the daughter of his uncle Jerimoth. Then he married the daughter of his uncle Absalom. Then he married sixteen more women...and took up with a total of 60 official girlfriends whom he went in unto a lot and generated a ton of offspring.

****

And I learned that at one point the soldiers of Judah killed a half million Israelite soldiers. We don't know what happened to the bodies.

****

And i learned that Jehoram was so wicked that Yahweh smote him with an intestinal ailment, and eventually his bowels fell out on the ground and he died. I suspect that alarmed his caretakers. Not his death: the other thing with the bowels.

****

Joash (you'll recall) was the kid who was rescued from Queen Athaliah's purge of her late husband's family, and was raised by the priest Jehoiada to become king of Judah. So long as Jehoiada was alive to keep him on the path of righteousness, Joash ran a tight ship of state. But as soon as Jehoiada died, things fell apart and people started worshiping idols and groves and whatnot. This did not sit well with Yahweh.

What is it about these people that makes them start worshiping new things, when they already have a perfectly serviceable god to worship? Every time we turn around, they're at it again. Do they just crave variety? Do they think they can maybe get a better deal from a different god? Are they slow learners about what happens (sometimes) when they do that? I don't get it.

Anyhow, Yahweh came down hard on them, and Jehoiada's son Zechariah took to scolding them about it, so to shut him up Joash had him stoned to death. It did no good, because the Syrians invaded Judah and tore up the place, and took everybody's stuff back to Syria and left Joash suffering from loathsome diseases contracted (somehow) from the Syrians.

Joash's people figured that the assassination of Zechariah had brought about the Syrian invasion, so they went up to the king's sick room and killed him, and that was that.
He was succeeded by his son Amaziah.

And here I ran across a passage that seems at odds with everything we've seen so far. King Amaziah killed the servants who had assassinated his daddy (and brought him to the throne). But he did NOT kill their children. Because, it says, the Law of Moses commanded: "The fathers shall not die for the children,

190

neither shall the children die for the fathers, but every man shall die for his own sin."

At this point you are supposed to say: What?? We have seen Yahweh routinely doling out punishments to transgressors and to their descendants down to the tenth generation or so. Indeed, on at least one occasion he has decided to punish, not the wrongdoer himself, but the sons and offspring of the wrongdoer instead. And now we are told that, according to the Law of Moses, that was a no-no.

Apparently, when Yahweh was handing down the Laws, it was "Do as I say; not as I do." You mustn't take Yahweh's behavior as a model for your own. When he does it, it's okay. If you do the same thing it's a sin. So sit down and shut up.

****

Anyhow, Amaziah decided to make war on the kingdom of Edom south of Judah. He began by amassing a local army, and augmented them with 100,000 mercenaries hired from up in Israel. But then a prophet came and told Amaziah that Yahweh didn't want him using foreigners in his fight with Edom, so Amaziah sent the mercenaries back home, without paying them. Which pissed them off.

Then Amaziah invaded Edom and killed a lot of people and took their stuff. He also captured ten thousand Edomite soldiers, and herded them up to the top of a mountain and pushed them off a cliff to smash onto the rocks below. He carried back the Edomite idols and started people worshipping them. As usual, this did not sit well with Yahweh. A prophet warned Amaziah about it, but Amaziah told him: shut up, or I'll give you what Zechariah got. So the prophet shut up, but had privately predicted disaster for Amaziah.

While Amaziah was fighting in Edom, the disgruntled army of unpaid Israelite mercenaries got even by raiding a bunch of northern Judean cities and killing everybody and taking their stuff. So Amaziah decided it was time to go to war with Israel.

He sent a challenge to the king of Israel, who was named Joash same as Amaziah's daddy. Joash wasn't alarmed, and told Amaziah he'd be better off leaving things along, or he'd get his ass kicked.

Amaziah ignored the warning, and went to battle, and got his ass kicked. The Israelites took him prisoner, and overran the cities of Judah, and took all their stuff back to Israel.

After king Joash died, Amaziah managed to escape from captivity, but his enemies tracked him down and killed him. He should have listened to that prophet, while he had the chance.

The Bible, Chapter 39

The Second Book of Chronicles
part 2

King Amaziah of Judah died, and was succeeded by his 16-year old son. But here there are certain discrepancies in this allegedly infallible work that I don't know how to deal with.

Back in II Kings, the son's name was Azariah throughout the story. Here in II Chronicles his name is Uzziah throughout the story. That's not just alternative spelling, because in II Chronicles Azariah is a priest who scolds Uzziah for wicked behavior. I do not know how to resolve this conflict. We'll call him Uzziah.

Uzziah got on Yahweh's bad side for what seems to be a minor technicality. Being the king, Uzziah went into the temple and made a burnt offering of incense to Yahweh. That did not please Yahweh, because according to the rules only priests were allowed to burn incense in the temple. So he smote Uzziah with leprosy of the face. Uzziah went into seclusion, and his son Jotham ruled as regent for the rest of Uzziah's life.

After Jotham was son Ahaz, who did the usual stupid stuff of worshiping other gods. Ahaz was followed by son Hezekiah, who did all kinds of good stuff and rebuilt the temple. To celebrate, he had 28,000 animals slaughtered and their blood tossed on the altar. I feel bad for that altar.

....

Egypt invaded Judah, captured the king, and made the king's brother Jehoiakim the puppet king of Judah. Jehoiakim was succeeded by Jehoiachin, who was succeeded by Zedekiah.

The Babylonians came and conquered Judah and killed men, women, old people, sick people, little kids, and took the rest of the people off to Babylonia to be slaves. Eventually, Babylonia turned into Persia, and King Cyrus let everybody go back home. And that was the end of the Second Book of Chronicles.

The Bible, Chapter 40

The Book of Ezra

Before we get too far into the Book of Ezra, I'd like to backtrack on the history in these stories so we'll have a clearer notion of what's going on.

Back a century or so before the events we're talking about here, there were still the two kingdoms: Israel to the north and Judah to the south. After a series of assassinations, Hoshea ended up as king of Israel. Israel had been paying tribute & taxes to the Assyrian empire. Hoshea decided he wouldn't do that any more. So the Assyrian armies invaded Israel, conquered it, dragged all of its people (the Israelites) off to Assyria, where they were never heard of again as a unified people. Eventually they dispersed throughout the region and became known as "the lost tribes".

So there was no more Israel, and the former Israelites were dispersed; there was only the southern kingdom of Judah. Its people were Judeans or "Jews".

A lot later, the Babylonians under king Nebuchadnezzar did a similar thing with Judah. They came in, occupied the territory and made it a colony of Babylon, and took their stuff including their temple appointments. Apparently (as far as I can tell) Nebuchadnezzar included Yahweh as a god to worship, so he respected the Judean culture as long as they behaved themselves and coughed up the required tribute to Babylon.

Judah's puppet king Zedekiah, appointed by the Babylonians, decided unwisely to rebel against them. Nebuchadnezzar took care of that. He sent in the troops and they killed all the Judeans they could lay their hands on: men, women, boys, girls, old folks, cripples, and whatnot. They took the rest of the stuff they hadn't taken before, burned the temple, destroyed the city of Jerusalem, and the Judeans they hadn't killed, they dragged back into captivity in Babylon.

That's where we are up to now: the former Israelites dispersed, and the Judeans in Babylonian captivity. We continue to see references to Israelites and Israel, but they now refer to the surviving remnants of all the original tribes (Children of Israel), not just residents of the northern kingdom.

****

As we plunge into the Book of Ezra much time has passed. The Persians have taken over Babylon, and Cyrus is the king of the Persian Empire.

Trying to follow the book as a sequential narrative is impossible, since the chronology is all bollixed up, and at times inconsistent. I suspect that different parts of it were written at different times by different authors, and were then shuffled together into a single book because of their common subject matter.

****

Jeremiah (about whom we'll hear more later) had prophesied that Cyrus would build a temple to Yahweh in Jerusalem, site of the former temple that Nebuchadnezzar had razed. So Cyrus released all of the captive Jews, telling them to go back to Judah and rebuild the temple. He ordered all of his subjects to assist them in their journey and in their work. The Israelites then packed up and went, and took the expropriated temple appointments back with them. Their various tribal leaders were in charge.

We are given a tedious enumeration of who-all went, totaling 42,360, not counting 7,227 slaves, 200 musicians, and livestock.

They set about rebuilding the temple, but the local neighbors opposed the idea. Efforts were made to sabotage the project, by bribing officials and intimidating the workers and one thing and another, so not much got done.

After their protector Cyrus died, the temple opponents got the new king Artaxerxes to put a complete stop to the temple project, on grounds that the Israelites were a wicked and rebellious people.

After Artaxerxes died, the Jews resumed work on the temple, without bothering to get permission. This put the local officials uptight, so they sent a message to the new king Darius, complaining that these rebellious Jews were building a temple without permission.

Darius searched the archives, found Cyrus' original decree to the Israelites, and told the complaining officials to shut up and give the Jews anything they asked for in rebuilding the temple to Yahweh. And if anyone complained or protested, he was to be impaled on a sharpened beam torn from his own house. That got the point across.

They went ahead and completed the project, and had a huge public festival to celebrate the dedication of the new temple. Later on, in recognition of the return of a unified Jewry to their homeland, they had a huge Passover celebration that lasted 4 days.

And they all lived happily ever after.

****

At this point in the book there's a chronological glitch:

Many years later (is what it says). when Artaxerxes was Emperor, there came a prophet named Ezra, who was the Great X 15 grandson of Aaron. He was a renowned teacher and scholar of the Laws of Moses, so Artaxerxes sent him off, with a retinue of leftover Israelites, to go to Judah with an assignment to oversee the religious well-being of the now-liberated Jews. He was given a ton of money to cover expenses, and authority to collect more along the way as he saw fit...an awful lot like the decree that Cyrus issued for the freed Babylonian captives.

(Was this the same Artaxerxes who, earlier, had shut down work on the temple? We thought he had died and been replaced by Darius, who sided with the Jews in rebuilding the temple. Or is it another later king with the same name? We are not told.)

Before setting out, Ezra combed the territory for priests and Levites and other similar types to help him when he got there. Then they headed for Jerusalem. When they got there, he organized people to handle temple business, and turned over gold and stuff to the temple. Then they had a big prayer session, and sacrificed a lot of animals to Yahweh, and all should have been well...

But then a bunch of busybodies went to Ezra and told him that the liberated Israelites had been making friends among the local populace, and intermarrying with them, and everything.

When Ezra heard this, he threw a tantrum and tore his clothes and gnashed his teeth and hollered and screamed and thrashed about on the ground, and generally made a spectacle of himself. His specialty, and his guidelines, were the Laws of Moses; and you may recall that, back when Yahweh's chosen people were heading for the Promised Land, they had been forbidden to have anything to do with the natives, except to kill them all and take their stuff. No alliances, no socializing, and especially no intermarrying. All non-Jews were a disgusting race who did unspeakable things, and contaminated everything they came in contact with.

Moses' jingoism hung right out for all to see: God Hates Gentiles.

To Ezra, such behavior was the epitome of wickedness and

disobedience to Yahweh. He went into a paroxysm of prayin', shoutin', singin', begging Yahweh's forgiveness of the children of Israel for this terrible sin they had committed. The only way to gain redemption and cleanse themselves would be to divorce all of the gentile wives and kick them out on the street. *(Presumably, there were no gentile husbands ...who would have presented a difficulty, since there seems to have been no way for a woman to obtain a divorce: that privilege was reserved for men.)*

To avoid having to take the time to do it one-by-one, they developed a system for doing gang divorces. Before long, all of the disgusting foreign wives and their disgusting half-foreign brats had been sent off to fend for themselves on the streets of Judah, with no husbands and no fathers and no visible means of support.

And Yahweh saw that it Was Good.

If anyone ever tells you that Yahweh disapproves of divorce, remind them of the Book of Ezra.

The Bible, Chapter 41

The Book of Nehemiah

The Back Story

The book of Nehemiah concerns roughly the same time period as the book of Ezra. Many years earlier, Nebuchadnezzar had laid waste to Jerusalem, destroying the temple, tearing down its walls, and burning its buildings. At the time of the book of Ezra it was still pretty much a ruin. King Cyrus allowed the captive Jews to leave Babylon, with a commission to rebuild the Jerusalem temple, which they did in the first part of the book of Ezra. But that was their only project. They had a restored temple and surroundings, but the rest of Jerusalem was still largely as it had been left by Nebuchadnezzar's army. It wasn't in friendly territory, either. The surrounding neighbors had no love for the Israelites, whom they regarded as troublesome and warlike. The Ammonites especially, had been more-or-less permanent enemies since the days of Moses, when they refused to allow the Children of Israel to cross their territory on their way to the promised land. They and others did their best to stop the restoration of the temple, and it only managed to get done after the Emperor put his foot down.

This is where Nehemiah comes in. Nehemiah wasn't a priest or prophet, like Ezra. He was one of the Jews who remained in Babylon when the rest headed back to Judah, and was what we would call an administrator. He was the wine steward in King Artaxerxes' court.

****

One day while Nehemiah was there in the capital, some of those who had gone to Jerusalem to rebuild the temple came back for a visit. They told him of the grim state of affairs back in Judah, where most of Jerusalem was in ruins and was surrounded by antagonistic unfriendlies who had it in for the Jews and picked on them.

Nehemiah broke down in tears at the news. Then he determined to do something about it, and prayed to Yahweh for some help. A while later he was pouring wine for the king, and the king asked him why he looked so moody. Nehemiah told him it was because of the condition of his homeland, and asked for permission to go do something about it. The king agreed, and gave him a retinue of soldiers to accompany him, along with a letter to surrounding governors to help him do something about it. Apparently, Yahweh had softened the king's heart, just as he had done the opposite with Pharaoh once upon a time. Or maybe the king was just a nice guy.

When Nehemiah got to Jerusalem, he soon had a run-in with a pair of neighboring bad guys: Sanballat and Tobiah (remember those names). Tobiah was an Ammonite. When they heard rumors he had come to improve the lot of the Israelites, they were immediately down on him.

Nehemiah didn't announce why he had come. But that night he sneaked out of the city and made his way around it, checking out the ruined walls that were mainly piles of rubble, and making plans.

The next day he got together with the leaders of the Jewish community and told them: Look, this is bloody disgraceful. Jerusalem, even with its temple, is a pile of crap. It's not even a city unless it has proper walls, and the first thing we need to do is rebuild them.

Everybody jumped in and started to work. Sanballat and Tobiah saw what was going on, and laughed and made jokes and ridiculed the Jews. Nehemiah and his folks paid them no mind, and kept on working.

At this point, Nehemiah tells us in dreary detail exactly which individuals worked on which section of the wall. No doubt he wanted to give them credit for posterity, but I can't see that it adds anything to the story. You want those details, go read them yourself.

Sanballat saw they were actually fixing to rebuild the wall, and pitched a conniption fit. Took to hollering and ridiculing and claiming there was no way a bunch of Jews could rebuild a city wall. Tobiah joined in and hollered even if they did build it, it would be so poor a fox could knock it down.

This pissed Nehemiah off, and he prayed to Yahweh to see to it that they were first robbed of everything and then imprisoned. *There's no indication that Yahweh heard or cared. At any rate nothing happened to the Bad Guys. Sometimes the prayer works, and sometimes it doesn't.* Meanwhile, Nehemiah and his crew kept on working.

When the Bad Guys saw how well the rebuilding was going, they were enraged and alarmed.

We aren't told exactly why, but here's my take on it. The Israelites of old had a reputation as rapacious and effective warriors, who liked to invade places and kill everybody and take their stuff. It looked to Sanballat and Tobiah and others that the Jews were rebuilding the city wall in order to fortify Jerusalem, as a base for eventually taking up their old ways. It was seen as an actual threat.

So they made preparations to come in with force, and put a stop to the rebuilding.

But Jews living out in the hinterlands kept Nehemiah informed of the plot, so he took steps to defend against it. All workers were provided with swords, and were told to be ready to fight at all times. The work schedule was divided between laying stones half the time, and standing guard the other half of the time. Other defensive measures were put in place, so the plot fizzled and Sanballat and Tobiah had to give up that idea. The Israelite military instincts hadn't been lost during the Babylonian captivity.

****

The Bible, Chapter 42

The Book of Nehemiah
part 2

A Break in the Rebuilding Narrative
The people came to Nehemiah complaining that their fellow Jews were chiseling them out of their livelihoods. They couldn't afford to buy grain at the prices asked, their farms and vineyards had been taken away in foreclosures, a few had been forced to sell some of their children into slavery in order to feed the rest of their families. This was being done to them by their own people.

Here we have the earliest manifestation of the reputation of Jews as being heartless money-grubbing Shylocks squeezing the life out of the poor...even other Jews.

Nehemiah called the leaders together, and royally chewed them out. "Here we've been working to get our Jewish brothers out of slavery to foreigners, and now you're forcing them to sell themselves back into slavery to their fellow Jews! Quit doing it."

He carried on in that vein, and got them to promise to cancel all debts owed them by Jews, and to give back all the foreclosed properties..."and if you don't keep that promise, Yahweh will come down on you like a ton of bricks." They kept the promise.

Then we are told about Nehemiah's generosity and unselfishness, as an example to the community of a non-Shylock Jew they should emulate.

Back to the Narrative
The walls were completely rebuilt except for putting up the

gates. The Bad Guys tried a new strategy, inviting Nehemiah to meet with them out in the hinterlands for a pow-wow. Nehemiah didn't fall for it. They tried a couple more times, with the same result.

Then they tried blackmail, sending out an open letter mentioning a rumor of the Jews of planning to revolt as soon as the city was completely fortified, and Nehemiah of plotting to make himself king of Judah. "When the King hears about this, you're in deep trouble, so I suggest we get together and talk it over."

Nehemiah didn't fall for it this time, either. They finished putting up the gates, and the city was secure.

There follows a reprise of the last half of the Book of Ezra, starting with an enumeration of the population (42,360, same as Ezra's number). Then Ezra shows up in Jerusalem, and reads the Laws of Moses to everybody.

Then there were a lot of religious celebrations, followed by a general Revival Meeting where people loudly confessed their sins in public, and wept and wailed and promised to repent and never do it again. (*I'm told that similar orgies of repentance are popular in Fundamentalist churches in America, and in the auditoriums of televangelists.*)

Then there was a great long prayer, where they praised Yahweh and summarized the Book of Exodus and told how the Children of Israel became wicked and disobeyed Yahweh, so he got even by letting them be enslaved by the Assyrians and Babylonians but because of his great mercy he didn't just destroy them outright.

Then everybody signed a pact promising to faithfully observe the Laws of Moses and Leviticus in all their grim detail.

****

Apparently, Jerusalem wasn't big enough to accommodate all of the returned Jews, so they drew lots to see who would live there, and everybody else got to settle elsewhere in Judah. Then we're given a listing of who-all lived in Jerusalem. Then we're given a listing of who-all lived elsewhere.

********.

Then the City Wall of Jerusalem was dedicated in a humongous ceremony involving music and parades followed by a cook-out.

Then Nehemiah set out to institute some reforms. He started by cleansing the temple.

During all this time, the general population had been quite friendly with Tobiah (yes, THAT Tobiah-- the Ammonite) because he was widely known as a doer of good deeds, and because he was married to a Jewish woman (I guess we can't use the word 'Jewess') and so was his son. That would have made him a sort-of Jew, a Jew-in-law, except for the part of Moses' law that said no Ammonite could ever become one of Yahweh's people, because of stuff that happened during the trek to the Promised Land a few centuries ago. The Law of Moses has a long memory.

Anyhow, up to now (before Ezra came along) nobody had been paying much attention to the picky details of the Law, so Tobiah was a respected member of the community. The priest in charge of Temple store rooms even allowed Tobiah to use one of them for his stuff. When Nehemiah heard about it, he freaked out and chucked all of Tobiah's stuff out into the street and had the room purified.

Then he started enforcing the law against doing things on the Sabbath.

People of Judah had apparently forgotten about the firewood-gatherer who was stoned to death for doing something useful on the Sabbath. They were treating it as just another day. Nehemiah put a stop to it, posting armed sentries everywhere to make sure nobody did anything on the Sabbath. It's not clear where the Sabbath-enforcing activities of the sentries fit into this, or whether they were violating the law by doing things to enforce it. Maybe it didn't qualify as useful work.

Then he started enforcing the law against intermingling with Gentiles, beginning by beating up some of the men who had foreign wives. Then he expelled people tainted by intermarriage. For example, a guy named Joiada was the son of a High Priest, and a Jew in good standing; but he was expelled simply because *one of his sons* had married a foreign woman. The old Guilt by Association business all over again.

And that's where the book ends.

Nehemiah doesn't tell us about the mass divorces mentioned by Ezra; but he didn't need to.

============

This reminds us again of one of the most distressing recurring lessons of the Bible: The segregationist attitude imposed by Yahweh (through Moses) on the Jews; the notion of a Chosen People, a race superior to all others and forbidden to have any social intercourse with any but their own. To me, it's 1930's Europe turned inside-out, with echoes of the American South in the 1800's (and in some parts even today). "It's unseemly — maybe even disgraceful— for a white person to marry a black person, or for a Jew to marry a Gentile." That's the view.

Nevertheless, it must be Yahweh's will because it's right there in the Bible

The Bible, Chapter 43

The Book of Esther

The events of this book are chronologically prior to the events in Ezra and Nehemiah. Ahasuerus (Xerxes I) is emperor of Persia, and the general exodus of Jews from Babylon/Persia to Jerusalem /Judah hasn't yet taken place. A large Jewish population remains in the Persian kingdom. The book reads like a novel, with plots and sub-plots and everything. It is noteworthy that Yahweh is never mentioned in the book of Esther.

===============

How Esther Became Queen

King Xerxes was a show-off. and an egomaniac, and a lecher. In the third year of his reign, he had a huge blowout for all of the princes, leaders, and power-brokers in the empire, followed by a 6-month show-and-tell where he displayed his riches and goodies for everybody to admire.

At the end of that event, he held another huge blowout to which everybody in the city, rich or poor, was invited to attend. It was another gaudy show of boasting opulence, with gold & finery everywhere and unlimited free drinks for all. It must have been a hell of a party. It lasted for a week. Then to cap it off, the king decided to display another of his beautiful possessions —the lovely Queen Vashti.

But when he sent for her to come forth and be shown, she refused. *We are not told why; maybe she just didn't like being treated like a bauble.*

This sent Xerxes into a towering rage. The gall of that woman! To disobey a command from her husband the king! He summoned his cabinet and asked them what they thought of the matter.

They agreed that it had to be answered. If the Queen started disobeying her husband, pretty soon other women would be doing the same and soon anarchy would ensue and society would crumble. Vashti had to be deposed as Queen, and that fact published everywhere. This would remind all women that they had to obey their husbands, or else. He then issued a proclamation to that effect: **the husband is absolute master and final authority in everything.**

I think this may be one of the things we are meant to learn from the Bible, but I'm not sure.

With Vashti out of the way, the king had no queen (though he seems to have had a harem full of girlfriends to help his through his loneliness). So his advisers suggested he order a search of the realm for young virgin hotties who might do as a replacement queen. Xerxes thought that was a great idea, and the search was initiated. As the candidates came in, they were placed in the care of Hegai, the head eunuch in charge of the king's harem where he kept his girlfriends.

****

In the city lived a Jew named Mordecai, with a young cousin he had adopted as a daughter after her parents died. Her name was Esther, and she was a real babe and was stacked. She was caught up in the search, and was sent off to Hegai to be prepped for an eventual interview with the king. She never let on that she was a Jewess.

Hegai took a shine to Esther, and gave her extra special treatment. Meanwhile, Uncle Mordecai hung out around the palace to keep up with how Esther was doing.

She was doing just fine.

The prepping of the candidates with beauty treatments lasted for a full year, involving unguents and perfumes and whatnot. When the girl was finally prepped, she was taken up to spend the night with His Majesty, and I do not suppose they spent the time playing cribbage. Next morning, she would be ushered off to a different harem under a different eunuch, to wait whether the king wanted her back or not.

When it came Esther's turn to snuggle with the king, afterwards he said "Oh! Wow!" or something like that, and promptly chose her to be his queen. She still hadn't let it out that she was Jewish, because Mordecai had warned her not to.

It's not clear exactly why she had such a powerful effect on him, but we may speculate that Hegai may have secretly taught her A Thing Or Two that would impress ol' Xerxes. He was head of the harem, and no doubt had a good idea of the king's preferences.

There was a big party to celebrate the new Queen. Then Xerxes decided to have another go at the girls who had been rounded up in the search; because, after all, he had probably missed a few...

Assassination Plot Thwarted
Since Esther was now queen, Uncle Mordecai was appointed by the king to be a doorman at the palace gate. While hanging out by the gate, he overheard a couple of disgruntled eunuchs who guarded the king's bed chamber, plotting to assassinate the king. He told Esther about it, and she told her husband about it, and after a short investigation he had the two plotters impaled, or maybe crucified, before they had a chance to assassinate him.

This episode will have great importance later on.

The Bible, Chapter 44

The Book of Esther
part 2

Haman Gets Promoted, and Forms a Plan

Along about this time, a guy named Haman (as full of himself as Xerxes was) got appointed to an office of authority higher than just about anybody except the king himself. This meant, by royal decree, that everybody had to genuflect in his presence.

And everybody did, except Mordecai, the Jewish gate-watcher. Whenever Haman passed the gate, everybody else knelt. Mordecai didn't. People reminded him of the king's command, but he said: I'm a Jew, and I don't kneel to rulers like Haman.

This really got under Haman's skin. This uppity gatekeeper needed to be punished for dishonoring (actually, for failing to honor) a bigshot like himself. When he heard that it was because Mordecai was a Jew, he decided if that's the way Jews are going to act, then all of them need to be exterminated.

So he set out a plan to kill every single Jew in the whole Persian empire. *One wonders if this is where a certain German dictator got his ideas from.*

****

I need to pause in the narrative to comment on this very odd thing that runs throughout the Bible: the notion of collective guilt. The individual, and the group he belongs to, are viewed as one. **If one did it, the group did it and must be collectively punished.** *That's the way these people think. It's the way Yahweh thinks. Take the Noachian flood: a lot of people are* *misbehaving, so Yahweh wipes out the entire human race except for Noah & Co. Take Sodom & Gomorrah: "The people are corrupt and the cities must be destroyed." Well, maybe some of the people were corrupt, but that makes the whole populace guilty. A man does something bad, and Yahweh smites him and all his descendants for many generations: the whole genetic line is guilty.*

Periodically, "the people" sin against Yahweh, and "the people" are punished for it...even though it was certainly a few individuals who sinned, not the entire nation.

It's not just Yahweh who thinks that way. We see it time & again in these narratives. If somebody offends you, the proper thing to do is to kill him and all of his family, or maybe kill him and everybody in his village. An offense by one is an offense by all.

David was offended by the tightwad farmer Nabal, and was moved to kill the farmer and his entire family, and his farm hands and their families. To him, that wasn't over-reaction; it was normal. And he would have done if it the lovely Abigail hadn't talked him out of it.

The Ammonite nation is forever guilty in perpetuity, down through the generations, for events that happened back during the trek to the promised land. The Israelites asked some Ammonites free passage, and were turned down. Bingo! Not only all the other Ammonites who were around at the time are condemned, but also every future Ammonite forever.

Regarding the individual and the group as one and the same when it comes to assessing guilt or responsibility, is standard Bible-think. No one ever acts individually; he always acts for some group to which he belongs.

This is nothing like the common fallacy of generalization: "That one is lazy, so they're all lazy." The Bible view is not that each member of the group is individually guilty of the offense of the one...they know that can't be true. The view is that the group as a

212

whole is as guilty as the one who actually did whatever was done.

There is probably a sociological explanation for this, but to me it is just plain weird. But this failure to differentiate between the individual and the group helps explain a lot of the really bad stuff that goes on among these Bible people.

****

Anyhow, Haman works up a plan to make sure that every single Jew in the empire gets offed: men, women, children, little bitty babies. First he needed permission, so he went to Xerxes and told him: There's this strange race of people dispersed throughout your empire. They keep to themselves and have their own laws and customs and don't respect the laws of the empire. It's not in your interest to have the likes of them in your kingdom. Give me permission to have them exterminated, and in return I'll put a whopping lot of money into your royal treasury.

The king told Haman to keep his money, but to do whatever he thought best, and entrusted the royal signet ring to him so he could issue proclamations in the name of the king.

The Decree for Annhilation is Issued

Haman's idea was to make sure that the slaughter of the Jews began on the same day everywhere across the Persian Empire. To decide which day, he got with his people and they cast lots, called "purim", to determine the date of the massacre. The date was decided as the 13th of the month of Adar, early Spring of the following year.

Then Haman drafted a proclamation decreeing that on that day, all Jews were to be killed, without exception and without mercy. There were to be no survivors. Those carrying out the decree would be entitled to confiscate the goods and property of the dead Jews as booty. It was sealed with the king's ring, to make it official. He had it translated into the language and dialect of every area in the empire. Scribes wrote it down, and couriers carried it throughout the kingdom, to be proclaimed to the people, including those in the capital city.

This news was not taken well by the people of the city, who weren't quite sure what to make of it, but were sure they didn't like it. Haman and Xerxes didn't notice or didn't care. They sat down and celebrated the issuance of the proclamation by getting drunk.

This presents a certain puzzle. It wasn't going to be a surprise attack; the decree was publicized everywhere, so everybody including the Jews knew about it. One wonders how they were expected to react to the news, and what they were expected to do about it. Here's my supposition (it's not made explicit in the narrative). They weren't expected to do anything about it, because they couldn't: as Jews they were forbidden to own weapons. So all they could do is sit helpless and await their fate. That's the only explanation I can think of for their supposed passivity.

Mordecai Gets the Word;The Plot of the Story Begins to Thicken

When Mordecai heard the proclamation, he went bananas and tore his clothes and put on sackcloth and ashes and went about the streets wailing and hollering and making a spectacle of himself. The same thing happened among Jews throughout the empire, as the proclamation was publicized.

When Esther heard how Mordecai was carrying on, she sent two people to find out what was the matter with him. He told them the whole tale, about Haman and the promise of booty to the treasury, and everything else, and gave them a copy of the proclamation that had been read in the city. He told them to give it all to Esther, and see if she couldn't intercede with the king to save her people.

Esther was more than willing, but there was a serious problem. It was forbidden for anyone to approach the king without being summoned, and the penalty was death. Esther had not been summoned. But there was an out; the king could excuse the intruder if he held out his scepter for the intruder to touch.

Esther said, "That's alright, I'll give it a try and approach him without invitation. If they kill me, I'll have died trying." She duded herself up in her royal robes, and went to see the king.

When he saw it was his beloved queen, he immediately held out his scepter, and asked "What have you come for? I'll give you anything you ask, even half my kingdom." But Esther was too cagy to come right out with it. Instead, she said, "I'd like you have you and Haman over to my place for dinner. I'll tell you then."

So they went. After dinner, the king said, "Now, tell me what it is you're going to ask for. Whatever it is, you can have it." But Esther said, "I'm not quite ready. If the two of you will come to dinner again tomorrow, I'll tell you then."

Haman's Fatal Blunder

Haman left for home, whistling and singing. With TWO invitations for dinner with the king and queen, he figured he was sitting in the catbird seat: he was surely the king's favorite, and could do just about whatever he liked. But as he passed through the palace gate, he saw Mordecai just sitting there: not rising and bowing, and not genuflecting, and not doing anything to acknowledge Haman's greatness.

And it really pissed him off.

He went home fuming, and gathered his friends and family and blew his own horn about how great he was, and how rich he was, and how many sons he had, and how the king had promoted him to powerful office...and how he had been invited to dine with the king and queen not once, but TWICE! But all happiness was driven out of him when he saw that insolent Jew sitting by the gate and not honoring him!

They told him, Here's what you need to do: Erect a huge gibbet, 75 feet high. Then in the morning, ask the king to have Mordecai impaled on it. That'll teach the Jew not to be insolent.

Haman thought that a splendid idea, and had the gibbet erected.

****

A point of clarification here. The King James translation, in several places including this one, speaks of people "hanging" or "being hanged." But scholars are pretty universal that they weren't talking about rope-around-the-neck hanging.

When a man was hanged on a tree or pole, he was nailed to it, or impaled on it, or fastened to it in some equally unpleasant manner. Back then nobody used rope-hanging as a means of execution. Maybe because it wasn't painful enough.

****

The Bible, Chapter 45

The Book of Esther
part 3

SYNOPSIS: Haman has had enough of that uppity Jew Mordecai, and decides to have him killed immediately, rather than waiting for the general massacre to get him.

The King Refreshes His Memory

That night, King Xerxes had trouble sleeping, so he had his secretary bring in the royal records and read them to him. When they got to the part where Mordecai saved his life by revealing the plot to assassinate him, the king asked, "What did we do to reward him for that?" They told him: Nothing had ever been done to recognize Mordecai's service to the kingdom. The king was amazed. Something had to be done about it, immediately. He asked the servants, "Are there any officials here in the palace?"

As it happened, Haman had just entered the palace, on his way to tell the king to have Mordecai impaled on a 75-foot pole.

"Haman's in the courtyard," They said. "Send him in," the king ordered.

When he came in, the king asked him, "What should be done for a man I am eager and ready to honor?"

Figuring, in his egotistical way, that the king was referring to HIM, he said,"He should be clad in royal robes, and seated on the king's favorite horse decorated with the king's crest, and a high government official should lead him through the streets, proclaiming, 'This man is one whom the king is pleased and delighted to honor for his service'."

"Splendid!," said Xerxes. "Have the robes put on Mordecai the gate watcher, and seat him on my finest horse. You yourself shall lead him through the streets!"

Haman almost shit a brick. All of a sudden, everything had turned upside-down for him. But he had no choice, so he went ahead and did it.

After he had delivered Mordecai back to the palace following the parade, Haman headed home in a blue funk. When he got home, he told everybody what had happened, and sat down to mope. His wife said, "Uh oh. With Mordecai the Jew now in the king's favor, I think you've got big troubles." But before he could do much more worrying, the king's servants came to escort him to Esther's second banquet.

Haman Dines with Xerxes and Esther

One can suppose that Haman hadn't much appetite right then, and would just as soon have skipped it. But there was no way out, so he joined the king and they went to Esther's for dinner. After they were done eating, the king asked Esther, "Now, finally, tell me what it is you were going to ask me for. If it's in my power, you'll get it."

Esther said, "Here's the deal. I'm a Jew, like my Uncle Mordecai. The Jews are my people. But a decree has been sent throughout your empire requiring that Jews be exterminated to the last man, woman, child, little bitty baby. These are my people who are fixing to be killed, and I ask you to keep it from happening."

The king said, "Decree? What decree? Who issued such a decree?" Esther pointed and said, "It was your top official, the despicable Haman." Xerxes blew his top and stormed out of the room in a rage. Haman could see that the fat was in the fire, and that running away would be pointless...he would just be hunted down. His only hope was to hang around and beg for the Queen's mercy and forgiveness.

In those days, royalty didn't dine seated in chairs. They lounged on sofas while eating. Haman went to the Queen's sofa and threw himself down on it, about to beg for mercy.

Just then the king came back in, saw what was going on, and screeched, "You lecherous wretch! First you order the Jews killed, now you're about to violate Her Majesty on her own couch in her own dining room!" As soon as he said it, the attendants grabbed Haman and slapped a blindfold on him. Then one of the servants told the king, "You know, he had a gibbet 75 feet high erected in his front yard, for Mordecai to be hanged on." "Good enough,"said the king. "Impale him on it instead." So they did, And the king's anger was appeased.

A Problem About Royal Decrees
King Xerxes gave the late Haman's estate to Queen Esther. He also appointed Mordecai to the office that Haman had recently vacated, and gave him the royal signet ring he had reclaimed from Haman.

A passing comment: Xerxes appears to have had trouble remembering stuff, or putting 2 and 2 together. Otherwise, when he got the ring back, he might have recalled why he let Haman have it in the first place. It was so that Haman could issue the same edict (with the king's okay, who said "Do whatever you think best") that now had the king in a lather. As a rule, kings aren't known for intellectual acuity. Maybe Solomon was an exception.

Esther renewed her plea to the king, begging him to cancel or negate the decree calling for the extermination of the Jews. The king said he'd love to, but you see there was this one problem: once a decree had been issued under the king's seal, it could never be countermanded or undone. it remained permanently in force.

But he COULD do something else. He could issue a second edict, saying that the Jews were free to arm themselves, and to defend themselves against the attack called for in Haman's edict. That wouldn't forestall the called-for massacre; but it would give the Jews a chance against it.

And so the second decree was issued.

The Bible, Chapter 46

The Book of Esther,
concluded

Mordecai's Decree
Mordecai, the Jew, was now the king's second-in-command. So the king told Mordecai to write up whatever he thought appropriate, and seal it with the royal ring, and send it off. *Virtually identical to the instructions he gave Haman earlier. Some kings never learn.* Anyhow, the decree that Mordecai dictated was a mirror-image of the one Haman had issued earlier. It authorized the Jews throughout the empire to organize and arm themselves against those who had been directed to wipe them out. And to be proactive about it. On the day that Haman had appointed for the Jews to be annihilated, the Jews were to attack their enemies and slaughter them without mercy, along with their wives and children, and to take their stuff as booty. *In other words, they were to revert to type: kill everybody and take their stuff.*

It was written up in the various languages and posted throughout the empire, which made the Jews very happy and others very nervous. When Mordecai rode out in his royal parade outfit, he was treated with cheers and huzzahs by the Jews. And with apprehension by others. A lot of gentiles quickly converted, so they'd be on the right side when the slaughter happened.

The Jews Rise Up
On the thirteenth of Adar, the Jews attacked with a ferocity that terrified everybody. They were abetted by all of the provincial officials, who were afraid of Mordecai now that he had become powerful. So the Jews killed everybody they thought might be against them (along with their wives and kids), but they didn't confiscate their stuff, at least not right then, though I don't know

why not since it wouldn't be doing the dead people any good.

In the capital city of Susa, they killed five hundred people, including the ten sons of Haman. When the king told Queen Esther the score (Jews 500, Gentiles 0), he asked her what she'd like next. What she liked was to have the slaughter repeated in the city the next day, and to have the corpses of Haman's sons hung on the gibbet that had impaled their daddy. So the corpses were hung, and the Jews killed another 300 in the city of Susa.

Out in the provinces, the slaughter was confined to just the one day, but they managed to kill 75,000 people all the same. The next day, there was no further killing. But there was celebration of their victory.

The Festival of *Purim*

Mordecai sent out a letter instructing Jews everywhere to observe the 14th and 15th of Adar every year, as a festival celebrating their victory over their enemies in the Persian empire. It was to be called the festival of *purim*, which —you may recall— was the name of the lots that Haman cast to determine the day for the Jews to be exterminated. Queen Esther added her authority to Mordecai's letter; from then on, all Jews and their descendants should celebrate the festival of *purim* in proper fashion and on the proper days.

Xerxes the king continued to do wonderful things. Esther continued to be his queen. Mordecai the Jew was second in rank only to the king himself.

And they all lived happily ever after.

The Bible, Chapter 47

Commentary

A noteworthy fact about these eighteen historical books of the Bible is the lack of any mention of a heaven, a hell, an afterlife, or any of that apparatus that forms the basis of most "Bible-based" religions.

Yahweh doesn't punish sinners with the fires of hell after they die, and he doesn't reward the righteous with streets of gold and unending bliss after they are dead. His punishments and rewards are right here on earth. If an individual misbehaves, he is smitten with leprosy, or a loss of family, or other misfortune. If a people misbehave, they get plagues and famine and drought. While they are alive.

Yahweh rewards those who deserve it with good fortune, good health, prosperity, fertility, and other earthly benefits. There's no hoping for a better life after this one. This one is the one you get, and then you die and that's that.

These Bible people do think of living on after their death. But not as spirits in some other realm. The way they live on is through their progeny, their descendants, their family line. It is crucial that a man have sons, to carry on the family line. If he has none, that's a serious misfortune; because when he dies, he is really dead and nothing of him survives. He leaves no legacy to live on after him.

When Yahweh wishes to inflict serious punishment on someone, he does it by extending the punishment to the sinner's descendants for many generations, while each of them is alive. Among the populace, you don't simply kill the man who has done you wrong. You also kill all of his sons, snuffing out any future legacy he might have had. That's how you kill someone for good.

The greatest reward Yahweh can issue is the assurance that a man will have a long and healthy family line. David was assured this kind of immortality, with Yahweh's promise that his family line would never end, and that his descendants would be persons of importance.

In a strange sense, all of these Bible people are Darwinians. Their golden rule, and their driving force above all, is to perpetuate their genes.

As I proceed onward in the Bible I'll be looking to see when, if ever, the notion of heaven and hell as destinations for souls in the afterlife, gets introduced.

The Bible, Chapter 44

The Book of Job

This may be the strangest book I've come to so far in the Bible. Its major premiss is weird; and the bulk of the tale, which consists mostly of dialogues, is rambling and laden with metaphors and allegories that usually fail to illuminate any definite point. Its conclusion is bewildering. If it is directed to any recognizable theological or moral point, I'm at a loss as to what they might be.

****

There was a man named Job, pronounced Jobe, and he was the finest of men. He was trustworthy, loyal, helpful, friendly, courteous, kind, obedient, cheerful, thrifty, brave, clean and reverent. And rich. He had a fine batch of sons and daughters and vast flocks of domestic animals, and was liked by everybody. He worshipped Yahweh wholeheartedly, and more often than necessary just in case he had missed anything.

One day Yahweh and Satan were chatting, and Yahweh said, "See that fellow Job? He's the most righteous man in the world. He worships Me and has nothing to do with evil." Satan replies, "That's just because you've been good to him and granted him a prosperous life. If you reversed course and treated him the opposite way, he'd stop worshipping you, and curse you to your face."

What Yahweh should have said is: "Of course. Nobody with any sense would worship somebody who systematically abuses them for no reason. Why should it be otherwise? He's earned the good fortune I've granted him by living a good and righteous life. If he earned only abuse for his righteousness, why should he worship me?"

But that's not what Yahweh says. He says, "I'll bet you're wrong. You go inflict misfortune on him any way you like, as long as you don't harm him physically, and we'll see who's right."

All of a sudden, Job has become a pawn in a wager between Yahweh and Satan. A wager that Job has no knowledge of. He's not going to know that his subsequent misfortunes have been inflicted by Satan. He's going to believe that Yahweh has turned from benefactor to abuser, whereas Yahweh has done nothing except to stand aside and watch Job's reaction while Satan systematically destroys his life.

The bet is whether Job, believing that Yahweh has blighted his life for no good reason, will continue to worship and honor his abuser. If he does, Yahweh wins. If he doesn't, Satan wins. Either way, Job loses.

The first thing Satan does is to arrange that Job's wealth disappears, his flocks of livestock are either killed or stolen, and his lovely family perishes in a windstorm. Job is left a pauper, subject to scorn and rejection by his neighbors.

Job wailed and tore his clothes and shaved his head and thrashed about, saying "I was born with nothing and will die with nothing. Yahweh gave, and now he has taken away. Blessed be the name of Yahweh".

So far, Satan is losing the bet. Job's response has been stoic acceptance of his lot, rather than condemnation of the Lord. He's still a faithful worshipper.

The next time Satan and Yahweh get together, Yahweh says, "See? Job is still as faithful and good as ever, despite what you've done to him." Satan says, "Yeah, but that's because you made me leave him his health. Let me work on that, and you'll see him turn against you." Yahweh says, "Go ahead. Do whatever you like, as long as you don't kill him."

So Satan goes to Job and inflicts him with boils and pus-filled sores all over his face & body, turning him into a pain-ridden repulsive-looking (and smelling) wretch. He goes and sits in a rubbish-heap to scrape his sores with a potsherd. His wife says, "You idiot! Why are you sticking with Yahweh? Just curse him and die!"

Job says, "Don't be ridiculous. When he sends us good things, we appreciate them. Why should we complain when he sends us troubles?" *Which I find a very odd thing to say, since there's no logical connection between the two. If I'm pleased when you give me gifts, does that mean I shouldn't resent it when you turn around and beat me up? But anyhow, Job continues to stick with Yahweh.*

Most of the remainder of the book turns into a series of dialogues among Job and three out-of-town friends named Eliphaz, Bildad, and Zophar. They speak in turn. Job makes a speech, and one of the friends replies to it. Job answers with another speech, and another of the friends replies to it, and so on.

Job's basic point throughout is this: He wants to know why Yahweh is punishing him this way, since he has always led a blameless life. He wants Yahweh to tell him the charges against him, so he can defend himself against them.

The other three speakers each starts from a common foundation, which I call The Basic Argument: *Yahweh Never Does Anything Unjust; Therefore You're Not A Victim of Injustice.* Each fleshes it out in a somewhat different rambling and disconnected way.

Eliphaz: *"You had some good times and now it's your turn to have some bad times. Yahweh doesn't think that anybody is completely righteous, not even his angels. Be grateful he's correcting you. Stick with him, and he'll restore your fortunes."*

Job: *"You guys supposedly came to comfort me, but you aren't* helping. You seem to be blaming me. What you said makes no sense. I need to know what I've done, for Yahweh to treat me this way. What's my offense, Lord? If I have sins, they can't harm you. Tell me the charges against me."

Bildad: "Yahweh always does what's right. Your children must have sinned against him. Plead with him and if you're righteous he'll restore your fortunes. Godless men are without hope. Evil men sprout like weeds. Yahweh never abandons the faithful, and never rewards wickedness. If you are good, he'll restore your fortunes." (The connection between these various points is not apparent.)

Job: "I've heard all that before. But even if Yahweh tells me the charges, how can I argue with him in my defense? No one can stop him from taking what he wants. The fact that I'm innocent is no defense in his eyes. All I can do is beg for mercy. if Yahweh were human, we could go to court to decide our quarrel. But there is no higher court to judge between is. And I have no idea what the charge is against me. Why wasn't I stillborn? Not ever existing would be better than my current condition. What have I done?"

You see the pattern, and it continues on for several chapters with little variation. I'm getting bored with rehearsing it, so I'll stop and remind us of some crucial things that have gotten lost in the dialogs between the afflicted Job and his apologist friends.

****

Job is pleading on the basis of a fundamental misapprehension: his belief that Yahweh is the author of his suffering, and that there might be a reason for it.

But that's not the case. It is Satan, not Yahweh, that has brought him to disaster. And not because Job has done anything to deserve it, but to settle a bet.

Nothing in Job's past life deserved condemnation. He was perfectly blameless, and both Yahweh and Satan were agreed on that point. Their disagreement was a hypothetical: **If enough undeserved suffering were inflicted on a righteous man, would he turn away from Yahweh, or not?**

All of Job's pleading is pointless at the start. Yahweh *can't* tell him what he's accused of, because he's not accused of anything. Rather, Job had been the most righteous man in the world. THAT is the **reason** for his suffering: to see if it would make him unrighteous. The bet would have had no point if the subject were a wicked man. It was because Job was a good man that he was chosen for the experiment.

No, Yahweh didn't inflict the suffering on Job. But he told Satan to do it. And then he stood back and watched this righteous man suffer, just to see what he would do.

All that crap that the three friends were spouting, "Yahweh never allows an innocent person to suffer," is all the more ironic since that is *exactly* what is going on. And Yahweh is a party to the deception, by allowing Job to believe that he, Yahweh, is the source of his suffering.

The underlying idea behind the bet, I suppose, it that it would be wicked for the righteous man to lose his loyalty to Yahweh because of his suffering...and then he would no longer be righteous. Which leaves Job in a bind; so long as he fails to curse Yahweh, the experiment and his Satan-induced suffering will continue. But if he finally gives up and loses his faith in Yahweh, he will become a sinner and Yahweh will smite him for it.

I find this whole scenario disgusting. It's like beating a friendly dog just to see how much abuse it will take to turn him mean, so you can shoot him. Yahweh is disgusting and Satan is disgusting and the bet is disgusting, and the notion that it would be wicked to turn against an abusing god, is disgusting. The whole tale is sordid, and it never becomes less so.

But back to the story. Yahweh finally answers Job, and his answer is to scold Job for being uppity. "Who do you think you are, to question me, you little pipsqueak. Do you think you are as great as I, who can create and destroy mountains..." and on and on and on, boasting about how powerful and great and wise and knowing he is. "Will you continue to challenge me?"

Job says Nope, I'm a worthless wretch. I spoke out of turn and I'd best say no more. Job is intimidated into silence. He hasn't been refuted; just scared silent.

But Yahweh continues his harangue. "Are you trying to prove that I'm unjust --that I'm in the wrong and you're in the right? Can you do any of the things I can do? Can you crush the wicked?" and on and on with more boasting. He ends up describing, in great detail, the mighty and terrible monsters he has created.

Yahweh is claiming that because he has a lot of power to do stuff, it's impossible for him to be wrong or to do wrong. Yahweh could use a good course in basic logic.

And the whole harangue is thoroughly hypocritical, since Yaweh KNOWS that Job has been treated wrong...that his life has been ruined, not because he deserved it, but just to see what he would do. Yet Yahweh is carrying on as if the opposite were true. He is pissed off about Job's accusations, but instead of telling Job the truth —"It wasn't me, it was Satan,"—he tacitly admits responsibility, then calls Job out for saying so.

Anyhow, confronted with Yahweh's tales of his land-monster Behemoth and sea-monster Leviathan, Job folds completely. He says: "I was complaining out of ignorance, and I was terribly wrong. Now I'll go sit in a trash pile and repent my sins."

This seems to satisfy Yahweh's ego, so he turns to those who had been arguing with Job, and scolds them "For not telling the truth about me, as my man Job has done." And he lays a penalty of sacrifices on them.

Which leaves me to wonder what exactly Yahweh has in mind when he says "Job has told the truth about me." Most of what Job has been saying for several chapters is that Yahweh has been punishing him unjustly. Is that the "truth" that Yahweh has in mind? But that's just what Yahweh has been dumping on Job for saying. I have no clue what Yahweh is accusing them of doing or not doing. It looks to me as if Yahweh, having decided to take Job to his bosom, feels he should give a little grief to those who had been criticizing him, just to show that Job is now back in his favor.

So Job prayed for his friends, and Yahweh restored his fortunes twofold. He got a new family of sons and daughters and twice as many sheep and animals, and gold and other goodies and his daughters were the fairest in the land.

And they all lived happily ever after, and Job lived to be a hundred and forty and died, "being old and full of days."

And that's supposed to make everything okay, but I don't buy it. The fact that Yahweh now decides to make nice with Job does not nullify the fact that Job suffered terribly for no good reason, and that his first family was killed for the sole purpose of making Job suffer. You can't beat someone up for no reason, and say it was really OK to do so because afterwards you gave him a new car and a hundred dollars. It may compensate *for the wrong...but it doesn't make it right retroactively. It was still wrong to beat him up in the first place.*

As far as I'm concerned, this Book-of-Job Yahweh is an unsavory character.

The Bible, Chapter 45

The Book of Psalms

The Book of Psalms isn't a unified whole. Rather, it's a collection of independent poems of two kinds: prayers addressed to Yahweh, and testimonials addressed to the reader. There are common, often conflicting, themes running through them, occurring in no particular order. If you try to read them as the connected serial thoughts of a single writer, you'll conclude that you have a mood-shifting paranoid-schizophrenic on your hands.

However, these poems were written by a lot of different people, at different times, in different circumstances, and not in the order in which they are collected here. There are 150 of them.

****

The subject matter of these poems falls into certain broad categories: (1) asking Yahweh for something, or (2) thanking Yahweh for something, or (3) complaining to Yahweh about something, or (4) praising Yahweh for something or other. Generally, any given psalm will include more that one of these themes.

What is **asked** for most is (a) protection from enemies or (b) rescue from misery, or (c) punishment of enemies, or (d) power to succeed in overcoming adversaries.

What is **thanked** for most is (a) Yahweh's protection from enemies, or (b)Yahweh's infinite wisdom and power, or (c) Yahweh's endless benevolence toward his worshippers, or (d) Yahweh's role in leading his people to the promised land.

What is **complained** about most is being forsaken by Yahweh and left in misery, broken physically and attacked by enemies.

What is **praised** most is (a) Yahweh's power, or (b) Yahweh's benevolence, or (c) Some particular thing Yahweh does or has done or is doing, or (d) Yahweh's punishment of the wicked -- meaning people he doesn't like. *Schadenfreude is common here...reveling in the way Yahweh makes those wicked people suffer.*

The Book of Psalms provides endless fodder for sermons. Overall it's a study in contrasts in the image of Yahweh presented. Sometimes he comes across as a loving and faithful protector of his people, who will never forsake them. Other times he is an uncaring overlord who ignores his people until they beg for his attention, or is a crushing tyrant who smashes those he doesn't like, or is downright cruel and inflicts misery for unknown reasons.

There are notable juxtapositions of these two views, such as the 22nd psalm, which is a cry of anguish, "My god my god why have you forsaken me?" followed by the 23rd, "The lord is my shepherd, I shall not want… he comforts my soul" and so on.

Throughout the book, there is a sameness of these two alternating themes that, after a while, caused my eyes to glaze over. Occasionally one of the testimonials, taken simply as a poem in isolation, is quite beautiful. But grinding through the book looking for occasional pearls of poetry can be a grim chore.

I'll comment on a few individual psalms that captured my attention.

The 38th psalm accuses Yahweh of cruelty. It might might have been uttered by Job: "Because of your anger, I am in great pain…my whole body is diseased…my sores stink and rot."

Psalm #10 accuses him of neglect and rejection:" Why are you so far away, O Lord? Why do you hide yourself? So does #13: "How much longer will you forget me, Lord? Forever?...How

234

long must I endure trouble?" And #60: "You have rejected us, God, and defeated us."

****

I found psalm 82 quite remarkable. It has Yahweh presiding in the heavenly council, in the assembly of the gods. He chides them for being corrupt, and revokes their immortality. *This may be the first we've heard of a council of corrupt gods. Though we did learn, back in Genesis, that Yahweh had a flock of godlet sons who were banging mortal girls. Maybe these were the same ones.*

****

Psalm #84 is noteworthy in that its message is positive from beginning to end. Most of them are not.

****

There are psalms where Yahweh seems to be saying: Knock off the sacrifices to me. I don't need your animals, and I don't eat the meat you roast on the altar. *Which leads one to wonder about all that stuff back in Exodus and Leviticus about the importance of sacrifices.*

****

There are psalms where Yahweh reaffirms his promise that David will always have descendants.

****

There is one psalm, #119, that is almost a book in itself. It runs to 176 verses, singing praises of the Law of the Lord and how wonderful and important it is, and so on.

****

There are psalms about all of the great things that Yahweh creates and makes happen: #145 is a good example: *"Great is Yahweh! Greatly praise him !His greatness is beyond discovery! Let each generation tell its children what glorious things he does. I will meditate about your glory, splendor, majesty, and miracles. Your awe-inspiring deeds shall be on every tongue; I will proclaim your greatness. Everyone will tell about how good you are, and about your righteousness."* ...and on in the same vein for several paragraphs.

****

There are psalms that are history lessons. Psalm 78 is seventy-two verses long, describing the events of Exodus through Joshua, and ends by saying that Judah is Yahweh's chosen tribe. *My guess is that it was written by a Judean. Most likely David.* Psalm 105 gives the history of the people from Joseph through Moses and the Egyptian captivity.

****

But the over-arching feature of this book, and the one I can't get away from, is the conflicting pictures of Yahweh contained in it. Yahweh is kind and benevolent and always watches over us. Yahweh can be cruel and punitive and often ignores us in our time of need.

After reading a few dozen of the psalms, it begins to seem repetitious.

You can get weary reading it.

The Bible, Chapter 46

The Book of Proverbs

Like the Book of Psalms, the Book of Proverbs is a collection of discrete elements and not a continuous discourse. Most or all of them are supposed to have been written by Solomon, the putative wisest man in the world. They give advice on various matters such as religion and morality and the importance of wisdom and getting along in the world and like that.

A running theme is the importance of obeying the teachings of those wiser than you, such as your parents and Solomon.

Proverb 1 contains advice worth commenting on. It says, "Suppose somebody tells you, 'Let's go find some innocent people and kill them and take all their stuff', don't listen to them; robbery always claims the life of the robber." *You may note however, that this is exactly what Moses, or maybe Yahweh, told the children of Israel on their trek to the promised land: "Let's go find some innocent people and kill them all and take their stuff and take over their land." The wisdom of Solomon is inscrutable.*

The first several Proverbs focus largely on Wisdom in the abstract, treating it as a commodity to be gained, or a preacher to be listened to. But when it comes to saying where this commodity is to be obtained, the answer is: from the teachings of men wiser than you. No advice is given on how to differentiate such men from the rest of the population, or how to tell when something is wisdom and when it isn't. They just hammer the reader with the value and importance and benefit of Wisdom, and how the Lord will be good to you if you have Wisdom, but will smite you if you haven't. Presumably, if you mistake something for Wisdom when it isn't, you can be in deep trouble.

You wouldn't have made that mistake if you'd had Wisdom.

Proverb 5 is an admonition against adultery, which is defined as getting it on with another man's wife. Her lips may be as sweet as honey and her kisses as smooth as oil, but they will lead only to bitterness and pain. It's not stated WHY they will have that consequence; only that they will. *History often proves otherwise. Consider David.*

Whenever the topic of adultery comes up, it is always the woman who is the seductress and temptress, out to lead a poor boy into sin and error. You know these women, always itching to cheat on their marriage vows. Never a hint that perhaps the seduction might just go the other way.

Proverb 6 contains a warning against laziness. Then it tells how worthless, wicked, lying people will always be struck with disaster, even though historical evidence would suggest otherwise. It lists seven things that Yahweh will not tolerate:
1. A haughty look
2. A lying tongue
3.. Hands that kill innocent people
4. A heart that devises wicked schemes
5. Feet that rush to do evil
6. A man who bears false witness
7. A man who stirs up trouble in the community

This last seems to put Thomas Paine, Jefferson, Frederick Douglas, the southern abolitionists, the leaders of the labor movement for better pay and working conditions, Vietnam war protesters, and the Arab Spring people, in deep trouble. I wonder where Jesus would fit in here? (But of course, we're a long ways from getting to Jesus yet.)

Then there's more about adultery.

Then **Proverb 7** talks about adultery some more, and how rapacious women drag young men into sin:

"Once I was looking out the window of my house, and I saw many inexperienced young men, but noticed one foolish fellow in particular. He was walking along the street near the corner where a certain woman lived. He was passing near her house in the evening after it was dark. And then she met him; she was dressed like a prostitute and was making plans. She was a bold and shameless woman who always walked the streets or stood waiting at a corner, sometimes in the streets, sometimes in the marketplace. She threw her arms around the young man, kissed him, looked him straight in the eye, and said, "I made my offerings today and have the meat from the sacrifices. So I came out looking for you. I wanted to find you, and here you are! I've covered my bed with sheets of colored linen from Egypt. 17 I've perfumed it with myrrh, aloes, and cinnamon. Come on! Let's make love all night long. We'll be happy in each other's arms. My husband isn't at home. He's on a long trip. 20 He took plenty of money with him and won't be back for two weeks." So she tempted him with her charms, and he gave in to her smooth talk. Suddenly he was going with her like an ox on the way to be slaughtered, like a deer prancing into a trap where an arrow would pierce its heart. He was like a bird going into a net—he did not know that his life was in danger."

Then **Proverbs 8 and 9** talk about Wisdom some more.

Proverbs 10 through 22 have a totally different structure. Instead of being sustained advisories on some topic or topics, each is a collection of short, one-or- two-sentence aphorisms. One is "Someone who holds back the truth causes trouble, but one who openly criticizes works for peace." How this fits with #7 above isn't clear. Others that seem to me problematic are:

—Wealth protects the rich; poverty destroys the poor.
—A man who hides his hatred is a liar. Anyone who spreads gossip is a fool.
—The more you talk, the more likely you are to sin. If you are wise, you will keep quiet.

Some others that have caught my eye:

—Never get a lazy man to do something for you; he will be as irritating as vinegar on your teeth or smoke in your eyes.
—Beauty in a woman without good judgment is like a gold ring in a pig's snout.
—Stupid people always think they are right. Wise people listen to advice.
—Unused fields could yield food for the poor; but unjust men keep them from being farmed.
—Better a small serving of vegetables with love, than a fattened calf with hatred.
—Only a man with no sense would promise to be responsible for someone else's debts. *Co-signers take note.*
—When some fool starts an argument, he is asking for a beating.
—A stupid son can bring his father to ruin. A nagging wife is like water going drip-drip-drip
—Some people are too lazy to put food in their own mouths.
—Think carefully before you promise an offering to God. You might regret it later.
—Better to live in the desert than with a nagging, complaining wife.
—The lazy man stays at home; he says a lion might get him if he goes outside.

Laced throughout this series of Proverbs are the same old homilies that history and experience show to be false: the righteous always prosper, the wicked are always punished. *It's a mystery to me how anyone could take these things seriously, and I find them downright annoying. If they are meant as statements of fact, they're patently false. If they are prophesies or predictions about how things are going to be, they are unsupported by experience. From what we've seen, Yahweh punishes whomever he pleases whenever he pleases, and rewards whomever he pleases whenever he pleases, and most of the time does neither, but ignores what's going on and just lets things happen*

The remaining **Proverbs, 23 through 30**, are often less brief in their statements. Among these are some examples of good sense, as well as some less so.

—Don't hesitate to rescue a man who is about to be executed unjustly. You may say it's none of your business, but God knows and judges your motives.

—People who promise things that they never give are like clouds and wind that bring no rain.

—Singing to a person who is depressed is like stripping off his clothes on a cold day, or pouring vineger into his wounds.

—If you can't control your temper, you are like a city without walls: ever open to attack.

—Getting involved in an argument that's none of your business is like going down the street and grabbing a dog by the ears.

—Gossip is so tasty! How we love to swallow it!

—You might as well curse your friend as wake him up early in the morning with a loud greeting.

—A friend means well, even when he hurts you. But when an enemy puts his arm around your shoulder —watch out!

—A man in authority who oppresses poor people is like a driving rain that destroys the crops.

—Prejudice is wrong. But some judges will do anything to get a bribe.

—It is a foolish waste to spend money on prostitutes.

—Stupid people express their anger openly, but sensible people are patient and hold back. *(Compare this with: A man who hides his hatred is a liar. Anyone who spreads gossip is a fool.)*

—You cannot correct a servant just by talking to him. He may understand you but he will pay no attention.

—A leech has two daughters, and both are named "Give me!"

—There are four things that are too mysterious for me to understand:
  —An eagle flying in the sky
  –A snake moving on a rock
  –A ship finding its way over the sea
  –And a man and woman falling in love

Proverb 31 says:
–How hard it is to find a capable wife! She is worth far more than jewels.

and then enumerates in great detail what makes a good wife.
–She's a good weaver and seamstress
–She gets up before daylight to cook the family breakfast
–She oversees the family's holdings, and buys land, and plants vineyards.
–She makes articles of clothing and sells them to merchants
–She speaks with gentle wisdom
–Her husband is a man of influence and a leading citizen (?!)

Finally, one of my favorites is **Proverb 28:26.** It says:
—It is foolish to follow your own opinions. Be safe, and follow the teachings of wiser people.

It intrigues me because it can be taken in either of two conflicting ways. On the one hand, it seems to be saying "Ignore your conscience in deciding what's right. If it conflicts with what authority tells you, just do what they say." On the other hand, it seems to be saying, "Don't get a big head and think you're an expert on everything. Listen to those who actually know what they're talking about ."

Many of these Proverbs are ambivalent in this same way. They are easy fodder for "Those Who Quote Scripture For Their Own Purposes."

The Bible, Chapter 47

The Book of Ecclesiastes

Ecclesiastes means "teachings". The book of Ecclesiastes was written by Solomon: it says so right at the beginning: "The words of the Teacher, son of David, King in Jerusalem." He was clearly in a blue funk when he started it. The opening theme of the book is pure nihilism: There is no purpose or meaning in anything. Life's a bitch, and then you die. Doing anything is like trying to catch the wind. As the book progresses he moves back and forth between that theme and less depressing matters, as he gets to feeling better for a time. It's almost a stream-of-consciousness essay, following wherever his thoughts lead him, but never abandoning the opening theme. One can almost see him grumbling though his long soliloquy. I find the mood shifts noteworthy enough to flag the different moods as A and B. Throughout there is only a casual occasional mention of Yahweh. Solomon is telling us how HE feels, not how Yahweh feels.

==========

A:
Meaningless, utterly meaningless. Nothing is significant, nothing is worthwhile. Everything is crap.

Nobody gets anything from his labor. The world goes on in its meaningless cycle. The same things happen over and over, nothing is for the first time. Men die and nobody remembers them and the world goes on. Anything you do is chasing the wind.

I sought and gained great wisdom and understanding, but in the end it meant nothing. Just chasing the wind.

I said to myself: Surely pleasure and happiness are worthwhile. But that was just babble. What does pleasure accomplish? I did great deeds, built palaces and orchards, amassed great wealth, had harems full of women, became the greatest man in the history of Jerusalem. And so what? When I looked at it I saw that it meant nothing, I had gained nothing in the end. Just wind-chasing crap.

Wisdom itself is pointless. So is folly.. Neither leads anywhere. In the end, the wise man and the fool both die.

Work and labor lead nowhere. A man works all his life, then he dies and takes none of it with him. It's is left for somebody else who never worked for it. It's utterly meaningless. There's no point to anything.

B:
The best thing anyone can do is eat and drink and find satisfaction in their work and their lives. Because those things are gifts from Yahweh.

A:
But in t he end they still mean nothing.

The world is an endless cycle of seasons. There's a season for everything: a time to be born and a time to die; a time to plant and a time to harvest; a time to destroy and a time to create; a time for sadness and one for laughter; a time to seek and a time to give up; a time to speak up and a time to shut up; a time for war, a time for peace, a time for love, a time for hate.

B:
There's nothing better in the world than to be happy and live a good life, because that's how Yahweh has arranged it. But people are no different from the other animals. They all operate on the same principles. They are born, live, die, and rot. In between, they enjoy their lives as best they can. But that too is

meaningless.

A:
Achievement is useless. Wealth is useless. As you come into the world, so you depart from it, and in the final analysis you have gained nothing. A corpse takes nothing with it. None of its achievements have any meaning to it.

When I look at all the injustice in the world, I envy those who are dead and gone. They are better off than those who are alive and suffering. But the most fortunate of all are those who have never been born to witness the world's injustice. *[A rather odd claim, given the difficulty of identifying —or even counting— the never-born, to congratulate them on their good fortune. How many fortunate never-born people are there?]*

The only reason people strive to succeed is envy; they want to do better than the Joneses, to show up their neighbors. But in the end, it all amounts to nothing.

B:
It's not good to be alone. Two are better off than one. They can help each other and care for each other, and comfort each other, and combine for defense against enemies.

A:
A king may rule over countless people, but when he dies there will be no gratitude for what he has done. His works were all useless wind-chasing.

B:
Some advice: Don't be frivolous in your promises to Yahweh. But when you do promise something, carry it out promptly. Yahweh is in heaven and you are on earth, so keep your promises scarce.

Here we see how Solomon's theology is radically different from that of Moses and the Levites. Back then Yahweh was concrete, and lived (in some state or other) in the tabernacle-tent made for him, fronted by the altar where blood-sacrifices were made to him. Solomon is no longer buying that. He sees Yahweh as living in heaven, which is Up. This theological shift was noted earlier, in the first book of Kings. It's complicated by the fact that Solomon built the first Temple as a refuge for Yahweh, so he could move out of his tent and into a real building.

Don't make idle talk with Yahweh. No matter how worthless your existence, you should still honor and worship him.

B: More advice. Don't long for wealth; you'll never be satisfied. The more you have, the more responsibilities you'll have.

A:
People labor and save, but in the end they lose everything and die. There's no point to anything.

B:
The best thing a person can do is eat and drink and enjoy his short pointless life.

A:
A man gains wealth and is unable to enjoy it. It doesn't matter how long he lives, if he dies unhappy without a decent burial. A baby born dead is better off.

Aphorisms for life:
B:
—A good reputation is better than gold.
A:
—The day you die is better than the day you were born.
—A home where there is mourning is better than one with joy. Remember death is always waiting.
—Sorrow is better than laughter
—A wise person dwells on death, not happiness.

B:
—Control your temper; don't bear a grudge.
—Gaining wisdom is as good an an inheritance.
—Nobody does what's right every time. We all make mistakes.

—I have striven to gain wisdom and understanding. And what I have learned is that there is nothing worse than a woman scheming to to run your life. You think she offers love, but it's just bait for a trap to get you into her claws. I have found countless men to respect and trust, but never a single woman.

This is a heartfelt cry from someone with great experience. A man with 700 wives and 300 concubines is going to be pussy-whipped from the get-go. He knows what it's like.

Some observations:
B:
—Obey the King and don't antagonize him. You'll get in a peck of trouble.
—There's no justice in the world. People commit crimes and get away with it because they aren't punished promptly. People say, "Yahweh will see to it that the wicked are always punished," but that's not true. Often as not, the righteous get punished and the wicked go scot-free.

So my best advice is to eat and drink and enjoy yourself as best you can, while you can.

A:
Nobody knows the future, and it doesn't matter. In the end, the righteous and the wicked end up the same. One fate awaits everybody, which is a dismal fact about the world.

B:
But as long as one is alive, one has some hope. A live dog is better than a dead lion. It's true, the living know they are going to die; but the dead don't know anything at all. So eat, drink, be

happy. Yahweh is okay with that. Enjoy life with the woman you love...

A:
...as long as you're going to live the useless life Yahweh has given you. Enjoy every useless day, because that's all you're going to get . Do your useless work, because you won't be doing anything when you're dead.

....

Are you getting tired of this? I certainly am. And it goes on the same for the rest of the book.
"You might as well live for the moment, because you can't know what the future will bring. Except in the end, you will be dead."
....

One of Solomon's final observations is this: **There are too many books. And too much study is a weariness of the flesh.**

The Bible, Chapter 48

The Song of Songs

The Song of Songs is a collection of love songs, or love letters, between a man and a woman. Sometimes the woman is speaking, sometimes the man. It is often claimed that the book is an extended metaphor about the love between Yahweh and his chosen people. Don't you believe it. This is about good old wonderful carnal human love. There is no mention of Yahweh anywhere in it.

The Yahweh interpretation comes out of the anti-sex view that nothing about actual human love could possibly have been included in the holy writings back when they were being assembled, because... well... because. It is also called the Song of Solomon, because of a claim that it was written by Solomon. I find that preposterous, given the misogyny he shows in Ecclesiastes, where he pretty much calls women the root of all evil.

In some of these songs or letters, the woman is addressing herself to her lover. In others, the man is addressing himself to her. In some of them, the woman is addressing nobody in particular, just ruminating to herself. The songs are rife with similes glorifying each other's persons and bodies. They are clearly hot for each other, in a way that Yahweh isn't hot for anybody. There is one odd song in the middle that has nothing to do with love, and seems out of place.

Summarizing a poem or love letter is a hopeless undertaking, but I'll do my best.

****

SHE
Your lips cover me with kisses all over. I love the smell of your

body. Let's run away...be my king, take me to your room and let's make love.

...Women of Jerusalem, don't scorn me because I'm dark; I am still beautiful. My color comes from working in the sun
---Lover, tell me where you'll be taking your flocks, so I don't have to hunt you out among the others.

HE
My lovely woman, you know the place; go there. You arouse me the way a mare arouses a stallion. Your hair is beautiful, the way it falls upon your neck. I'll bring you a gold and silver necklace.

SHE
We were lying on his couch. The fragrance of my perfume filled the air. He has the scent of myrrh as he lies upon my breasts. He is like the wild flowers that bloom in vineyards.

HE
How beautiful you are! Your eyes glow with love.

SHE
How handsome you are! We can make love right here. The green grass will be our bed, the trees will be the beams of our house. Here, I am just a lily in a mountain valley.

You are like an apple tree in a forest compared to other men. I love being near it, its fruit is sweet to my taste. I am in his banquet hall where he has brought his cloak of love over me... Restore my strength with raisins and apples. I am exhausted from love-making. His left hand is under my head, his right hand caresses my body... *Women of Jerusalem, promise you won't try to take my lover from me.*

****

SHE
I hear his voice racing over the hills to meet me, running like a young deer...now he standing here at my window...he speaks to

251

me...

HE
Come then my darling, come with me. It is springtime, the flowers are in bloom, the birds are singing, fruit is ripening, the air is fragrant with blossoms. Come out to me, my love...you are acting like a dove hiding among the rocks. Let me see your beautiful face, hear your beautiful voice.
....
Catch the little foxes, before they eat up the new crop of grapes.

It's not easy to tell what this is about, coming in the midst of a tender speech to his beloved. If it is addressed to her, it must have some symbolic meaning that is totally obscure. But it seems to be addressed to somebody else. I'll leave you to figure it out.

****

SHE
I had a terrible dream! I dreamed my lover wasn't there and I went looking for him throughout the streets and alleys. I asked the watchmen "Have you seen my lover?" But then I found him, wrapped my arms around him, and wouldn't let him go until I took him to my mother's house, to the room where I was born... *Women of Jerusalem, promise you won't try to take my lover from me.*

****

Here is the strange passage I mentioned, that seems to have nothing to do with what is going on elsewhere in the book.

SHE
What's this I see coming from the desert? It's King Solomon, carried on his throne, surrounded by his finest soldiers, hardened in battle, each armed with a sword! What a throne! The finest wood! Its posts are covered with silver, its canopy is cloth of gold, its cushions are covered with purple cloth made by the women of Jerusalem.

Women of Zion! Come see King Solomon! He's wearing his royal crown!

****

HE
My love, you are so beautiful, your eyes shining with love behind your veil! Here's what you are like:
-Your hair bounces like young goats bounding down the hills.
-Your teeth are white as sheep, perfectly matched, and none missing.
-Your lips are like a scarlet ribbon.
-Your neck is like the tower of David
-Your breasts are like gazelles, feeding among the lilies.

Until daybreak I will go to the mountain of myrrh and the hill of incense. *[Are you thinking what I'm thinking?]* You are SO beautiful, in every respect, in every way.

****

Then there's a lot more of the same thing, with him reciting her virtues on and on. Just try to make out the following as meaning something other than carnal love.

HE
Your love is better than wine, your scent more fragrant than spice. The taste of honey is on your lips, my darling, your tongue is milk and honey to me. My sweetheart is like a garden...

SHE
Let my lover come to his garden and eat the best of its fruits.

HE
I have entered my garden, my lover, my bride. I am gathering my spices, i'm eating my honey and drinking my wine and milk.

253

****

Then she has another dream. Her lover disappears. She seeks him frantically. The city watchmen beat her up. She never finds him.

SHE
Women of Jerusalem, promise you won't try to take my lover from me.

Then she takes her turn at telling what HE's like, praising his face, his hair, his eyes, his cheeks, his lips, his hands, his body, his thighs, his mouth. "Everything about him enchants me."

The 7th and 8th chapters of Song of Songs are openly erotic in their message. It's also quite beautiful poetry, and I won't spoil it by trying to summarize it.

Go read that part yourself.

The Bible, Chapter 49

The Book of Isaiah
part 1.

Then there is a sermon against those who are mean to widows and orphans, and a promise that they will be punished. Go figure.

Then there is a long condemnation of Assyria, in which

The book of Isaiah purports to be the thoughts of the prophet Isaiah concerning the people of Judah in general and Jerusalem in particular, a couple of hundred years down the road from the time of Solomon, during the reigns of Uzziah, Jotham, Ahaz, and Hezekiah. It is a very long, rambling, hodgepodge of prophecies, condemnations, threats, stories, poems, etc. It has no narrative structure, and no evident principle of organization. No overall synopsis of its content is possible. Toward the end, it moves ahead a couple of centuries after Hezekiah, well past the life span of Isaiah, to the time of Ezra and Nehemiah and the Babylonian Captivity.

A prominent early theme is that the Judeans have fallen out of favor with Yahweh, and are therefore doomed. We are given no clear catalog of their offenses, but a primary one seems to be Lack of Humility, since one of Yahweh's major goals, according to Isaiah, is to bring down the lofty, humiliate the proud, uglify the beautiful, and in general Teach Them A Lesson for Being Uppity.

******

The opening chapters have Yahweh giving the Judeans a thorough chewing out for their misdeeds, telling them to take their burnt sacrifices to him and Shove Them; they are no longer pleasing to him. He is fixing to smite them the way he did Sodom and Gomorrah...and on and on, until the land is cleansed and he can institute a New Deal of Prosperity among the righteous.

His condemnation of the women is a perfect example of the chaotic nature of the writing. I quote:

The women of Zion are haughty, walking along with outstretched necks, flirting with their eyes, strutting along with swaying hips, with ornaments jangling on their ankles. Therefore, the Lord will bring sores on the heads of the women of Zion; the Lord will make their scalps bald. Instead of fragrance, there will be a stench. Instead of a sash, a rope. Instead of fine clothing, sackcloth. Instead of beauty, branding. Your men will fall by the sword, your warriors in battle. The gates of Zion will lament and mourn; destitute, she will sit on the ground. In that day seven women will take hold of one man and say, "We will eat our own food and provide our own clothes: only let us be called by your name. Take away our disgrace."

(1) The women of Zion are —surprisingly— acting like women. (2) Yahweh will punish them for it. (3) The menfolk will be killed in battle. (4) Multiple women will be in need of a husband. One supposes they will have a hard time finding one, given how they look and smell after Yahweh is done with them.

Then more general scolding and prophecies of doom. Real estate acquisition is condemned. Drinking and partying are condemned. Asking Yahweh to hurry up with what ever he's going to do is condemned. Belief in one's own wisdom and cleverness are condemned. Knowledge of drink-mixing is condemned, along with bribery.

Then Isaiah has a mystical experience in which he confronts

Yahweh directly, which sounds somewhat like an acid trip. Yahweh sits on a throne, wearing a robe so huge that it fills the temple. He is attended by creatures with six wings, singing his praises loud enough to shake the building. Isaiah is scared shitless. Then one of the creatures takes a pair of tongs, grabs a burning ember from the sacrificial fire, flies over and jams it against Isaiah's mouth, saying "There! Now all your sins are forgiven."

Then Yahweh commissions Isaiah to go forth and make the people stupid, so they won't have a clue how to get back into Yahweh's good graces. *This seems an odd instruction, but that's what it says.*

Then he prophesies a coming war, and says that Yahweh will send a sign; to wit: a young virgin, or maybe just a young girl, will give birth to a son to be named Immanuel. Then Judah's enemies will be laid waste and everything will be alright. *(Several centuries down the road, a New Testament writer will try to make much of this prophecy.)*

Then Isaiah prophesies an Assyrian invasion of Israel and Judah. When the time comes, Yahweh will whistle as a signal for the Assyrians and Egyptians to come swarming in. Then he'll commission a barber from out of the country to shave everybody's head and beard and pubic hair.

Then Yahweh told Isaiah to take a large scroll and write a name on it. Then Isaiah Went in Unto the prophetess, who may have been his wife, and she conceived, and bare him a son which they baptized with the name on the scroll., which meant something like "quick to the plunder, swift to the spoil", in honor of the Assyrian's raid on Judah. Why this was done we are not told.

Then there are more threats of punishments, and warnings not to consult spirit mediums or communicate with the dead, and then promises of a brighter day to come.

Then there's a poem or song promising the arrival of a Messiah, which may or may not have something to do with the baby named Immanuel that the young virgin or young girl gave birth to. This passage will achieve great popularity a few hundred years down the road, when we get to the New Testament, since it seems to foretell events recounted therein...unless those events were foreordained. But we shall get to that in due time.

Then Yahweh gets mad at Jacob, aka Israel, who's been dead and gone for many centuries, and takes it out on the local people and promises to bash them all, including orphans and widows, because they are all wicked and deserve it.
Yahweh threatens to do a whole bunch of things to them that apparently never got done in actuality.

Then there's a long prophecy about the people of the tribe of Jesse, who you may recall was the father of King David a long time ago. They will witness a new Eden in which wolves and leopards and lions and bears will make friends with lambs and goats and calves, and lions will eat hay like oxen, and a little child will lead them, and babies will play with vipers without getting bit.

A new king of the house of David will take over, and the lost tribes that were dispersed around the world when Assyria conquered Israel will all come back, and Israel and Judah will be allies instead of enemies, and together they will go out and invade surrounding cities and kill everybody and take their stuff.

The Bible, Chapter 50

The Book of Isaiah
part 2.

Prophecies of doom continue. Isaiah predicts horrendous disasters will befall Babylon. The Lord will gather his armies, and when they strike, Babylonians will die in horrible agony akin to birth pains. The earth will be made a desert. The stars will go out, the sun will go dark, the moon will give no light. All who are sinful, or arrogant, or proud will be destroyed by Yahweh's anger. Litle bitty babies will have their brains dashed out before the people's eyes. Their houses will be looted, their wives and daughters will be gang-raped. Babylon will be a desolation, fit only for ostriches and wild goats. And so on and so forth.

This time Isaiah prophesied right, except of course for the astronomical anomalies that never happened. The Assyrians invaded Babylon, reduced the city of Babylon to rubble, and killed everybody and took their stuff. It took a while for Babylon to recover so that Nebuchadnezzar could conquer Judah and destroy the Temple and drag a bunch of Jews into captivity back in Babylon.

Then there's more grisly predictions about how the Babylonians will suffer, and the Kings of Babylon will be killed and left in the field to rot along with dead soldiers.

Then Yahweh will destroy the Assyrians.

Then Yahweh will destroy the Philistines.

Then Yahweh will destroy the Moabites.

Then Yahweh will punish Syria. Damascus will be a pile of burning ruins.

Then Yahweh will see to it that Israel comes to an end of its days as a power.

At the time Isaiah was writing, during the reign of King Hezekiah, the northern Kingdom of Israel had already been overrun by the Assyrians, who dragged all the Israelites off to Assyria, where they would eventually turn into the Ten Lost Tribes dispersed throughout the world .Looks to me like Isaiah is just reporting on current event, not prophesying.

Then Yahweh will punish Sudan.

Then Yahweh will punish Egypt. He will arrive riding on a cloud. He'll foment internal strife so the Egyptians will fight each other. Then he'll make the Nile gradually dry up. The Egyptians will be terrified of Judah, and will begin to speak Hebrew and will convert to Judaism.

Then Yahweh told Isaiah to throw away his shoes and clothes and go about naked and barefoot. He did that for three years, and apparently it never got much notice --maybe the people were accustomed to prophets wandering around doing crazy stuff. When the Assyrians conquered the Philistine city of Ashdod, Yahweh announced "See what I made Isaiah do? That's what will happen to Egypt and Sudan...the Assyrians will shame everybody by making them go naked and barefoot with their buttocks hanging out for everybody to see,"

We aren't told whom Yahweh made the announcement to. Or what Ashdod had to do with it. Or why it was shameful for the Egyptians to go about bare-assed, when it wasn't for Isaiah. *Some Bible events remain wrapped in mystery.*

Then Isaiah had a bunch of visions about various peoples. *I especially like the one about Edom:*

Somebody calls to me from Edom: "How soon will the night be over. How soon will it end?" I answer, "Morning is coming, but

260

night will come again. If you want to ask again, come back and ask."

Say what?

Then Isaiah gets all over a guy named Shebna, the administrator of the royal household, for being uppity. He says, "Who do you think you are, carving a tomb for yourself in the hillside? You think you're a big shot, but Yahweh will fix you! He'll fling you into the desert like a ball and leave you there to rot. Then Eliakim will take over your job and run the houshold until his dependents start hanging on him and wear him out." All because Shebna was digging a tomb for himself.

Then there is another doleful prophecy of doom for Phoenecia.

Then there's a prophecy that Yahweh will get mad and lay waste to the whole Earth, and turn it into a desolation. Then he'll fix it up again.

Then Yahweh will destroy the Moabites again.

Then he'll give Judah peace and prosperity.

Then he'll get mad again and punish everybody for their sins. He'll take a sword and kill the sea-monster Leviathan that he bragged about creating in the book of Job.

Then Isaiah predicts doom for the northern kingdom of Israel, which had already happened. Then he complains about the prophets of Judah getting too drunk to make sense of their visions. They sit around their table and puke all over it and make a general mess and never clean it up. Shame on them.

Then he predicts a bunch of bad stuff that's going to happen to the people of Jerusalem.

****

And I am getting bored with this same-old same-old over and over again. Isaiah, in my estimation, is a windbag. He needs to learn a new tune. There are 66 chapters in the Book of Isaiah, and we are only up to 28.

I have no idea what sort of life guidance I'm supposed to be getting from all this. I don't think it means I should go naked and barefoot for three years. And I no longer see Babylon as a serious threat.

The Bible, Chapter 51

The Book of Isaiah
conclusion

I have had it with this bombastic turkey Isaiah. It's the same thing over and over. Somebody is doomed. Yahweh will protect his people. Yahweh is getting ready to blast somebody. Yahweh is great. Babylon is doomed. Yahweh loves his people. Yahweh despises his people as sinners. Somebody is doomed. Yahweh promises that Israel will rise again. All of the evil people will be blasted. Yahweh promises things that never happened and never will. Yadda yadda yadda.

Then at one point he repeats, varbatim, the Hezekiah story from the book of Kings. And doesn't bother to footnote it.

Then it's off again on the same old track.

****

Reading onward, I found an item worthy of mention.

Yahweh's servant whom he has sent is a wholly unremarkable man, plain in appearance or even homely— nothing desirable about him. He has grown up in misery and suffering, despised and rejected. We believed Yahweh was punishing him for his wrongdoing, but he was punishing us THROUGH his servant. The servant was enduring OUR punishment for our transgressions, not his own. He suffered mildly and uncomplaining. He wil be buried with the wicked, even though he never did anything wrong. It was Yahweh's will to crush him and cause him to suffer. But after he has suffered he will see the light and be satisfied.

I'm pretty sure, when we get to New Testament times, some will hark back to this and see it as a prophecy about Jesus-bar-Joseph of Nazareth…or according to some, Jesus-bar-Yahweh…even though it's not recorded that Jesus was especially ugly or grew up in misery and suffering or was buried with sinners. We shall see what comes.

****

I found this next item of interest for a different reason. Yahweh says that when Jerusalem achieves its rightful place of glory among nations, it and its people will be given new names. "The people will be called Hephzibah…and the land will be called Beulah."

There's an old hymn called "Beulah Land", and I had often wondered where the reference came from. Now I know.

> Oh Beulah Land, sweet Beulah Land
> As on the highest mount I stand
> I look away across the sea
> Where mansions are prepared for me
> And view the shining glory shore,
> My heaven my home forever more

Except the hymn takes its premise from modern theology, and sees Beulah Land as *Heaven*: the place where good people's souls go after they die. There's no hint of that metaphysic in Isaiah, or any other book of the Old Testament I've read so far.

I'm still waiting to see when they start talking about heaven and hell and afterlife.

The Bible, Chapter 52

The Book of Jeremiah
part 1.

> JEREMIAD *noun*: A long literary work, in which the author bitterly laments the state of society and its morals in a serious tone of sustained invective, and always contains a prophecy of society's imminent downfall. More generally, a long condemnatory or pessimistic complaint. Named after the Biblical prophet Jeremiah's writings.

This may be the most incoherent book I have yet found in the Bible. I'll do my best to illuminate it.
....

Jeremiah was in business during the tail end of the Judean kingdom, from around 620 bc to 587 bc —a period when the people once again were going off and worshipping Baal and other idols, and not paying attention to Yahweh. Nothing annoyed Yahweh worse that having "his" people worship some other god. He laid claim to their being his, due to the mutilated-genitals covenant made a long time ago. As I recall, the deal was that if the (male) children of Israel would cut off their foreskins, Yahweh promised to take care of them forever. But if you ask me, he hadn't done a very good job of holding up his end of the bargain. "His" people had been assaulted by Egyptians and Assyrians repeatedly, without Yahweh doing anything much about it. Instead, he sat back and said they had it coming, it was their punishment because they hadn't been worshipping him enough. My guess is, the people figured that if Yahweh wasn't going to do his job of protecting them, they might as well look for another god who might.

Despite the lack of anything like a plot in Jeremiah's carrying-on, it's possible to discern a timeline of sorts within them, as he references various events taking place during his career. I'll try to mention that.

****

When Jeremiah was a little kid, Yahweh came to him and appointed him to be a prophet to preach to all nations. Jeremiah complained that he didn't know how to preach because he was just a little kid. But Yahweh said: Don't worry, we'll take care of that. He reached out his hand and touched Jeremiah's little mouth, and said: I have put my words into your mouth. Now I appoint you over kings and nations to oversee their destruction.

Then Yahweh asked: What do you see? The kid said: I see a boiling pot tilted toward us from the north. Then Yahweh said: This means that disaster will come to Jerusalem from the north, and their kings will come and take over, and it will be the people's punishment for turning to other gods.

But Yahweh (or Jeremiah) had a limited grasp of geography, since the threat wasn't to come from Assyria to the north, but from Babylon to the east or Egypt to the west. I suppose it didn't matter to him WHERE it came from, as long as it came...he couldn't bother with details. What was important was the punishment to come.

Then Yahweh told Jeremiah to go and tell the people of Jerusalem: "There was a time, way back, when your ancestors were faithful to Yahweh and everything was rosy for them. But then they lost trust and drifted away to worthless idols. They defiled my land. Therefore, because of those ancestors, I shall punish YOU for what they did."

The old "inherited guilt" thing again. Somebody did something bad, so let's put the hurt on somebody else instead. One of the more dismal Biblical principles.

266

Then Jeremiah goes into long rant in fiery rhetoric worthy of Isaiah, condemning the people of Judah for their sins of unfaithfulness and idolatry.

•*Long ago you abandoned me. You lay down and spread your legs like a prostitute. You can't wash away with soap your sins against me.*

•You are like wild, donkeys, smelling a mare in heat and chasing after her. "I lust after foreign gods and I must go after them."

•Why do you look to stone and wooden idols. Haven't I been good enough for you? Why have you rebelled against me?

•Can't you people learn? I've punished you and punished you and you still turn against me. *("The flogging will continue until morale improves.")*

•You've forgotten what I've done for you like a bride forgets her wedding jewels.

•Mark my words: Egypt and Assyria won't help you.

****

.

•If a man's wife leaves him and marries another man, would he have her back after she's been defiled? You are like a prostitute, who has been had by every man that comes along.

The metaphor continues: Yahweh as the cuckolded husband, Israel and her sister Judah as faithless sluts awash in promiscuity, copulating indiscriminately.

•I thought that after the whoring and adultery Israel would return to me. But she didn't, and neither did her faithless sister Judah. I divorced Israel because of her adulteries. But Judah didn't learn from that. Israel committed adulteries with idols of stone and wood. Judah did the same. She only pretended to be faithful to me.

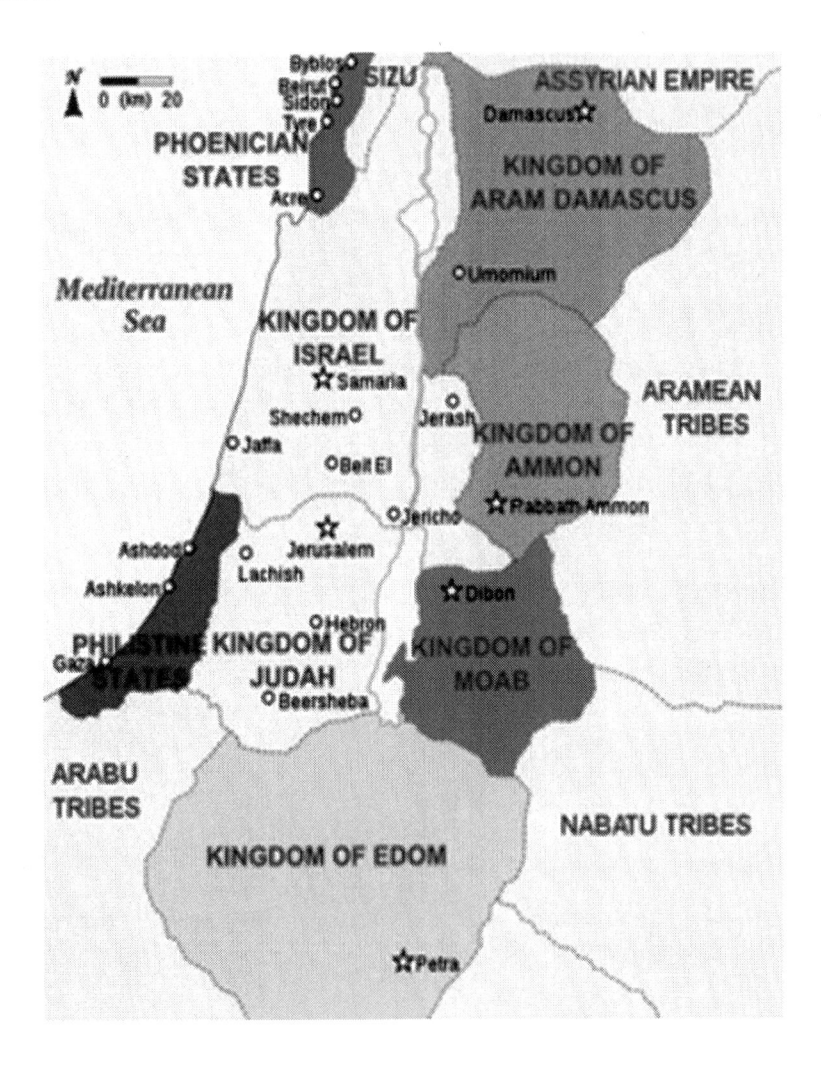

****

Let's review some history here, for a better grasp of what's going on. 300 or so years before Jeremiah, King Solomon ruled the entire territory occupied by the twelve tribes of Israel (named for the twelve sons of Jacob, aka Israel). When Solomon died, there was a revolt against his son Rehoboam, who turned out to be a jerk who vowed to be a ruthless tyrant. The kingdom divided along an east-west Mason-Dixon line. Ten tribes north of the line refused to accept Rehoboam, and chose Jeroboam, a man outside the lineage of David, to be their king. Their territory became the Northern Kingdom of Israel. The other two tribes, Judah and Benjamin, stuck with their Davidic king Rehoboam (because, after all, David has been a Judean.). Their territory, south of the line, became the Southern Kingdom of Judah. . The name "Jews" derives from the name of the homeland, Judah or Judea. The two kingdoms didn't get along at all, and fought back and forth a lot for the next couple of hundred years through a succession of different kings.

With no descendant of David to keep them in line, the Northern Kingdom started looking to gods besides Yahweh for something to worship. The Southern Kingdom, with periodie lapses, stuck with Yahweh-ism.

While these two tiny kingdoms were yapping at each other, the Assyrian Empire moved in from the north and started taking over. Eventually, both kingdoms became vassals of Assyria. The Northern Kingdom didn't go quietly, and continued rebelling against their Assyrian conquerors. Assyria soon got tired of that, and solved the problem by massively invading Israel, taking the entire population captive, and hauling them en masse back to Assyria, where they were never heard of again. They became "the lost tribes of Israel". The Northern Kingdom ceased to be. The Southern Kingdom managed to get along quite well with their Assyrian overlords, until the Assyrian empire began to fall apart and the authority structure began to change.

Jeremiah's stint begins in the middle of the 30-year reign of King Josiah. You can read about him in Kings and in Chronicles. Josiah was a confirmed Yahwhe-ist, and worked hard to purge the kingdom of paganism and Baal-worship. Fifteen years into Jeremiah's career, Josiah died. His successors started again to fall away from Yahweh. During this time, Babylonian king Nebuchadnezzar invaded, took over the Southern Kingdom, and installed a puppet king. After a while, the puppet got too big for his britches, so Nebuchadnezzar came back, sacked the city of Jerusalem, destroyed the Temple, and hauled much of the Judean populace back to Babylon as captives. Jeremiah remained in business throughout this period.*

****

At the time Jeremiah is writing, Israel —the northern kingdom— had been extinct for a century. Yahweh's method of divorce had been to send the Assyrians to overrun Israel, drag its people back to Assyria, break up the tribes and disperse the people out into the world. For Jeremiah, Israel is only a dim memory carried in legend in the story of her destruction. What remained was Judah. And Jeremiah is forecasting a similar fate for her. But for some reason, he continues to carry on as if Israel were a currently existing entity, speaking to (or of) both Israel and Judah.

•I thought you, Israel, would be true to me, but you turned away from me like an adulterous wife.

•As for you, Judah, Circumcise your hearts to the Lord...otherwise you'll feel my wrath.

Jeremiah preaches on, predicting in great detail the disaster that will come from the north. Verse after verse after verse of dire threats and preaching of doom to come.

The message never varies. He repeats the same thing over and over. *You people of Judah have turned away from Yahweh, and have been fooling around with other gods. So Yahweh is going to bust your chops, but good. Invaders from the north will lay waste to your lands and sack your cities and kill everybody and take your stuff. You have misbehaved in the sight of t he Lord, and he is going to punish you for it. You haven't been faithful to Yahweh, so he's not going to be faithful to you. He's going to smite you for what you've done. If you repent and return to Yahweh, he'll make it all okay ...after he's done punishing you for what you've done. I see destruction coming. Yahweh says he's going to lay waste to the whole earth...but not completely destroy it, You have rejected his authority, and he's going to make you pay for it.*

...And on and on and on, saying the same thing over and over. Jeremiah is just as big a windbag as Isaiah. He writes as though he's being paid by the word. If the people of Judah didn't get the message after the 20th time he's said it, the 21st would likely be no more successful. And yet he carries on.

§: **The people of Judah have worshipped false gods, so I will turn their land into a desert, ands dig up the bones of their kings and prophets and strew them around the country like manure.... Watch out! the Lord is sending poison vipers to bite you! ...**
He says, Why have you made me angry by worshipping idols?...

§: **I wish I could get away from these people of Judah, they are all traitors, they are all wicked, liars, killers, deceivers. The Lord says: I will take revenge for these things.**
I ask: Why is this land devastated? Yahweh answers: Because the people have disobeyed me and worshipped Baal and other gods...

§: **The Lord says: don't follow the religions of other nations, they worship sticks and idols like scarecrows. Those aren't real gods, and can't do anything for you. Yahweh is the only god. He is going to expel you from this land and crush you until none are left. Armies from the north will turn Judah into a desert....**

§: **Yahweh reminds Jeremiah of the ancient covenant with Abraham after he brought the children of Israel out of Egypt: If they would obey my commands, I would be their god and take care of them. I warned them and warned them to keep the covenant, but they wouldn't listen...they have set up other gods...when they cry for help, then I won't listen.**

****

Well, Jeremiah was talking to, and about, the people of Judah in around 620 bc, trying to scare them into behaving like he thought they should.

But what are modern day followers of the Bible supposed to get from it? Is there a lesson to be learned? I believe there is, and it's this:: If you stop worshipping Yahweh, he'll bluster and threaten, but he'll let you get away with it for a whole long time before doing anything about it, and won't do anything until after you've quit doing it. Then he'll punish your descendants. See, the heyday of Baal worship in Judah was pre-Jeremiah, during the 55-year reign of Josiah's predecessor King Manasseh, and Yahweh did nothing to stop it while it was going on. He vowed a lot of punishment, and that's all. The practices went on. Then Manasseh died and Josiah became king. Josiah cleaned house, and got rid of the idols to Baal and rediscovered the Laws of Moses and steered the country back to Yahweh. And it was while Josiah the reformer was in office that Jeremiah came along and started his fulminations against idolatry and Baal-worship... which was no longer going on. Yahweh began issuing ominous new threats against the people for something they weren't doing, and hadn't been doing for a long time. And if punishments were inflicted now, they wouldn't fall on the Baal-worshippers of long ago; they'd fall on the Yahweh-worshippers of Josiah's time. Which by the way, didn't happen. The threats weren't fulfilled until a whole lot later. And they weren't nearly as severe as Jeremiah had made them out to be.It was just bluster.

But I digress

....

The people of Judah didn't like what Jeremiah was prophesying, and decided to have him killed. So he prayed to Yahweh, and Yahweh took care of it by having the plotters killed in combat, and their children die of starvation.

§: Jeremiah raises the age-old question with Yahweh: *Why are wicked men allowed to prosper?* Yahweh has no answer. Instead he changes the subject to something about men racing against horses.

§: We get parables.

The Bible, Chapter 53

The Book of Jeremiah
part 2.

I'm going to have to change my approach to this long (52 chapters) and tediously repetitive book. It is much of a muchness, as somebody said about something else. If I'm ever to complete my project of Reading the Bible and reporting on it, I must deprive you of many delicious details and get right down to brass tacks.

In Chapter 13:1, Yahweh directs Jeremiah to go buy a linen sash, wear it for a while without getting it wet, then go hide it in the rocks by the river. When Jeremiah goes back for it a few days later, it is ruined and useless. Linen is one of the most durable fabrics, almost insusceptible to rot. Conclusion: the condition of the sash can't be from natural causes. *Yahweh did it as an object lesson.*

He tells Jeremiah: *That's what I'm going to do to the pride of Judah and Jerusalem. They go after other gods, and I shall ruin them the way I ruined the sash. I adopted them as my people in order that they would praise and honor me, but they have failed in that duty...* letting slip his true motive for taking the Children of Israel to his bosom: He wanted his own personal cheering section, to boost his ego and make him feel good.

When they fail to do that, they are of no further use to him and can be discarded. He tells the people, *For your sins, I will pull your skirts up over your face and expose your private parts, to shame you for your adulteries and prostitutions and other abominations.*
....

Chapter 14: Yahweh sends a drought. The cisterns of Jerusalem go dry. Farmland lies dry and parched. Does abandon their fawns. Wild donkeys pant like jackals. He tells Jeremiah: **Don't pray for these people. No matter what they do, I shall destroy them.**

Jeremiah: But their local prophets keep telling them that you will rescue them and protect them.

Yahweh: **Those prophets lie. I never told them that. They are just making it up or imagining it. I never told them I would protect the people. They will perish along with the people. I'll give them the calamity they deserve.**

He carries on that same vein, in grim and graphic detail, for nthe next couple of chapters.

I'd give something to know just how Yahweh and Jeremiah communicate. Yahweh's instructions, threats, and warnings are so detailed and explicit, it's as if they had email or telephone connections or meetings for lunch. "Go buy a linen sash." Furthermore, Jeremiah is just about the only one that has this access. According to Yahweh, all the other prophets who are telling the people what Yahweh has in mind are either just making it up and lying, or are mistaking dreams and imagination for communion with the Lord. They haven't really been in touch with him, and the people who follow them are being misled. At least, that's what Yahweh tells Jeremiah.

I note again that Yahweh is fixing to blight the people of Judea because of what their ancestors did. These early chapters were written when Josiah was king. I think I mentioned that his predecessor Manasseh had been a Baal-worshiper. Josiah was a reformer, who brought the people back to Yahweh-ism. No matter: it was too late to punish the Manasseh generation, so he'll settle for the current one.

The obvious question to ask is: **Why did Yahweh wait until now to exact his punishment?** Why didn't he do it back when Manasseh was king and the people were still worshipping Baal?

He could have done it as easily then as now. *The ways of Yahweh are unfathomable.*

Chapter 18: Jeremiah is ordered to go down and watch the potter at work at his wheel. He sees the potter start to make a vessel, but the clay collapses; so he simply reshapes the same clay, and makes it into a different pot. Yahweh says, "See what he did with his clay? I can do the same thing to the House of Israel. I can crush it or raise it back up, whenever I please. If I decide to destroy a nation, but they repent, I' can change my mind and leave them alone. If I decide to reward a nation, and it turns to evil, I can change my mind and rain punishment on them."

****

A couple of kings down the road from Josiah, Jehoiakim occupied the throne, and he was bugged by Jeremiah's constant braying about imminent disaster. Jehoiakim had abandoned the reforms of Josiah, so he was already on Yahweh's shit list. But he disliked Jeremiah's message , and so took steps to shut up the messenger. Details show up later in the book.

When Jehoiakim started a campaign of harassment against Jeremiah, Jeremiah went whining to Yahweh, asking him to punish them for being mean to him: . *Let the children die of starvation, let the men be killed in battle, let the women be childless and widows and let them scream in anguish when you bring invaders to break into their homes and overrun them. Bring disaster to them for being mean to me. Please.*

But Yahweh didn't do it. Instead, he told Jeremiah to go get a clay pot, preach to the people about their iniquity, and smash the pot, saying *"This is how Yahweh is going to smash Judah for its wicked ways."* That should scare them.

It should have, but it didn't. It just made them mad. When the high priest Pashtur heard him carrying on that way, he had Jeremiah beaten and put in the stocks overnight, to teach him a lesson. It did no good. Next day when he was let out of the stocks, he cut loose with another batch of the same threats and invective, this time directed at Pashtur as well as everybody in Judah. Then he went off into a flood of self-pity, complaining that Yahweh had let him down, and cursed the day he was born and everybody that had anything to do with it."Why did I ever come out of the womb to see trouble and sorrow and end my days in shame."

****

To recapitulate a bit of history: This Jehoiakim had been installed as king by the pharaoh of Egypt. In the middle of his eleven-year reign, Babylon swept in, kicked the Egyptians out, and took over. Jehoiakim wisely shifted his allegiance to Babylon. But Egypt kept fussing around,trying to regain power over Judah. Eventually Jehoiakim unwisely shifted his allegiance back to Egypt. At that point, King Nebuchadnezzar roared back from Babylon, definitively established Babylonian rule, deposed Jehoiakim, deported a bunch of his followers to Babylon, and appointed Zedekiah as king of Judah. We shall have more to say about Zedekiah in a bit. Note that shortly after this point, Jeremiah's narrative moves ahead a few years, from Jehoakim to Zedekiah

Jeremiah got along well with Zedekiah, and from time to time was asked for advice. But at a crucial point, he failed to take it. Jeremiah advised against Zed's decision to revolt against Babylon, And we know what happened.

****

During the siege of Jerusalem, Zedekiah told Jeremiah, *We're in trouble here. See if you can't get Yahweh to intercede for us against the Babylonians.*

Jeremiah's answer was, *Not a chance. If you go against Babylon, you'll be going against Yahweh's wishes, and you'll suffer disaster and defeat. Yahweh's advice to the people is to surrender to the Babylonians, and go along with whatever they want. If you do that, you'll be okay. But Babylon is going to win this fight, and if you've gone against them, you'll be doomed.*

Nebuchadnezzar is Yahweh's instrument and ally in disciplining miscreants. Yahweh calls him, "My servant Nebuchadnezzar." Jeremiah's plan was this:*Advise the people of Judah to save themselves by surrendering meekly to Nebuchadnezzar. Those who follow Yahweh's advice will be safely taken as captives to Babylon, where they may settle down and resume a normal life for a while. Those who fail to follow Yahweh's advice will be slaughtered, as Yahweh's punishment for their disobedience. It'll serve them right.*

And here's what happened. Nebuchadnezzar's response to Zedekiah's treachery was to swarm in with his armies, sack and burn Jerusalem, tear down Solomon's Temple, confiscate all of its goodies, and drag most of the Judean population back to Babylon as captives. He had Zedekiah's sons slaughtered before his eyes, then had Zedekiah's eyes put out and hauled him in chains back to Babylon to finish out his days. It wasn't smart to mess with Nebuchadnezzar.

****

But at this point, Jeremiah is still talking as if the above hasn't happened yet; he's just prophesying about it, apparently from a long time previously..

The Bible, Chapter 54

The Book of Jeremiah
part 3.

Before moving along, I'd like to say a few words about this supposed collusion between Yahweh and Nebuchadnezzar. That whole thing sounds fishy, and I'm inclined to think that Jeremiah just made it up. According to him, Yahweh set the whole deal up as a test of faith: those who follow his orders (to surrender to Babylon) will turn out OK; those who disobey his orders will be in a world of trouble.

Let's get real. Jeremiah is writing this at the time that Jerusalem is under siege by an overwhelming Babylonian force. It's inevitable that it will fall before long. It doesn't take a Yahweh for people to figure out what's in their best interest and what's not. When the Babylonians overrun the city, the prudent people will lay down their arms, surrender, and be taken captive. Those who don't will get their asses kicked. Jeremiah is just stating the obvious, and pretending that it's a dictum from Yahweh. Those who refuse to surrender aren't going to suffer because they disobeyed the "dictum". They're going to suffer because they were stupid.

****

Now, on with the story.

Chapter 22: Jeremiah jumps back in time several king's-worth, and begins strapping on about wicked kings prior to Zedekiah, and how Yahweh will oversee the destruction of Judah because of them. Jeremiah isn't prophesying here; he's relating what happened, though phrasing it in the future tense. Jeremiah was in business well past the fall of Zedekiah.

****

The first of the bad kings after Good King Josiah is his #2 son Shallum, also called Jehoahaz. History-wise, he's pretty insignificant: he just ruled for 3 months before the Egyptians came and dragged him off to Egypt. Jeremiah's prophecy (attributed to the Lord): "He's not coming back. He'll die in the land where he's held captive."

Followed by a jeremiad: "Woe to him who builds his palace by unrighteousness, making his countrymen work for nothing...your eyes and your heart are set only on dishonest gain, on shedding innocent blood..." and so on. *Hard to tell where this is coming from, since Jehoahaz wasn't in office long enough to seriously do any of the stuff that Jeremiah lays on him.*

Next he sets his sights on the next king Jehoiakim, Josiah's #1 son placed on the throne by the Pharaoh. Says Jeremiah, "They won't mourn for him when dies; they'll treat his corpse as they would a dead donkey, and dump it out over the walls for the buzzards." Which had indeed happened: Jehoiakim had unwisely changed allegiances one time too many.

Jeremiah's next target is Jehoiachin, who briefly succeeded his father Jehoiakim. According to Jeremiah, the Lord says, "Even if you Jehoaiachin were a signet ring on my right hand, I would still pull you off and turn you over to Nebuchadnezzar."
What happened is that 3 months into Jehoiachin's reign, Nebuchadnezzar's army overran the city, hauled Jehoiachin and his retinue off to captivity in Babylon, and set up the next king as a puppet. There's no record that Jehoiachin did anything to warrant the wrath that Jeremiah pours on him. I think he just needed the fall of Jerusalem to somehow be the fault of Yahweh's fury at somebody, rather than due to superior military forces.

I want you to keep that signet ring thing in mind, when we get

280

around to the tray of figs.

§: Jeremiah has Yahweh make a promise and prediction that didn't happen, hasn't happened, and won't ever happen: The promise that ALL of the descendants of the Children of Israel, scattered in exile, will all return to Judah and Israel, and will be ruled wisely by a king from David's line.

Didn't happen. Ain't going to. Eventually a lot of Judean exiles in Babylonian Captivity returned to Judah. But the Israelites swept up in the Assyrian Captivity were dispersed throughout the world, and were never heard of again. And won't be. So much for Yahweh's promise.

....

Then Jeremiah has Yahweh spend a LONG time explaining that Jeremiah's competitors in the prophesying-business are all frauds and bad people. *These other prophets are wicked and evil, and practice or at least condone adultery, and some of them prophesy by Baal, and others prophesy by Yahweh, but these are fraudulent, because they never talk to Yahweh to get his opinions the way Jeremiah does. They claim Yahweh comes to them in a dream. Bah!* "Let the prophet who has a dream tell his dream, but let the one who has my word [like Jeremiah here] *speak it faithfully."* All other prophets are doomed for their wickedness and mis-prophesies about me.

But just between you and me, I'm skeptical that Yahweh actually told Jeremiah to preach that stuff. I think he just made it up, to one-up the competition with the audience: *Yahweh says you shouldn't listen to those other guys. Just listen to me. I actually have Yahweh's ear; they only have dreams about it. If you listen to them, you'll be in deep doo-doo.*

****

§: After King Jehoachin had been carted off to exile, Yahweh came along and showed Jeremiah two baskets of figs. One had good figs, the other had bad figs. Then Yahweh says: *Like these good figs, I regard as good the Judean exiles I sent away to Babylon. I will watch over them and bring them back home. Like the rotten figs, I will reject Zedekiah and his followers and destroy them for disobeying my orders and fighting back.*

I need to stop and comment on this remarkable passage. I'll pass over Yahweh's reassertion that he colluded with Nebuchadnezzar to get the people of Judah herded off to Babylon. What I'm interested in are those baskets of figs.

Yahweh has hands, capable of wearing signet rings. He said so a while back. Yahweh shows up at Jeremiah's doorstep with baskets of figs and says "Look at these." Yahweh has long conversations with Jeremiah...not in dreams, but straight ahead.

THIS Yahweh is the one from Genesis and Exodus —a walking living being, of whom Adam and his descendants are copies. He has a body. He carries fig baskets. He's not the Yahweh of Solomon, who was sort of nowhere and sort of hovered and communicated by telepathy. This one lives someplace, but manages to hide from everybody except Jeremiah. Presumably, he lives in his chamber in the Temple, as he did back before Solomon when it was a tent; but he comes out occasionally, to deliver figs and chat with Jeremiah and NOBODY ELSE NOTICES HIM.

Maybe so, but here's what I think. I think Jeremiah is a man with a fertile and creative imagination, and he's making all this stuff up. Yahweh isn't really telling him what to say. Rather, he's saying what HE THINKS Yahweh would want him to say. Yahweh didn't show him fig baskets. He saw some fig baskets and made up the rest, to use as a metaphor. Yahweh didn't send him to watch the potter work with clay; he saw the potter re-shape a ruined pot into another one, and used it as a metaphor.

Jeremiah is a fire-and-brimstone preacher who knows what he wants Yahweh to be like, and who makes up preachings to fit his own model. Much like modern-day evangelists. All of his direful threats and prophecies are just verbal pyrotechnics, and have no more real significance than poetry.

Is what I think. But I'll continue to go along with the gag, for the remainder of this account.

§: Jeremiah predicts that the people of Judah will remain captive in Babylon for 70 years; then Nebuchadnezzar's regime will fall, and they will return to Judah. For that part of the story, go back to Ezra and Nehemiah. Then he predicts doom and destruction for all the kingdoms in the neighborhood of Israel and Judah. Same as always.

§:We go back to the time of King Jehoiakim. Yahweh instructs Jeremiah to go and preach the usual stuff to the people of Jerusalem and surrounding towns. That gets on everybody's nerves, and they suggest that he needs to be lynched. It doesn't shut him up. He just preaches more and harder, and eventually they said: *Maybe we ought not to kill him —he says he speaks for the Lord.* So they didn't kill him.

Another prophet named Uriah wasn't so lucky. His prophecies were in the same vein as Jeremiah's. When they threatened him, he hightailed it off to Egypt, but they tracked him down, hacked him to death, and flung his body into the local common pit.

§: We proceed to the time of King Zedekiah. Yahweh doubles down on his alliance with Nebuchadnezzar.

Jeremiah has Yahweh saying this: *I am going to give all countries and peoples —even the wild animals — over to MY SERVANT Nebuchadnezzar. All nations will serve him (until he falls from power). I will deliver deep doodoo --sword, famine, and plague-- on all who fail to serve him.*

Those who surrender to him should go ahead to Babylon, settle down, raise families, and bide their time. Eventually I will see to it that the reign of My Servant Nebuchadnezzar is destroyed, and you will return to Judah under a king from David's line.

....

I'm not sure what to think of this. The prophecy describes something like treachery on the part of Yahweh, turning against His Servant when he has no more use for him: Is it true from the mouth of a double-dealing Yahweh, or made up by our televangelist Jeremiah?

The Bible, Chapter 55

The Book of Jeremiah
.part 4

Jeremiah is SUCH a repetitive windbag that I have a hard time convincing myself to keep working with him. But let us endeavor to persevere.

§: Time frame: reign of Zedekiah. A false prophet Hananiah predicts that in a couple of years, Yahweh is going to visit his wrath on Babylon, and get back all the people and treasures that had been hauled away. Jeremiah said: Wrong-o. Jeremiah was wearing a symbolic yoke Yahweh had prescribed for him, symbolizing the servitude to Babylon that (he said) Yahweh was demanding. Hananiah yanked off his yoke and broke it, saying "This is how the Lord will break the yoke of Nebuchadnezzar." Jeremiah: "For preaching these falsehoods, you will die before the year is out." Hananiah died before the year was out. No mention of whether foul play was involved. Nebuchadnezzar carried on, unscathed.

§: Jeremiah dictates a letter to his scribe Baruch, to be delivered to the Judeans in Babylonian exile and still in Judea. It's a re-hash of stuff said before. Yahweh wants the about-to-be exiles to settle down and get comfortable, and raise families and build houses, and carry on with their business. Yahweh predicts the usual horrible fate for those who fight back against the Babylonians, accusing them of adultery with their neighbors' wives, though its not clear how adultery relates to fighting back against the Babylonians. It's just Jeremiah fulminating as always.

§: Jeremiah repeats and amplifies the stuff from earlier: Yahweh is going to bring back all the Israelites and Judeans scattered in captivity, and they will all live in prosperity under the rule of a king from the house of David.

§: Yahweh continues his speech to the people. His opening salvo is one I find remarkable. Yahweh says, to the Children of Israel: "I have loved you with an ever-lasting love; I have drawn you with loving kindness. I will build you up again and you will be rebuilt, O Virgin Israel."

This ever-lasting love claim has me saying What?

§: Zedekiah is king of Judah. Jerusalem is under siege by the Babylonians. Yahweh tells Jeremiah to buy some real estate. *(Recall Yahweh's antipathy to real estate ownership back when he was talking to Isaiah.)* Anyhow, Jeremiah buys it. Then there's a lot of dialogue on The Usual Topic between Jeremiah and Yahweh.

§: Jeremiah is confined under guard. Yahweh promises to bring widespread slaughter, followed by rebuilding and renewal. Same old same old.

§: Yahweh warns Zedekiah that he is about to be overrun by the Babylonians. An emancipation proclamation for slaves is issued. Yahweh promises horrible disaster for the people of Judah, because they haven't been worshiping him enough.

§: Flashback: Jehoiakim is king again. He's the one before Jehoiachin, who was the one before Zedekiah. There was a tribe of people called Recabites because they were descended from some guy named Recab. Their doctrine requires them to be teetotalers and nomads, abstaining from wine and living in tents, rather than building settlements and planting crops. Because of this, they find favor in Yahweh's eyes while he proclaims his plan to blast the rest of Judah into perdition. This is the first mention of Yahweh's having become a Prohibitionist. Nor is it clear why he favors tent living. He's supposed to have LIKED the temple Solomon built for him, to get him out of tent city.

§: Jeremiah is in custody. He has his scribe Baruch write on a scroll all of Yahweh's dire threats against Judah et al., from the time of Josiah forward. Then he has Baruch go read the scroll to everybody, to scare them into behaving themselves. When the king heard what it said, he wasn't scared a bit. He cut up the scroll into pieces and burned it. Then he commanded the arrest of Jeremiah and Baruch; except they were in hiding and couldn't be found. So Jeremiah has Baruch write a new scroll, with all of the old threats plus new ones against Jehoiakim. We are not told whether it was ever published.

§: Flash forward to the reign of Zedekiah. Egyptian armies have come to the defense of Judah against the besieging Babylonians. Jeremiah warns Zedekiah that the Egyptians were only in for the short term; after they leave, Nebuchadnezzar will come back and sack Jerusalem. Jeremiah is no longer in custody, but when he tries to leave town he's arrested, accused of treason, and clapped in a dungeon. The king gets him out and gives him a pension.

§: The people are miffed at Jeremiah's continued harping that those who remain in Jerusalem are doomed, and only those who submit to Babylonian captivity will be saved. They complained to the king that he was preaching sedition and discouraging the soldiers. The king told them to do whatever they liked to Jeremiah, so they dumped him into a cistern with a mud bottom. A Cushite court official named Ebed-Melech, with the king's permission, took a squadron of men and hauled Jeremiah back out of the cistern. Then king Zedekiah asked Jeremiah to do some prophesying, so Jeremiah gave him the same rap as before: surrender to the Babylonians or you are doomed and Jerusalem will be put to the torch. Zedekiah didn't listen.

§: *This and following sections are remarkably free of Jeremiah's usual bombast. They are written narratively, much more in the style of the earlier Histories, with very little preaching. I'm inclined to doubt that Jeremiah actually wrote them.*

§:In the 9th year of Zedekiah's reign, Nebuchadnezzar's armies overran Jerusalem. Zedekiah and his guards snuck out the back gate at night and tried to get away, But the Babylonians tracked him down and hauled him back in front of Nebuchadnezzar. The

Babylonian king showed his displeasure by having Zedekiah's sons slaughtered before his eyes. Then he blinded Zedekiah, put out his eyes, clapped him in manacles, and ordered him dragged back to Babylon in chains.

All of the Judean people of any substance were taken back to Babylon in captivity; but Neb left the poor folks there, and gave them vineyards and fields liberated from their erstwhile owners. Nebuchadnezzar took Jeremiah under his wing (no doubt having heard of the gist of Jeremiah's pro-Babylonian prophesying) and gave him carte blanche to go wherever he wished and stay wherever he wished.

The Bible, Chapter 56

The Book of Jeremiah
part 5.

We are still talking about what happened after the fall of Jerusalem to Nebuchadnezzar's armies. This is some very exciting historical stuff; to me, at least.

§We get more details of Jeremiah's peace with Nebuchadnezzar, who had appointed a fellow named Gedaliah to be the new governor of Judah. Gedaliah established his headquarters in the town of Mizpah. The head general of the Babylonian troops, named Nebuzaradan, found Jeremiah manacled with the other captives and quickly cut him loose. He said "You can come with me to Babylon if you like, otherwise go wherever you like." Then he added, "But I recommend you go hang out with Gedaliah." So that's what Jeremiah did.

There were still a lot of Judean officers and troops scattered about the territory after their defeat, one of them being a certain Ishmael (watch him). They heard about Gedaliah, and came to see him to find out what was up. Gedaliah seems to have been a decent bureaucrat. He told them, "Don't be afraid; we aren't going to punish you as long as you behave yourselves. Get on with your lives, conduct your autumn harvest, and I'll be your representative and intermediary between you and the Babylonian government."

When all the Jews who had fled to neighboring kingdoms heard about the Babylonian governor, they retuned to Judah to join the remnant who had stayed there. The Judean army officers, appreciating Gedaliah, warned him that the Ammonites had commissioned Ishmael to assassinate him. They offered to go take out Ishmael for him, but alas! Gedaliah didn't believe it.

§: Shortly thereafter, Ishmael and companions showed up on Gedaliah's doorstep. The governor invited them to dinner, and while they were eating, Ishmael jumped up and jammed his sword through Gedaliah, and that was that. They also killed everybody else who was there, Jews and Babylonians alike, dumping the bodies into a cistern. This ought to have included Jeremiah, since he was supposed to be there, but there's no mention of it.

The next day, eighty Jewish pilgrims showed with stuff to make Temple sacrifices to Yahweh. Ishmael ordered his troops to annihilate them and dump them into the cistern. (It must have been some cistern). Ten of them were saved when they said they knew where supplies were hidden. Ishmael took everybody he could in Mizpah as captives, and fled toward the kingdom of Ammon.

Meanwhile, the Judean officers and troops outside the city heard about Ishmael's atrocities, and headed off under the leadership of Johanan, to deal with Ishmael and his bunch. When Ishmael's people saw what was coming, they promptly released their captives and surrendered. Ishmael managed to get away. Johanan took the people of Mizpah who had been released, and headed toward Egypt for refuge. They were afraid of what would happen when Babylon got the news about Gedaliah.

§: Jeremiah and the scribe Baruch were among the people of Mizpah who had been rescued. Johanan's people asked Jeremiah to pray to Yahweh for them. Jeremiah had a conversation with Yahweh, and ten days later he told them: "Here's what the Lord says. If all of you stay here in Judah and help it to recover from its defeat you'll be OK; the Babylonians will let you alone. But if you abandon Judah and retreat to safety from attack in Egypt, Yahweh will bust your ass." Yahweh/Jeremiah didn't want the remnant of Jews left in Judah to be abandoned. He wanted their brother Jews to hang around and help them recover. Under threat of dire punishment: "If you got to Egypt you will die in war or of starvation or disease there."

§: Johanan's faction didn't buy it for a minute. They saw Jeremiah as a shill for the Babylonians, and figured he was setting a trap so they wouldn't be on their guard when the Babylonian hordes returned to kill them all. So they took all the Jews they had rescued from Mizpah, including Jeremiah, and headed off into Egypt.

When they got there, they settled in a place called Tahpanhes (which has various spellings). Yahweh had Jeremiah bury some stones in the entrance to the Pharaohs palace, and prophesy: "Nebuchadnezzar will send his armies and overthrow Egypt and set his throne right above these very stones. He will demolish Egypt and its culture. And I (Yahweh) will burn down the temples to Egypt's gods. And y'all Jews who disobeyed this warning to stay in Judah will die in misery."

****

§: Jeremiah-ish bombast returns. Yahweh is really bugged that the contingent of Jews who had followed Johanan into safety in Egypt, had abandoned the remnant of their fellow Jews who had been allowed to stay in Judah. To show his displeasure, he avows to destroy ALL of Judah, both those who went to Egypt and those who didn't... because he is really pissed off, and when you're really pissed off, it doesn't matter who's to blame. He accuses them, without real evidence, of all sorts of idolatrous behavior including humping their wives while burning incense to other gods, and of proclaiming their determination to disobey the instructions that Jeremiah has claimed to be giving them from the mouth of the Lord himself.

I'm not on Yahweh's side here. He hadn't done anything to warrant their respect. These are people who had felt abandoned by the their official god Yahweh, and been left to the mercies of the Babylonians. Having found refuge in a foreign land, they followed the customs and worship of the people who had granted them refuge. So Yahweh, the "everlasting love" guy who

291

had failed to protect them from the Babylonians because they hadn't worshiped him enough, is now busting them for getting along in the society where they WERE protected. I do not approve of Yahweh's actions nor his motives. So far as I can tell, he has no concern for the well-being of "his people", but only with whether they are giving him enough ego-grease. His everlasting love is paper thin. What he really wants is to sustain a viable population of Yahwehists in Judah to keep his name and his worship warm.

The Jews in Egypt felt about the same way. They said, "Why listen to you? When we were making sacrifices to the Queen of Heaven [*probably Ashtoreth*] in Judah, we were happy and prosperous. But when we stopped doing that, we had nothing but grief. So we intend to go on doing it. It seems to do some good. All Yahweh has done is give us a bad time."

Jeremiah's response was to double-down on the threats made earlier: "For your wickedness and abominations you will all die horribly, in war or of disease. The Lord will destroy Egypt and hand its king Hophra over to his enemies, just as I handed Zedekiah of Judah over to Nebuchadnezzar. So there!."

But I wish to interject an historical comment. I've done some research on the matter, and so far as I can tell, Yahweh's dire promises and threats about Egypt never came true. Nebuchadnezzar never conquered Egypt. He never even came close. His one attempt at invasion was a failure. He never set his throne on top of Jeremiah's buried stones. He didn't bring destruction and disease to the Jews in Egypt. His only victory over Egyptian troops happened not in Egypt, but in Mesopotamia, where the Babylonians, the Egyptians, and the Syrians all fought each other trying to take over some territory. Yahweh never burned Egypt's temples to its own gods. Pharaoh Hophra was never handed over to his enemies. He was eventually deposed in an insurrection, went and allied himself with Babylon, and was killed by Egyptian solders when he tried to reclaim the throne.

You can take it either of two ways. Yahweh is full of bluster and threats, like The Man Behind The Curtain, but is unable to follow through. Or Jeremiah is a fulminating blowhard who has no clue what Yahweh actually wants or will do.

The Bible, Chapter 57

The Book of Jeremiah
part 6.

As you can tell, I am having a hard time following my determination to slog all the way through this endless and repetitious book. But let us move onward to the end.

§: This is a short and very strange chapter. Baruch the scribe has just got done taking some dictation from Jeremiah, when Jeremiah prophesies at him: You complain that your troubles and woes are more than you can bear. But Yahweh says to you: "Hey, I'm fixing to wreak disaster on all of humanity. Why do you think I should leave you out? At least I'm not going to kill you."

§: Most of this and succeeding chapters are in poetic form. It begins with an account of the Battle of Carcamesh, where the pharaoh's forces got their butts kicked by Babylon. Then there's a long Jeremiad against Nebuchadnezzar. Then one where Yahweh tells the Jewish people at large what he already told Baruch: "I'm going to wreak terrible punishment on everybody, including you, but you'll survive and flourish once again."

Then a prediction of disaster for Philistia. Then a similar one about Moab. Then similar prophesies about Ammon and Edom. And Damascus. Then a prophesy that Kedar and Hazor will be crushed by the Babylonians. Yahweh will destroy Elam, but it will rise again.

§: Jeremiah predicts the fall of Babylon to "a nation from the north" (which turned out to be Persia), and the return of the Children of Israel to their homeland. Then a detailed account of all of the bad stuff that is going to happen to Babylon.

Yahweh says: "I'm going to repay Babylonia for all the evil they did to Jerusalem. I am its enemy, and I shall reduce it to ashes."

This is the same Babylonia that, under Yahweh's servant King Nebuchadnezzar, overran and destroyed Jerusalem. It was with Yahweh's approval, and at his bidding. It was Yahweh's way of punishing Judea for its wickedness. Nebuchadnezzar was Yahweh's instrument in the matter. And now the Babylonians are being punished for doing it. Go figure. *Nobody has seriously accused the Lord of being consistent in his behavior.*

§: The book ends with a reprise of the account of the fall of Jerusalem, related elsewhere in the book of II Kings 24.

And that's it for Jeremiah.

The Bible, Chapter 62

The Book of Lamentations

The Book of Lamentations is exactly what it's name says it is: a series of poems keening and wailing about the general awfulness of things.

Chapter 1: This is a lament about the fall of Jerusalem and the conquest of Judah, at the hands of unnamed parties but most likely Babylon. The blame for the awfulness is laid mainly on the conquering forces.

Chapter 2: This is another lament about the destruction of Jerusalem and the conquest of Judah. But this one lays the blame squarely on Yahweh, who has created the awfulness in his anger at the people for something or other. It's not a military defeat, so much as punishment for wickedness. A lot of the imagery is upsettingly graphic. Children and babies are fainting and dying from hunger in the streets of the cities. Women are eating the bodies of their children. Corpses litter the streets. And so on.

Chapter 3: This is a lament, not about what has happened to Jerusalem and its people, but primarily about the fate of the lamenter himself, bewailing all the terrible stuff that has happened and is happening to him. Having catalogued the many evils befalling him, he nevertheless says, without noticing the irony, "My hope returns when I remember that the Lord's unfailing love and mercy still continue, fresh as the morning, as sure as sunrise." *Yeah, right.* He says, "They threw me alive into a pit and closed the opening with a stone. Water began to close over me, and I thought death was near." This suggests that the author may be Jeremiah, who was imprisoned for a while in a cistern. Then he carries on, pissing and moaning about how badly people have been treating him, and ends up by entreating the Lord to bash his tormentors. Typical Jeremiah-ish stuff.

Chapter 4: This lament is about conditions in Jerusalem after the fall. It carries on in lurid detail: "People mistreat their young, letting them die of hunger and thirst. Once vital young men now lie as blackened shriveled mummies in the streets." Then it harks back to the conquest itself: "Her leaders wandered through the streets like blind men, so stained with blood that no one would touch them." It ends by inveighing against surrounding kingdoms that had failed to rescue them: "Laugh while you can, Edom and Uz. Your disaster is coming as surely as ours has. You're gonna get yours."

Chapter 5: This is not a lamentation, but a long plea for Yahweh to be nice to them for a change. It re-lists the awful conditions in Judah, and ends by saying "You O Lord, are king and will rule forever. Why have you abandoned us so long? Will this go on forever? Is your anger at us without end?" *So much for "...hope returning at the thought of Yahweh's unfailing love."*

As with Jeremiah and Isaiah, I haven't found any guidance for the conduct of life in this book. Unless it's "Complaining is good for the soul."

The Bible, Chapter 63

The Book of Ezekiel
part 1

Ezekiel saw the wheel
Way up in the middle of the air
Ezekiel saw the wheel
Way in the middle of the air
The big wheel run by faith, my Lord
The little wheel run by the grace of God
A wheel in a wheel in a wheel
Way in the middle of the air.
--Negro spiritual

The Book of Ezekiel is the epitome of Biblical weirdness. Ezekiel is Jeremiah on acid. His Jeremiads (or "Ezekielads") are accompanied by wild surrealistic hallucinatory visions. Ezekiel thinks they are real, and that they mean something. I'm not sure what. The "visitors-from-outer-space" crowd think they describe Ezekiel's Close Encounter of the Third Kind.

The setting is with the first crop of Judean exiles in Babylonia ca. 592 bc. Ezekiel is 30 years old. Zedekiah is still king of Judah. Nebuchadnezzar hasn't yet destroyed the city of Jerusalem. But he will. Throughout this book, when Ezekiel refers to Israel, he means "the House of Israel" –the descendents of Israel/Jacob, rather than the long-gone Northern Kingdom.

....

Within a flashing lightning storm he sees four figures that are

more or less humanoid --they have hands and legs-- but the human resemblance stops there. They have four wings apiece, and each has four faces, a different one on the each of the four sides of its head: a human's face, a lion's face, a bull's face, and an eagles face. Their legs are straight, apparently without knees, and they have hooves like a bull instead of feet, which appear to be made of bronze.
.

These living Beings arrange themselves in a square, facing outward, with spread wings touching at each corner. With their other two wings, they cover their bodies. Whenever they move, the whole square moves as a unit. It moves in each of the four directions without turning, something like the King or Rook in chess. Except they move lightning fast. They appear to be on fire.

In front of each of them is a glowing wheel, intersected by another wheel at a right angle, like the cage of a toy gyroscope, so it can roll in any direction without falling over. But the wheels don't roll; they stay in front of their Beings. Their rims are covered with eyes. The Beings forming the square, and their wheels, are all parts of a single assembly which always moves as a unit, horizontally and vertically.

I hope you get the picture: A square each side of which consists of a stiff-legged four-winged creature with multiple faces and spread wings who is on fire, with a compound wheel sitting stationary in front of him. When the square moves about it always moves as a unit, and always in a straight line perpendicular to one of its four sides. Or straight up or down.

Above them, he sees a crystalline vault or canopy or something. With the Beings' outer wings touching at the corners to form the square, and their inner wings covering their bodies, he hears the beating of their wings, like the roar of the ocean or the voice of Yahweh or the marching of an army. Exactly how this works isn't explained. Perhaps, they flap their wings without breaking their square formation.

Above the vault or canopy, he hears a voice. It is coming from a throne made of sapphire, upon which sits a man-like figure. From his waist up he looks like glowing molten metal; from the waist down, he looks like fire. Ezekiel recognizes the figure as that of Yahweh himself, and falls prostrate on the ground. This does not seem to be the same Yahweh as the one back in Genesis, that walked and talked with Adam and Eve. That one didn't glow.

Here's one artist's interpretation of this complicated situation:

Here's another, more elaborate one:

But that's not the end of Ezekiel's acid trip. It continues.

Yahweh speaks to Ezekiel about the Israelites (the Judeans, the remaining Children of Israel). He calls them a "rebellious lot", and repeats it in about every third or fourth sentence, in case

301

Ezekiel should forget. Ezekiel is sent to go among the rebellious lot and preach the word of Yahweh and get captured and abused by them, but just keep on preaching and keep the faith.

Then (if you didn't think it was weird before), Yahweh hands him a scroll, which he unrolls so Ezekiel can see the writing on both side of it. But Yahweh doesn't tell him to read it; he tells him to EAT it, and then go do his preaching. So Ezekiel eats the scroll, and says it is very tasty. Yum.

Then Yahweh repeats his instructions to go preach to the rebellious Israelites and get captured and tied up but Yahweh won't let him yell or anything: just preach, when the Lord tells him to.

Then (we are up to Chapter 4 in this vision), Yahweh instructs Ezekiel to do a bunch of stuff even weirder than eating a scroll. Yahweh tells him to draw a plan of Jerusalem on a clay tablet, and to put miniature siege works around it, and then hold an iron skillet between himself and the model of Jerusalem. Then he is to pretend to besiege it. He says, "This will be a sign to the house of Israel."

Then Ezekiel is told to lie on his left side and assume all the sins of the Kingdom of Israel He is to lie on his left side for "the same number of days as the years of their sin", namely 390. So Ezekiel is to remain lying on his side for just under 13 months, as penance for the sins he has assumed. Eating and taking care of bodily functions during those months will present difficulties.

When he's done doing that, he is to turn over onto his right side, assume the sins of the southern Kingdom of Judah, and stay that way for 40 days --the number of years of its sinning. *(This dates back to when Josiah the reformer was king, when things were to Yahweh's liking. Go figure.)* He will be tied with ropes to keep him from turning over.

He is directed to take a stash of wheat, barley, beans, etc. and somehow cook and eat food for himself during the 390 days he is lying on his left side, and the 40 days he is lying bound and immobile on his right side. This will represent the food of the rebellious Israelites and the sin-ridden Judeans and will be in severely rationed portions since they will suffer a shortage of food. And he is to cook it on fires made from human dung, so they will be eating defiled food as part of their punishment.

This last part is more than Ezekiel can stomach. He says "No Way. I have never eaten non-kosher in my life, and don't intend to start now." So Yahweh says, in that case make the fires of cow dung instead. (*The dietary laws of Moses are inscrutable.*)

This takes us to the end of Chapter 4 of Ezekiel. Remember, we are still in the midst of this vision/hallucination/dream/whatever. Ezekiel is still chatting with the molten-metal god from the sapphire throne above the crystal canopy over the winged square assembly of Beings and wheels.

The Bible, Chapter 64

The Book of Ezekiel,
part 2

We left Ezekiel (still in his hallucinatory state) having received from Yahweh instructions to spend a total of 430 days lying on one side or the other, as penance for the misbehavior of Israel and Judah. You would expect Chapter 5 to find him doing that. But not so.

Instead of giving him a chance to do his penance, Yahweh gives him a new set of instructions. Ezekiel is to take a sword (yes, a sword) and hone it to a razor sharpness. Then he is to use the sword to shave his head and his beard and save the hair.

Let us pause to consider. Swords in those days were not huge; probably no more than 2 feet long. But that's long enough to present Ezekiel difficulties. Try to imagine a man using a heavy 2-foot razor-sharp sword to shave his face. And then his scalp. And to make it a dry shave, so he can save the hair. And to do this without serious damage to himself. But that's what he was commanded to do.

Then Yahweh tells him to divide his shaved-off hair into thirds plus a bit. He is to burn one third of it in the middle of the city (meaning the model city that Ezekiel constructed on the clay tablet); strike a third of it over the city with the razor sword, and scatter a third of it to the wind. He is to tuck the leftover bit into his clothing. Then take a few of them back out and throw them onto the fire.

All of this is supposed to represent a dress rehearsal of what's going to happen to the real Jerusalem and its people. The fate of the hairs represents the fate of the people.

At this point, Yahweh takes over the conversation and begins a long, repetitive, Jeremiad against Judah and its people, explaining in graphic detail what he, Yahweh intends to do to them. There will be bloodshed and disease and famine and men will eat their sons and sons will eat their fathers, and everything will be destroyed and the rotting bodies and bones of the Judeans will lie before the altars to their idols and the rest of the world will hate them and they will become loathsome, and on and on for two and a half chapters.

And do you know what got Yahweh's dander up? The people of Jerusalem had been worshiping other gods. And do you know why they were worshiping other gods? It was because Yahweh was doing zilch to protect them from the Babylonian invasion and siege. They had figured they could rely on Yahweh as their protector. But when that proved false, they turned otherwhere for help. And that pissed Yahweh off. Instead of being ashamed of himself for having failed to protect his people, he gets mad at them for realizing that he wasn't going to do anything for them about the Babylonians. He thinks they should have continued to worship him as their protector, even though he was deliberately withholding protection from them (remember Job). He wants his people to reward him (and only him) with worship, even when they get nothing in return except frequent abuse. This Yahweh seems to be of low character. He has shown these traits before.

I note, in passing, the fixation with cannibalism that both Jeremiah and Ezekiel seem to have. They repeatedly speak of famished people eating their babies, or eating their parents. We might think this is just a hyperbole, part of their overwrought way of writing...but I suspect there may be something to it. Remember the lady, back in Kings II, who complained to King Ahab about another lady who failed to keep a bargain: They had cooked and eaten the first lady's baby, but then the second lady hid hers so they couldn't eat him. If it went on up in Israel, it might well be going on down in Judah as well. Ewww.

****

This concludes Ezekiel's first dream/vision/whatever. Chapter 8 begins some time later. He is sitting in his house with the elders of Judah, when another vision begins. He sees Yahweh, the molten metal and fire version, approaching him. The figure takes him by the hair of the head (since grown out), lifts him into the sky, and takes him —in a vision— to Jerusalem. They hover over the city, and Yahweh directs his attention to the goings-on below. The people are worshiping idols.Then he has Ezekiel burrow into a wall, where there are images of fabulous disgusting monsters, and into a chamber where the elders are burning incense and worshiping an idol. Then he takes Ezekiel back up over the city and points out similar things everywhere.

In Ezekiel's continuing vision, Yahweh hisownself hollers out in a loud voice, "Bring the city guards here, and have them bring their swords!" And here come a half dozen soldiers armed to the teeth. They bring a scribe with them, and stand at attention, waiting. Yahweh tells the scribe, "Go through the city, and make a mark on the forehead of all those who have rejected the worship of idols,"

Then he tells the guards to follow the scribe and slaughter everybody he doesn't put a mark on. Kill everybody: old, young, men, women, boys, girls, little bitty babies.

So the guards head out, and begin killing everybody, Yahweh urging them on: "Pile the bodies in the courtyard, fill the temple with corpses!"

While this was going on, Ezekiel had been left behind and he collapsed face down, hollering "Lord! Do you intend to wipe out all of those remaining of the House of Israel, sons of Jacob? Are you gonna obliterate your chosen people?"

306

Yahweh answers: "The city is full of bloodshed and injustice. These people say, 'The Lord has forsaken us' *[which he had]*, so I'll have no mercy on any of them; they're toast, victims of my mighty wrath."

****

The vision then moves to another dimension. Ezekiel sees the sapphire throne from before, above the canopy over the Beings from the earlier vision, whom he now calls Cherubim. Yahweh tells the scribe, "Go in among the wheels of the Cherubim, fill your hands with coals from the Cherubim and scatter them over the city." So the scribe did as he was told.

Ezekiel gives a reprise of his earlier description of the Beings, but with a new feature: Their entire bodies, front, back, hands, wings, are full of EYES! Before, just the rims of the wheels were infested; now the Beings themselves have caught the infection.

I need to comment on these "Cherubim". Ezekiel's version embellishes them far beyond what was said of them before. Earlier, back in Exodus and since, Cherubim were seen as human figures with wings, prototypes of the Angels depicted in Renaissance paintings. One of them guarded the gate of Eden to prevent Adam and Eve from going back in. But the main role of Cherubim was to guard the Ark of the Covenant. A pair of them knelt at the sides of it, facing each other, and spread their wings toward each other, providing a canopy over the Ark. They had no wheels, no infestation of eyes all over their bodies, no multiple faces, no bronze hooves, no burning fire. And they didn't face away from each other in all directions.

Ezekiel isn't following tradition. He's just making stuff up for dramatic effect.

They are creations of his bizarre hallucinatory world.

This brings us to the end of Chapter 10. But, not to the end of Ezekiel's current dream. There's lots more of it to come.

The Bible, Chapter 65

The Book of Ezekiel
part 3

This continuing dream is like a screen-play for a Cecil B. DeMIlle movie, complete with special effects. Ezekiel would be as tedious as Jeremiah, except for the remarkable fantasies that make it interesting.

Chapter 11 continues from where we left off; but in many ways it seems to be a flashback to Chapter 9. Back then, they hovered over Jerusalem and Yahweh addressed the city guards directly, instructing them to go and kill everybody, and fill the streets with corpses, which they did. And then Ezekiel asked if Yahweh intended to wipe out the last remnant of Israel, and Yahweh said he would destroy the city without mercy.

Then there's an episode with the Cherubim.

This time, Yahweh lifts Ezekiel up (it doesn't say by the hair), and they float over the city. They spot a crowd of city leaders, and Yahweh says they are wicked men plotting evil...for they say, "Will it not soon be time to build houses" or maybe "This is not the time to build houses", and then they say "This city is a cooking pot, and we are the meat" —a metaphor that I don't fully grasp. Then Yahweh tells Ezekiel to go prophesy at them. Tell them:

"That's what YOU think. But you've killed people wholesale and littered the streets with corpses. And so the Lord says: "The bodies in the streets are the meat and this city is the pot, which I shall drive you out of...the city won't be a pot and you won't be the meat in it, because foreign invaders will come destroy you because you have failed to obey my commands."

So...Yahweh first gets the city guards to kill everybody and litter the city with corpses, and then he turns around and rails on the city leaders because everybody got killed and the streets were littered with corpses. Go figure.

Then Ezekiel, just like last time, falls down on his face and says "Lord, do you intend to destroy the last remnant of Israel?"

But this time Yahweh tells him, in so many words, that it's OK for him to destroy Jerusalem, because that WON'T be the last remnant of Israel: There are those in exile and scattered among nations. So after he has Dealt With these rebellious Jerusalemites, he'll bring back those descendants of Israel (aka Jacob) who are exiled and scattered, and they will rebuild Jerusalem and will fall back in line with the Lord's commandments and all will be ducky once again.

Then there's an episode with the Cherubim.

Then Ezekiel awakens from his vision, and somehow finds himself back with the exiles in Babylon and tells them everything he has dreamed. This ends the chapter.

Yahweh regularly addresses Ezekiel as "Son of man." I'm not sure what it means exactly...maybe something like "You human", or "You mere mortal". Or maybe something else entirely.

Chapter 12 finds Ezekiel in Jerusalem, getting instructions from Yahweh. We are not told how he got there from Babylon. Walking, it took Ezra four months to travel between the two. If it took Ezekiel the same, there's a lot of time unaccounted for. Why doesn't Ezekiel tell us what he did during that time? What is he covering up?

Anyhow, once back in Jerusalem, Yahweh tells him to pack up his stuff as if he's heading into exile, and to let everybody see him do it. Then he is to go dig a hole with his hands through the city wall, and to do it in one night, even though the walls of Jerusalem were about 8 feet thick, which he does.. Then he takes his stuff upon his shoulders and creeps out through the hole, making sure the people are watching him.

When they ask him what he's up to, he's to tell them, "I'm a sign to you; just as I'm heading off to exile, you'll be dragged off as captives into exile."

Then Yahweh takes over and starts fulminating about what-all he's going to do to the wicked Jerusalemites, and how he's going to make them suffer, and on and on, because of his mighty wrath.

Chapter 13 continues the message, with Ezekiel taking over as messenger, continuing and repeating and amplifying the threats for an entire chapter. His main target at first is the local prophets who have been prophesying falsely;
•They have been prophesying peace, so Yahweh will make sure there isn't any.
•Then he turns his attention to the women, "who sew magic charms on all their wrists and make veils of various lengths for their heads in order to ensnare people." *(I do not understand this veil business. But he's clearly seeing women as a bunch of tempters and seductresses.)*

Then he seems to be talking to the prophets again, and tells them, "By lying to my people, who listen to lies, you have killed those who should not have died and have spared those who should not live." Then he issues some more threats of the familiar kind. I find this bothersome, since so far in the narrative the only ones who have been killed are the ones Yahweh directed the guards to kill in the earlier vision.

Chapter 14 is a tirade against idolatry and the worship of gods other than Yahweh, with the standard threats, and Yahweh giving assurance that none shall escape his wrath.

The Bible, Chapter 66

The Book of Ezekiel
part 4

I'll have to start condensing this stuff better if I'm ever to get done with Ezekiel (34 chapters to go) and move along to Daniel.

Chapter 15: An allegory. Just as the wood of the grape vine is fit for nothing except to be burned as fuel, so the people of Judah are fit only to be consumed by Yahweh's holy wrath.

Chapter 16: A metaphor that is flogged to death. Jerusalem is likened to an abandoned infant girl who was rescued and raised by Yahweh. He pampered her and sheltered her, and raised her to be a queen, with Yahweh now being her consort. But instead, she used her beauty to become a whorelady, and went whoring around and sold the jewelry she had been given to hire men to be her customers...*the opposite of an ordinary whorelady*. And she took the children she had borne to Yahweh, and sacrificed them to idols. And she stood on street corners like a hooker, offering her body to every passerby...even with Egyptians and Assyrians and Babylonians but her nymphomania was never satisfied. And because she was unfaithful to her husband and had been promiscuous and had flashed her body around, Yahweh was going to gather all her lovers and strip her naked in front of them, and give her the punishment due an adulteress, and then turn her over to the lovers, who would tear her to pieces. And on and on.

I'll leave it to you to unpack the metaphor. Hint: The johns to whom she gave herself were Egypt and Assyria and other surrounding non-Yahweh-ist nations. The rest you can figure out for yourself. But I'll mention in passing that Yahweh's method of rearing his "daughter" consisted mainly of bashing her when she stepped out of line.

That's what you gets from "spare-the-rod-an-=spoil-the-child"

312

methods of parenting. Generally not what you wanted.

The context of **Chapter 17** indicates that it was written during the time of Jerusalem's puppet king Zedekiah, who unwisely dropped his alliance with Babylon and took up with Egypt instead. Ezekiel recounts the first Babylonian conquest of Jerusalem, the removal of Jehoiachin, the installation of Zedekiah, and Zedekiah's ill-fated alliance with Egypt. These are recounted as having happened.

He then turns to prophecy about what is to come. Yahweh predicts that Jerusalem will be overrun, Zedekiah will be hauled off to die in Babylon, the Pharaohs armies will be ineffectual against the Babylonians, and Jerusalem will be obliterated. Then, in a complicated metaphor, Yahweh promises to eventually restore Jerusalem to greatness.` The prophecy turns out to be pretty accurate, except for the last part which is exaggerated.

Chapter 18 contains a remarkable abandonment of a fundamental principle that has been observed and enforced throughout the Bible up to now: The principle of Associative Guilt. In countless instances we have seen whole populations punished for the sins of a few of their members, generations of descendants punished because of their ancestors. It has been Yahweh's stock in trade ever since Genesis. But now Ezekiel tosses it out the window. He declares that "the one who sins is the one who will die." If a righteous man has an unrighteous son, the father will not suffer for it. If a righteous son has an unrighteous father, the son will not suffer for it. The guilt lies squarely on the head of the sinner, and nowhere else. *(A similar deviation appears in 2 Chronicles.)* Absolution is also recognized. If a sinner rejects his evil ways, is "born again" so to speak, and continues to live a righteous life, he won't be punished for his earlier sins.

Yahweh says to the house of Israel, "I will judge you each one according to his ways. Repent, turn away from your offenses, then sin will not be your downfall. Rid yourselves of all the

313

offenses you have committed, and get a new heart and a new spirit...repent and live!"

This is enough to make one's head spin. As early as Exodus, Yahweh was afflicting the entire Egyptian people with plagues and stuff, because of the Pharaoh's behavior. Later, when King Sihon of the Amorites refused to allow the Israelite hordes to pass through his territory, Moses took care of him by killing Sihon and all of the other Amorites they could catch including women and kids . Thereafter, for centuries, the descendants of those Amorites remained on Yahweh's shit list for what their ancestors had done.

There was Sodom and Gomorrah, where Yahweh blasted the entire populations — adults, children little bitty babies —for the behavior of some.

Yahweh told Jeremiah to go and tell the people of Jerusalem: "There was a time, way back, when your ancestors were faithful to Yahweh and everything was rosy for them. But then they lost trust and drifted away to worthless idols. They defiled my land. Therefore, because of those ancestors, I shall punish YOU for what they did."

Just a couple of chapters ago, Yahweh was proclaiming his determination to wipe out the entire population of Jerusalem because some of them had been worshiping other gods. And here, all of a sudden, we have Yahweh denouncing the very principle that he has used to justify indiscriminate mass killings.

I don't believe it. I don' t think Yahweh told him that. I think Ezekiel wrote this chapter when he was drunk.

****

Then there are several chapters of Yahweh fulminating about the misbehavior of the Israelites ever since back when he brought them out of Egypt and about what rotten people they are, and that they never learn and keep worshipping other gods and how he's going to smite them in his righteous anger, and on and on.

At one point, he returns to the metaphor of Jerusalem as an adulterous slut, and says "I'm going to turn you over to the Babylonians and the Assyrians and they will cut off your noses and your ears and leave you naked and bare and the shame of your prostitution will be exposed."

****

Yahweh tells Ezekiel that his beloved wife is about to die, but not to mourn for her. She dies and he doesn't mourn for her. This is a sign to the Judeans of what is in store for them. *I don' get it.*

....

Yahweh rails against Ammon and Moab and Edom and Philistia and Tyre and all the surrounding nations for one thing or another. Then he rails about Egypt. Then he laments for Pharaoh. Then he says that if a watchman warns the people that an invading army is coming, and they don't heed him, the blood is on their own head for ignoring the warning. Then he says that Ezekiel is the watchman, and if the people don't heed him and stop their wicked ways, their punishment will be on their own heads. Then he likens their leaders to shepherds who are irresponsible and don't take proper care of their flocks. He will take their flocks away from them and give them to a new shepherd —his servant David. Or, since David has been dead for going-on 400 years, a descendant in the Davidic line.

Then Yahweh rails some more against Edom. He says that since the long-ago Edomites had turned the Israelites over to their enemies, he would now turn their descendants over to their enemies, and make their land a desolate waste. *So much for the enlightenment of Chapter 18. Now we're back to good old inherited guilt.*

....

Again, let us pause and catch our breath.

The Bible, Chapter 67

The Book of Ezekiel
part 5

We enter a period when Yahweh is concerned about convincing folks that he is the Lord.

Instead of prophesying at people, Ezekiel addresses his next prophecy to the mountains of Israel. Yahweh promises that just as Israel's mountains have been scorned by surrounding nations, those nations will be scorned in return. The he compares the transgressions of the people of Israel to the uncleanness of a woman menstruating. Then he promises again, for the umpteenth time, that he will eventually return all the scattered children of Israel to their homeland, and they will flourish and prosper and sin no more and it will be like the garden of Eden.

And that will prove to the outlying territories that Yahweh really is the Lord.

Chapter 37: Ezekiel has another vision. He finds himself wandering in a valley littered with human bones, which are old and dry. Yahweh asks him if he thinks the bones might live again. Ezekiel says: I don't know, but maybe you do. Then Yahweh tells him to prophesy his words at the dry bones, and tell them:

"Bones, I'm going to bring you back to life. First I'll cover you with flesh and with skin, and then I'll breathe life into you."

"Then you'll know that I am the Lord."

So Ezekiel prophesied at them, and the bones began to reassemble themselves into skeletons, and the skeletons were covered with flesh and then with skin, but they weren't yet alive.

Then Yahweh commands the four winds to come breathe life into the creatures, and the winds did, and the creatures came to life and stood up and were a great army.

Then, still in the vision, Yahweh makes one of his more remarkable promises: When he reassembles the children of Israel in their homeland, as promised above, it won't just include those currently living: it will include all of the dead Israelites and Judeans, who will arise, zombie-like, from their graves and acquire flesh and skin and the breath of life and will join their living brothers (and sisters) in enjoying Yahweh's new Eden.

This is the first we've heard of any mass resurrection. I suspect that this is one source of the latter-day notion that at the End of Days there will be a great gettin' up morning, and all of the dead will come out of the ground and come alive with newly endowed flesh.

Note that what Ezekiel is talking about is a physical resurrection of corpses, who will occupy the land of Israel. Not unearthly heaven, not streets of gold, none of those latter-day embellishments. They will walk the streets of Jerusalem just as they did in life, and they will be ordinary streets, except cleaner and nicer than before, as befits Eden.

This far along in the Old Testament there is still no hint of the doctrine of heaven and hell and afterlife in some non-physical realm. Punishments are physical punishments and rewards are physical rewards, and "afterlife" is the physical resurrection of the corpse to walk the earth.

....

In the next vision, Ezekiel is taken to a mountaintop and is shown a man with measuring and surveying instruments laying out the plans for the new Jerusalem that will be built when the children of Israel return to their homeland. The plan goes into great detail, describing the buildings and rooms and giving measurements in cubits. But it's not clear that the people of

Nehemiah, who actually carried out the rebuilding, followed Ezekiel's plat map or even knew about it.

After this, we are given various rules of conduct for the new Jerusalem. Much of this seems to be a rehash of rules laid down in Leviticus. These concern the altar, and sacrifices, and rules for using or not using certain gates. Only the Levite priests may enter the Lord's sanctuary, and they can wear only linen...no wool allowed. They can't wear anything that might make them sweat. And when they depart the sanctuary, they have to leave their holy robes and turbans and underwear in a special anteroom, and put on street clothes, to avoid consecrating the townsfolk with their holy garments. They must keep their hair nicely trimmed ...no shaved heads. There are rules about whom they may marry. Rules for the allotment of land. Rules for sacrifices and for holy days. Rules for festivals.

Then there's a description of the Jordan River valley. Finally, there are a lot of rules about division of the land, and we are at the end of this long, threat-laden and repetitious book. And I'm glad.

****

*The only constructive advice for the conduct of life I've gotten from the whole Book of Ezekiel is***: Don't worship idols***. Which I wasn't planning to do anyway.*

The Bible, Chapter 68

The Book of Daniel
part 1

The first part of the book of Daniel is largely narrative, which is a refreshing relief from the tedious string of fire-and-brimstone sermons of the last two books.

The book was written in the period after the destruction of Jerusalem and during the second Babylonian Captivity. It begins with a brief description of those events.

Daniel is living in Babylon with the other exiles.

King Nebuchadnezzar has his chief-of-staff go out among the captive Israelites and round up a bunch of worthy young men from their nobility and royalty. He wants to train them in the Babylonian language and customs, so they can become servants in the palace. *It says "some of them" were from Judah, but I wasn't aware that any from the Northern Kingdom had ended up in Babylon. They had all been hauled off to Assyria and dispersed several centuries earlier. But that's what it says.*

Four of these Judeans were Daniel, Hananiah, Mishael, and Azariah. They were given new Babylonian names: Shadrach (Hananiah), Meshach (Mishael), Abednego (Azariah), and Belteshazzar (Daniel). *Don't confuse him with Belshazzar, who is a different dude that comes along later.*

Daniel rebelled against eating the non-kosher palace food, and asked to be excused. The guy in charge said, "The king has assigned you guys' food, and if you don't eat it and start losing weight and the king sees it, it will be my ass." Daniel said, "You don't have to *starve* us. Instead of the palace food just give us veggies and water for a few days, and see whether we look skinnier."

After a week and a half of the vegan diet, the four looked healthier that the ones eating the palace food. So they were allowed to stick with it.
****

Daniel especially flourished , and developed wisdom and the ability to interpret dreams. When Nebuchadnezzar finally held an audience with his chosen Judeans, he was immediately taken by these four, and took them on as advisors (they did better advising than the others).

And Daniel remained there until the first year of King Cyrus.

This casual throw-away line is fairly significant, and needs some fleshing out because a whale of a lot of history is condensed here.
*•**Nebuchadnezzar** finished off Jerusalem in about 586 BC, and continued to rule for another 19 years.*
*• He was succeeded **by Amel-Marduk** (or evil-Marduk) who ruled for 22 more years. •After him was somebody named **Neriglissar** for 4 years,*
*•then a short-timer **Labashi-Marduk** who lasted just a few months. Finally, there was •**Nabonidus** and his son*
*•**Belshazzar**, who ruled for 17 years, until the Persians came and took over Babylon in 539 BC.*
*•**Cyrus the Great** of Persia became Babylon's king in 539, or about 47 years after the destruction of Jerusalem and the second Babylonian captivity.*

This is what's sandwiched into that one sentence.

There's a certain amount of chronological jumping-around in this book that I'll try to keep track of.

321

****

Daniel had his first chance to show his stuff when Nebuchadnezzar had a troubling dream. The king summoned all the magicians and astrologers and dream-interpreters and told them "I've had this dream. Tell me what it means." They said, "Sure, tell us the dream and we'll tell you what it means." Neb said, "No no, you don't understand. YOU tell ME what the dream was, and THEN tell me what it means. And if you don't, I'll have you sliced and diced like stew-meat. But if you do, I'll reward you handsomely."

They said,, "Hey! Nobody but you can know what was in your dream!" But Neb said, "Quit stalling. If you don't tell me my dream, I'll know you're conspiring to tell me bad things in your interpretation. The only way I'll know you're not fudging is if you yourselves relate the dream and then relate its meaning."

They replied, "But that's impossible!", which pissed off the king, so he ordered that all dream-interpreters be rounded up and hacked to death. Among those rounded up were, of course, our four Judeans. But before the hacking commenced, Daniel up and volunteered to interpret the king's dream and save everybody.

Then Daniel went home and prayed, and had a vision, and went back to the king and told him what he had dreamed (he could do that because Yahweh had told him in the vision). Then he told he king what the dream meant.

The dream was a series of images of a gigantic statue made of various metals that got smashed by a boulder which grew into a mountain that filled the earth.

According to Daniel, the dream foretold a series of kingdoms after Nebuchdnezzar's. Bad stuff will happen to them along the way. The final kingdom will be instituted by Yahweh himself, which will crush and destroy all the previous kingdoms. Yahweh's kingdom, however, will endure forever.

Nebuchadezzar was duly impressed, both with Daniel and with Yahweh, whom he called "the greatest of all gods." He appointed Daniel to be in charge of the entire province of Babylon, and appointed the other three to be his deputies.

****

The Fiery Furnace

Neb's appreciation of Yahweh's power wasn't permanent, however. Before long, he had a humongous image of pure gold constructed, 90 feet high and 9 feet wide. *Supposing it was a foot thick, that would be somewhere between 500 and 800 cubic feet of solid gold. At 1,204 pounds to the cubic foot, that's something between 300 and 500 tons of pure gold. I wonder where he got it?*

Anyhow, he had the statue set up out in a field, with a furnace nearby. Then he summoned all government officials to come attend the dedication of the statue. When they were all there, he said, "Here's the deal. When the musicians start playing, all of you fall down and worship this here statue. Anybody who doesn't will be tossed into yon blazing furnace to teach them a lesson."

So the music played and *almost* everybody fell down and worshiped the statue. But some ornery astrologers went to the king and told him, "Those three Jew deputies of Daniel's — Shadrach, Meshach, and Abednigo— didn't do it. They refused to worship your humongous golden statue."

When he asked the three if that was true, they said "Indeed it is." He told them, "Then do it now, or it's into the furnace with you!" They said, "Nope. And if you put us in, we think our god will save us from burning. But even if he doesn't, we ain't worshiping no stinking statue."

So they stoked up the furnace and tossed the three into it. Nebuchadnezzar watched, expecting to see them sizzle and fry and turn crisp. Instead, he saw what looked like FOUR figures walking around in the flames, completely unharmed.

He went over and hollered for the three to come out, and out they came, without a sign of scorching.

The king said, "Praise be to your god, who sent his angel to protect you in this way. This convinces me of his power. So I decree that anybody who ever says anything against the god of Shadrach, Meshach, and Abednigo will be sliced and diced like stew-meat, and his house will be reduced to rubble." Then to seal the deal, he gave each of them a promotion.

Which brings us to the end of **Chapter 3**.

The Bible, Chapter 69

The Book of Daniel, part 2.

Chapter 4: Nebuchadnezzar's Madness

Eventually, Nebuchanezzar has another disturbing dream. None of the other necromancers were able to make sense of it, so Daniel (aka Belteshazzar) got called in again. The dream involved a tree with certain marvelous features that eventually got chopped down, leaving its stump and roots behind for shoots to grow from.

Daniel proceeded to tell the king its meaning, and it was not good news. King Neb would fall out of power and descend into madness. He would be driven out of the city to live like an animal, going on all fours and eating grass along with the cattle. He would remain in that condition for seven years (or seven somethings) until he acknowledged Yahweh's greatness...and meant it. Then his madness would be lifted and he would be restored to power.

A year later, the king was up on the roof admiring the city he had created, and admiring himself for creating it, when he had a revelation from Yahweh, repeating the same prophecy Daniel had given the year before.

At that moment, Nebuchadnezzar went mad, dropped to all fours and began eating grass alongside the sheep and cows. The people chased him away. His hair grew long and longer, and his fingernails and toenails grew out until they looked like claws. William Blake painted a really cool picture of it.

At the end of seven somethings, maybe years, his sanity was restored and he took to praising Yahweh as hard as he could. I assume he went back to being king. And that was that.

Chapter 5: The Moving Finger Writes

Abrupt time-shift here. We jump ahead several decades and several kings, to the time of Belshazzar (who wasn't really a king: he was just holding down the job while his daddy King Nabonidus was off doing something or other.) At the time, Babylon was under siege by the Persian and Medean armies, but Belshazzar blew off the danger, figuring the city was impregnable.

This Belshazzar decided to throw a huge banquet for a thousand of his nobles and their wives. To make it extra fancy, he had the sacred silver and gold Temple goblets Nebuchadnezzar had liberated from Jerusalem brought in, so the guests could drink out of them while carrying on and getting drunk and praising the idols that served as their gods.

In the midst of the party, a ghostly human hand appeared, and wrote some stuff on the wall.

This scared the crap out of Belshazzar, who called in all his necromancers and offered a huge prize to the one who could interpret the writing on the wall. None of them could do it, which scared him even worse. While he was in a tizzy of fear, the queen came along and reminded him that there was this person called Belteshazzar, who was really Daniel, who had a long-standing reputation for his ability to interpret stuff.

The king had Daniel brought in, and offered him the prize if he could interpret the writings. Daniel said, keep your prize, I'll interpret them for free.

Daniel related the tale of Nebuchadnezzar's fall from power and madness because of his arrogance and pride. Then he predicted a similar downfall for Belshazzar, for defiling the sacred cups while partying with them and worshipping false gods with them. The words on the wall, he said, were

MENE MENE TEKEL UPARSIN

Daniel interpreted them as follows:

1. Your days and your bones are numbered, and the end of your kingdom foretold.
2. You have been weighed in the scales of justice, and have been found unfit.
3. Your kingdom will end, and be given over to the Medes and the Persians.

Sure enough, that very night the Persian armies entered Babylon, Belshazzar was killed, and the kingdom was taken over by Cyrus The Great. Cyrus appointed Darius of Medea as governor.

Chapter 6: The Den of Lions
Darius appointed a bunch of locals to important office, including

Daniel. Daniel quickly distinguished himself, to the point that the others became envious, and developed a plot to have him brought down.

They got together and urged Darius, who was not a humble man, to cement his greatness by decreeing that, for the next month, anybody caught worshipping a god other than Darius himself would be tossed into a cave inhabited by hungry lions, to be torn to pieces and eaten. Darius thought that was a peachy keen idea, and the edict was issued.

We aren't told whether it was a wild pride of lions that just happened to have settled in the local cave, or a sort of zoo that Darius maintained for shredding wrongdoers. Whatever...

When Daniel heard about the decree, he went up to his room facing Jerusalem, and carried out his usual prayers to Yahweh. The conspirators saw him and went and told Darius that Daniel was praying to Yahweh, and asked what he intended to do about it. Darius was fond of Daniel and tried to figure out a way to avoid giving him to the lions; but the conspirators reminded him that according to his own law, a royal decree could never be annulled or reversed.

So Darius stuck Daniel in the lions' cave, saying, "I hope your god may keep you safe." Then they sealed up the opening of the cave with a stone. Darius continued to worry about Daniel.

Later artists had different views on the question of a zoo versus a natural cave. Rubens depicts Daniel as a young man in what looks like a natural cave infested by lions.

Riviere shows Daniel as an old guy with a bald head, and the venue looks more like a zoo setting, with brick walls and a paved floor devoid of lion droppings, suggesting a keeper or janitor..

Daniel himself says nothing to settle the matter.

Anyhow, next morning at daybreak, Darius went to the cave and hollered, "Hey Daniel, did your god manage to keep you from being eaten?" Daniel hollered back, "Yes indeed. Yahweh sent an angel, and the angel made the lions keep their mouths shut, so I'm okay. The Lord knew I hadn't done anything against you."

So Darius had Daniel released from the lions' cave. Then he rounded up the conspirators, along with their wives and children, and had the lot thrown to the lions where they were promptly eaten up....once again honoring the principle of associative or inherited guilt: the wives and kids hadn't done anything, but that didn't matter.

Then Darius issued another decree, saying that everybody had to show reverence for Daniel's god (Yahweh), who had shown his power by keeping Daniel safe. And that was that.

The Bible, Chapter 70

The Book of Daniel
part 3.

The Book of Daniel has been more difficult to report on than any so far. I've had to do a lot of outside reading just to get a handle on it. At this point —chapter 7 onward— the entire character of the book changes. It ceases to be an account of events in the life of Daniel, and becomes a series dreams and visions and revelations and prophecies, all concerning events in the far future and all saying pretty much the same thing. These "prophecies" are so remarkably accurate that either we must suppose Daniel to have been truly clairvoyant, or that these chapters were written, not by Daniel, but by someone writing at a time when those events were history.

The Book of Daniel has probably received more attention by Bible scholars, Bible historians, and other serious researchers, than any other book in the Old Testament. The overwhelming consensus is that the last half of the book, from chapters 7 through 12, could not have been written in the times identified in the earlier chapters –the time of Nebuchadnezzar and Belshazzar and the Persian conquest of Babylon. Those events happened in the 5th century BC. Nebuchadnezzar razed Jerusalem and destroyed the temple in 587 BC. The Persians conquered Babylon in 539 BC.

That is the claimed time-frame for the writing of the first 6 chapters by Daniel.

The final "vision/revelation" chapters are thinly veiled accounts of events that happened mainly in the 3rd and 2nd centuries BC. They are so accurate that they only could have been written after those events, by some historian who knew of them. Devout believers stick with the notion that 5th century Daniel was clairvoyant, that the future had been revealed to him by or

331

through Yahweh.

Serious scholars dismiss that interpretation. Either the last chapters were written hundreds of years after Daniel wrote the first chapters, but were laid out as earlier prophecies attributed to him...or perhaps the entire book was written later than it claims!.

Briefly, the events in question begin around the time of Alexander the Great (Macedonian by nationality, Greek by culture), and onward for another century or so. Alexander began his conquest of empire in 336 BC, and within a few years he ruled everything from India to Eastern Europe, including all of Asia Minor and Egypt. When he died, his empire was divided into several parts, the most powerful being the Seleucid (Asia Minor, including Persia) empire and the Ptolemaic (Egyptian/Libyan) empire, which would war back and forth. Events thereafter would have a great effect on Judea and the Jews. The Seleucids set out to force Hellenistic (Greek) culture and practices on everybody, and forbade the worship of Yahweh, and so on. Now, back to the Bible.

****

Chapter 7: Daniel's Dream
Another time jump: we are back in the early days of Belshazzar's rule, before Babylon fell to the Persians.

Daniel's first dream is a masterpiece. Try to imagine it in Technicolor.

Four huge beasts are disgorged from the sea.

The first one looks like a lion, except it has wings. Then the wings are torn off, and it arises up and erect, and morphs into a humanoid form. It somehow receives a human heart.

The second beast is a gigantic bear, standing up on its feet. It is crunching three ribs between its teeth. A voice tells it, "Go out and eat flesh until you can't eat any more."

The third beast resembles a leopard. It has four wings growing out of its back. "Like a bird," says Daniel, but four wings sounds to me more like a dragonfly or something. It has four heads. We are not told where or how they are attached, but it seems to me they would interfere with its resemblance to a leopard. Maybe the spots were enough.

The fourth beast is terrifying in an unspecified way. It has iron teeth, and it chomps and stomps everyone and everything in its path. It has ten horns. Then it starts growing another horn in their midst, which uproots three of the old horns. The new horn is equipped with human eyes, and with a mouth that speaks.

Artists differ in their interpretation of Daniel's dream. Here's one:

Here's another:

The scene then shifts to an arrangement of thrones, with Yahweh sitting in one of them. He has white wooly hair and wears white robes. The throne he's sitting in has wheels and is made of fire. A river of fire flows from it. He is attended by thousands upon thousands. They all sit down and open their books. Their books were probably scrolls, and they "opened" them by starting to unroll them.

Meanwhile, back at the last beast, the horn with eyes and a mouth is spouting boastful stuff. Then something or other kills the beast and tosses its corpse into the fire.

Then a human shows up, approaching the throne of Yahweh. He

is given divine authority over everything forever, and everybody worships him.

That concludes the dream.

At the conclusion of his dream, Daniel hits up a bystander to interpret it for him. Daniel is a renowned expert at interpreting stuff, but apparently in this case he is unsure of himself.

The interpreter tells him that the four Beasts represent four kingdoms that will arise, yada yada yada. Then Daniel presses him about the fourth beast, the one with iron teeth that grinds and stomps everything in its path and has ten horns and an eleventh horn that grows and pushes 3 of the others out of the way and had eyes and a mouth that talks. Daniel supplies more details of his dream: the new horn "was waging war against the saints and defeating them," until Yahweh intervened on the side of the saints.

Who are these "saints" are that Daniel refers to?. In the later era of Christianity the notion has a pretty clear definition; but not here. Two translations use the phrase "God's people" instead of "saints". But in King James it's "saints", when "God's people" would have been clearer. I'd give something to know the meaning of the Hebrew or Aramaic word in the original.

But in the second place, I get no mental image of how a horn can wage war on anything. A horn, after all, is just a horn. We're told that this horn can see and talk, but nothing else. It's only mode of attack would be verbal, so maybe "waging war" came down to a shouting match between the talking horn and the "saints", with the horn winning the debate ("defeating them") until Yahweh got into the act and declared the saints to have the stronger side of the argument. But the whole thing is so weird that Daniel may have dreamed that the horn actually jumped off the Beast's head, and went and started beating up the saints. I'll leave this riddle unresolved.

Here's the bystander's interpretation of the fourth Beast. The

Beast itself represents the fourth and final kingdom that will eventually crush and conquer the entire world. The ten horns represent ten kings who will rule during this kingdom. (The eleventh horn is a different king, who overcomes three of the other kings (displacing three other horns) This king will oppose Yahweh, and oppress Yahweh's people, and try to institute new laws and norms of behavior. Yahweh's people will adopt the changes for a while. Then the heavenly court will sit in judgment and take away the horn king's power and destroy him completely. The world kingdom will be given to Yahweh's people, and everyone will worship Yahweh forever.

Daniel was troubled by this interpretation, but doesn't admit it.

The details of this and subsequent "visions" are important, so I shall list them again.

1. A fourth and final kingdom will conquer the entire world.
2. It will be ruled by ten different kings.
3. An eleventh king will overcome several of the others.
4. This king will oppose Yahweh, and institute new laws and forms of behavior.
5. Yahweh's people will conform for a while.
6. Divine intervention will destroy this last king.
7. Yahweh's people will be ascendant.
8. The whole world will come to worship Yahweh.

Chapter 8
Still in the time of Belshazzar, Daniel has another vision involving a ram and a goat. Again, to get the full flavor, imagine it in Technicolor like a scene from *Fantasia*.

Daniel is sitting next to a creek. He spots a nearby ram, with one horn longer than the other, and continuing to grow. The ram ran in all directions, cowed all the other animals, grew in power, and did whatever he pleased.

Suddenly, out of the west, came a magical goat with a single horn between his eyes. He crossed the whole earth without touching the ground. In a rage, the goat attacked the ram and broke off both its horns. Then he proceeded to kick the crap out of the ram, showing it who was in charge.

The goat grew in power (as the ram had) but at the height of his power his central horn broke off and four new ones grew in its place. Then one of these grew a horn of its own, which grew until it reached the sky and knocked some stars down and tromped on them. The horn set itself up to be as great as Yahweh, assumed Yahweh's sacrifices for itself, and took over the Temple. It continued to prosper, and Yahweh got displaced. The appearance of this takeover by the horn, including its method of tromping, are never made clear.

Then Daniel hears voices of holy men. One asks the other, "How long will it be before this goat-horn vision gets fulfilled and the Lord's people get trampled?" The other says, "It'll take 2,300 days. Then Yahweh will return to power and the sanctuary will be re-consecrated." Which doesn't exactly answer the first one's question. It seems to say how long the trampling will last, but not how long before it starts.

Then, if I read it right, the vision fades and Daniel looks and sees what looks like a man approaching, and a voice comes from the creek where he is sitting: "Gabriel, tell the man the meaning of his vision." So it's not really a man, but the angel Gabriel. The voice was presumably Yahweh hisownself.

Except that we're not actually in real life (as opposed to experiencing a vision), because Daniel says he was lying on his face in a deep sleep during this time. Gabriel has told him (in his sleep) that the goat vision " concerns the time of the end of the world."

Then Gabriel pokes Daniel to wake him up and tell him all about it.

Says Gabriel: "The two-horned ram is Medea and Persia. The

goat is Greece, and his single horn is the first king (of somewhere, probably Greece). The four horns represent the fragmentation of the Greek kingdom into four smaller kingdoms. In due course, as these descend into wickedness, a mighty new, stern, king will arise. He will bust everybody's chops, espouse evil, and claim to be the supreme power. Eventually, he'll get in a fight with Yahweh, and he'll be defeated (but not by human power)." Then he tells Daniel not to tell anybody about the goat vision or its meaning.

The whole episode makes Daniel sick to his tummy, and he stays that way for several days.

The details of the vision:
1. Greece will overcome Medea and Persia.
2. The Greek empire will be broken up into separate kingdoms.
3. These will descend into wickedness
4. One of the separate kings will become most powerful.
5. He will conquer the other kingdoms.
6. Divine power will defeat him.

Chapter 9.
Time shift again. Daniel moves ahead from the Belshazzar period to the time when Darius is governor of Babylon.

Daniel quotes Jeremiah, to the effect that the Babylonian Captivity will last 70 years. He then launches into a great long prayer to Yahweh, which consists of a lengthy declamation of how naughty and wicked and unworthy the Judean captives have been in the sight of Yahweh, and how Yahweh has repeatedly whacked them for their misbehavior...and they haven't yet reformed. But in spite of their endless iniquity, he asks Yahweh to look in favor on them...

While he's doing this praying, the angel Gabriel shows up again offering to give him insight and understanding. Then Gabriel gives a long rap involving sevens.
"Seventy sevens are decreed for you to atone for your evil ways and achieve everlasting righteousness. ...from when the time

comes for you to rebuild Jerusalem until an anointed king comes to you, there will be seven sevens and sixty-two sevens...after the sixty-two sevens, the king will be deposed and destroyed. But first, war will ensue until the end of time. He will confirm 'a covenant of many for one seven'. In the middle of the seven he will put an end to religious offering, and will set up a den of evil in the Temple until he meets the end that is decreed."

Thus ends the chapter.
I know not what these sevens mean. And Daniel doesn't tell us. I don't think he knows either.

The Bible, Chapter 71

The Book of Daniel,
part 4.

Chapter 10

Now we're up to the third year after King Cyrus took over Babylon, and the first year that Darius was governor, making it 536 BC. Daniel has another visionary episode, possibly brought on by malnutrition (he hadn't eaten for three weeks).

In these final chapters, Daniel refers to various ones as "princes"; but they are clearly supernatural beings, not ordinary human sons-of-kings. It doesn't seem proper to think of them as angels; I think of them as what the Arabs called "djinns" —spirits or demigods whose main aim is to give humans trouble.

In this vision, Daniel sees himself standing by the river bank when he spots what he claims is a man...except that it's dressed in white linen with a golden sash, its body is translucent like a gemstone, its face is like lightning, its eyes like flaming torches, its arms and legs are burnished bronze, and its voice is as loud as a multitude. I personally would not in a minute have mistaken this thing for a "man".

Nobody else could see it, but all the others ran off, terrified by something or other. Daniel got weak in the knees and fell into a trance. The creature tells him the following curious tale.

"I have been sent in response to your devotion to Yahweh. But the demigod of the Persian kingdom kept me away from you for three weeks until the angel Michael came and provided me reinforcements. So I'm here to foretell your future."

Chapter 11

The man-creature (not exactly an angel, either) gives Daniel pretty much another version of the same predictions that came from earlier visions.

The man-creature says:

"Before long, I'll go back into battle with the demigod of Persia; and after I go, the demigod of Greece will show up. My only support will be from your demigod Michael [who probably really *is* an angel, but nevermind].

"Three kings will arise in Persia. Then a fourth greater king [***Daris I***]will assume power. He will stir up his people against the Greeks. A fifth king, mightier than the others, will take over and rule as an absolute despot. [***Alexander the Great.***]

"Eventually, his dynasty will end, , his empire will be broken up into smaller kingdoms. and none of them will be ruled by his heirs. [***The empires ruled by Seleucus, Ptolemy, Lysimachus, and Cassander.***]

One of them, the king of the South [***Ptolemy, king of Egypt***], will achieve great power, but one of his officers eventually will take charge of his own kingdom.

The two kingdoms [***Ptolemaic and Seleucid***] *will become allies [**312 BC**]*. The daughter [***Berenice II ?***]of the king of the South will attempt an alliance with the king of the North, but it will be rejected.

"A war [***274-271 BC***] will ensue between the South [***Egypt***] and the North [***Seleucids***]. The South will win and will carry off all of the North's treasures and stuff to Egypt..."

"There will be another war between the North and the South [***Battle of Raphia,217 BC***], to be won by the South. The North will sustain massive casualties."

[*I'm tired of inserting historical dates. Look them up yourownself if you're interested.*]

"Eventually, there will be rebellion within the Southern Kingdom. The Northern king will come in force and establish an alliance with the South. He will give his daughter in marriage to the king of the South. After further campaigns, he will return to his country where he will be overthrown and seen no more."

"His successor will institute taxes to preserve royal splendor, but will soon be deposed. HIS successor will be a despicable person who will wage wars with Egypt yada yada yada. He will invade Judea, destroy the latest temple, and undertake to eradicate the worship of Yahweh. He will set himself up to be greater than any god. He will extend his power over many countries. But he will eventually meet his end."

Chapter 12
"The angel Michael, who protects the children of Israel, will come to the rescue. At that time, everyone will be delivered. The dead will all arise from their graves. Some will receive everlasting life, others everlasting misery."

Here ends the man-creature's interpretation of the dream.

Then Daniel looks and sees two men, one on each side of the river. One of them says to the man-creature, who is hovering above the water, "How long before these things come to pass?" The man-creature says, "It will be for a time, times, and half a time. When the power of the holy people has finally been broken, those things will happen."

Daniel says, "Huh? I don't get it."

The man-creature tells him, "Go on your way Daniel, and don't worry about it. The meaning of that prophecy will remain hidden until the time of the end. None of the wicked will understand, but those who are wise will. From the time that the religion of the Jews is stamped out and forbidden, there will be 1,290 days. Blessed be the one who waits for and reaches the end of the 1,335 days."

"Carry on as usual Daniel, for the rest of your life. Then at the end of days, you will be resurrected and receive whatever you deserve."

Thus ends the Book of Daniel

****

I hear tell of people who claim that the "prophecies" in the Book of Daniel aren't really about long-ago events in the Middle East, but rather are encoded predictions about out own time. I think not. But a skilled interpreter can probably interpret anything to mean anything other than what it says.

.

The Bible, Chapter 68

The Book of Hosea
part 1

In Hosea we move back in time a century or two from Daniel, before the destruction of the Kingdom of Israel, when Jeroboam II ruled Israel, and Uzziah ruled Judah. Two hundred years before, the United Kingdom of Solomon had divided, with the northern kingdom of Israel being ruled by Jeroboam, who had no royal background and the southern kingdom of Judah being ruled by Rehoboam, who was a descendant of David and therefore had some legitimacy. He was also cruel and stupid. From the get-go, the northern kingdom had fallen away from Yahweh, and taken to worshiping Baal and being materialistic and other bad stuff, while the southern kingdom had played it pretty straight.

So here we are, two hundred years later, with Israel under Jeroboam II still pretty much ignoring Yahweh while Judah under Uzzziah is pretty much sticking with him. That's the setting. Hosea himself is obviously an Israelite. The time is around 750 BC.
....

The book of Hosea is one weird book. It begins with Yahweh telling Hosea to go marry a whorelady, or a woman who will become one and will bear him children by other men she's been a-whoring with. He is supposed to do this because the Kingdom of Israel is like a whorelady in being unfaithful to Yahweh. I fail to understand the point, but that's what he's told to do.

So Hosea goes off and marries a woman named Gomer, who either is a whorelady or will become one, and he goes in unto her and she bears him a son. Then Yahweh tells Hosea to name the kid Jezreel, "because I will soon punish the house of Jehu for the massacre at Jezreel and I will put an end to the kingdom of Israel."

Which is weirdness #2. Let us refresh our memory.

A century or so earlier, Jezreel was the home base of the wicked King Ahab and his wicked wife Queen Jezebel. Ahab was killed when an errant arrow happened to miss his armor and hit his bod. He was succeeded by his wicked son Joram.

Meanwhile, the prophet Elisha had secretly anointed a guy named Jehu to be the rightful king of Israel, and ordered him to eradicate the house of Ahab. So (to shorten the tale) Jehu took care of Joram by shooting him in the back with an arrow. Then he killed the king of Judah who had witnessed it. Then he and his army occupied Jezreel and had the wicked Jezebel defenestrated, where she splattered on the pavement and the dogs ate her. Then Jehu had all 70 of wicked Ahab's descendants rounded up, and beheaded, and piled their heads in the courtyard. Elisha, Yahweh's prophet, had anointed Jehu as king, and told him to go and do all this stuff. This was the massacre of Jezreel, carried out with you-know-who's approval.

Now, here in Hosea a hundred years later, Yahweh absolutely reverses himself, condemns the Jezreel massacre, and promises to avenge it by destroying the kingdom of Israel. Remember, Ahab's reign was as corrupt as they come, and under Jezebel had encouraged the worship of Baal, which is why Jehu was commissioned to do away with the whole lot. So Yahweh now is going to punish Israel for getting rid of a kingdom of Baal-ites. Go figure.

But why any of this is a reason for the naming of Hosea's child (of the whorelady Gomer) is not explained.

Then Gomer has a daughter, and Yahweh tells Hosea to name her Lo-Ruhama, which means "unloved", because, Yahweh says, he will no more show love for the house of Israel, but he will show love for the house of Judah. He later vacillates on both of these claims.

Then Gomer has another son, whose paternity is questionable. and Yahweh says to name him Lo-Ammi, meaning "Not my people" *[Get it? Not Mine],* because Yahweh proclaims "You are not my people and I am not your god." Then he gives a cryptic prediction that someday the two kingdoms of Israel and Judah will reunite under one leader, and all will be well.

I personally wonder what it would be like for a kid to go through life with a name like "Not my people." I'll bet the other kids would make fun of him.

Chapter 2
In a very long soliloquy, Hosea tells his children to coax their mother to give up her whoring ways. "Until she does, she is no longer my wife and I'm not her husband. I'm not going to support her children conceived by other men. I'll strip her naked and leave her destitute. She will blow it off and say 'Then I'll just go get support from my lovers. They'll be glad to give it.' So I'll set up roadblocks of thorns in her way so she can't get to them. Then she'll decide to come back to her husband for support. But I won't give it. I'll strip her naked and let her lovers see what a whore she is. I'll destroy the orchards and vineyards they gave her so she can't support herself. I'll punish her for idolatry..." saith the Lord.

Saith the *Lord*?

So was it Hosea, talking about his unfaithful wife Gomer, or was it Yahweh, speaking metaphorically about his unfaithful people the Israelites? Or maybe both. In the continuation of the soliloquy, it is clearly Yahweh speaking, not about reconciliation with a wife, but reconciliation with a people.

"I will restore her fortunes, and she will be glad, and will accept me as the Lord. She will give up worshiping other gods. I will make a covenant for them..."

*[The only plural noun that can plausibly be the antecedent of 'them' is 'other gods'.
The ways of Yahweh are mysterious. So...]*

"...I will make a covenant for those other gods with the birds and animals. I will abolish the means of warfare from the land, and peace will reign. I will treat you with love and compassion...

"Then I will respond to the heavens and they will respond to the earth, and it will respond to the grain and the vine and the olive; and they will respond to Jezreel."

You make sense of it; I can't.

"Then those I called Not My People will be my people and I will be their god."

Chapter 3
The Lord tells Hosea to go reconcile with his adulterous wife, who at the moment is apparently shacked up with somebody else. He says, "Love her just as I love the Israelites, even though they were unfaithful to me."

So Hosea goes and buys her for 15 shekels of silver and several bushels of grain. Why he has to buy her, or whom he has to buy her from, is not explained. My guess is that she was working in a brothel, and he had to pay the Madam to get her out. Then Hosea tells her, "You're going to give up whoring and be faithful to me, just as the Israelites will give up Baal-worship and be faithful to Yahweh."
 This is the last we hear of Gomer.

The Bible, Chapter 69

The Book of Hosea
part 2

We hear no more of the adventures of Hosea. From here on out it's straight preaching.

Chapter 4
This is the first of a series of Jeremiads from Yahweh against Israel, covering the usual suspects: unfaithfulness, cursing, lying, murder, ignoring God's law, prostitution, idol worship, sacrificing at the wrong altars, adultery, stubbornness, etc. He is going to bust them for it.

Chapter 5
Another Jeremiad giving Yahweh's judgment against Israel.

Chapter 6
Another one, with a whack at Judah for good measure.

Chapter 7
A continuation of Chapter 6.

Chapter 8
Accusations against Israel; its fate prophesied. Israel has rejected what is good, they have set up kings without Yahweh's consent, made idols of gold and silver, including another golden calf (didn't learn from Aaron's similar venture). Those will get broken up, Israel will be swallowed up by Assyria. They conduct sacrifices not pleasing to the Lord. For punishment they will return to Egyptian captivity. How this will happen when they are swallowed by Assyria is not explained.

And the fortified cities of Judah will be consumed by fire.

[Though so far I haven't seen any accusations *leveled against Judah that would warrant punishment; just Israel. I suspect that Hosea made that part up, because he wanted to get the rival southern kingdom on Yahweh's shit list too. Why should they get off scot-free, when Israel is about to take it in the shorts?]*

Chapter 9
Punishments for Israel. Yada yada.

Chapter 10
Nothing new. More fulminating against Israel. Same old accusations, same old threats.

Chapter 11
After all this, Yahweh professes his love for Israel. First he lists all their transgressions, beginning with the Flight From Egypt. Then he says, "How can I abandon you? Compassion has overcome my anger. So I'm not going to follow through on any of those threats I made. Instead, they will return from Assyria and Egypt like docile obedient children, and I will settle them in their homes." *Go figure.*

"But Israel has surrounded me with deceit, and Judah is unruly against me."

Chapter 12
All that merciful jive seems to have lasted for only one chapter. Now he's back to blaming and punishing. Israel is practicing deceit, and is making alliances with Assyria and Egypt. And the Lord has a charge to bring against Judah, though it isn't specified. Instead, he starts talking about punishing Jacob for his deeds. This makes better sense when we recall that Jacob had his name changed to Israel.

Says Yahweh: "Jacob wrestled and angel and whupped him. He begged for his (my) favor and talked with me at Bethel." None of which seem deeds calling for punishment.

Then he says:
"The merchant uses dishonest scales to defraud. Ephraim [by which he means Israel, since it's the largest tribe] claims that its wealth and success prove how righteous it is."

Then he says:
"I brought you out of Egypt and I will make you live in tents again. The people of Gilead are wretches who sacrifice bulls in Gilgal, using piles of stones for altars."

Then he says more stuff about Jacob and how he (Yahweh) used prophets to help his people, and how Israel has pissed him off and will suffer for it.

Chapter 13
Then he expounds some more about how angry he is with Israel. "There was a time when the tribe of Ephraim spoke, the rest of Israel trembled in fear. But when they went to worshipping Baal, they fell out of favor and died. (?) But they keep on sinning, making idols of silver. and offering sacrifices to them and even kissing them. Their doom is coming."

"When I cared for them in the desert they honored me. But when they got rich, they forgot me. So I intend to come down on them like a mother bear defending her cubs. I'll rip them open, and eat them like a lion. Israel, this time you've had it!"

...and on and on and on,

Chapter 14
Then he changes his tune and starts talking about redeeming them instead of disemboweling them, using botanical metaphors. "If they just beg nicely for forgiveness and promise to renounce their sinful ways, I will take them back. I'm not mad at them any more. Israel will blossom like a lily and put down roots like a Lebanon cedar. It will be as beautiful as an olive tree and will have the fragrance of cedar. It will grow and flourish and smell like Lebanese wine [or cedar, or something from Lebanon]."

"The ways of the Lord are right, and the just shall walk in them but the transgressors shall fall therein."
....

And that's it for Hosea.

Yahweh's back-and-forth mood shifts are something to think about.

The Bible, Chapter 70

The Book of Joel

Joel is the mystery book of the Old Testament. Nobody knows who Joel was, except that he was a son of Pethuel. However, nobody knows who Pethuel was, except that he was Joel's daddy. And nobody knows when he was; guesses and estimates differ by centuries. His book contains no narrative. It's all prophecy and preaching, that has to stand on its own, since it has no provenance. His writing is a series of long poems, which are repetitious. He appears to be addressing the people of Judah, even when he slips and says "israel". You can tell by his focus on Jerusalem.

Chapter 1
He starts out by commanding the elders to tell their children and descendants about a series of insect plagues that has occurred or is about to occur...the tense isn't clear. First a swarm of locusts covers the land and eats pretty much everything they can. Then a second swarm of a different kind of locusts follows them and eats what the first swarm had left. This is followed by a third and a fourth swarm, and when they get done there is nothing left.

Then he describes the devastation the locusts have left, followed by a killing drought that affected even the wild animals. Then he calls upon the priests to wear sackcloth and to mourn and to declare a holy fast and for everybody to weep and moan and beseech Yahweh for relief.

Chapter 2

Then he tells about the mighty hordes of locusts again and how they devour everything in their path and overrun cities and come in through the windows.

Then he tells everybody to return to the Lord and to blow trumpets and declare a holy fast and assemble everybody...old, young, little bitty babies, bridegrooms on their wedding night...and for them to weep and moan and beseech Yahweh for relief.

If they do that, Yahweh will take pity on his people and will get rid of the invading hordes and will call off the drought and allow the crops to flourish. He will repay them for the damage he inflicted on them, and everybody will praise and worship Yahweh who works wonders for them. They will know that he is back in Israel and there is no other god but Yahweh.
****

Then there will come a day of armageddon when Yahweh will call down fire and smoke from the heavens to kill everybody except those who worship him. Those will be okay.

Chapter 3

Then when he has restored the fortunes of Judah and Jerusalem, he will call a conclave of all the nations, and gather them in the Valley of Jeshoshaphat and chew them out for mistreating his people and scattering them among nations and for using boys as prostitutes and selling girls to get money for wine.

That's not all. Yahweh is mad at them for stealing his gold and silver treasures out of his temple and carting it off to use in their own.

So he proposes to turn the tables on them. First he will bring all his people back together in Judah, and he will sell the foreigners and their sons and daughters to the people of Judah, and to other far away lands, and see how they like it.

Then he tells the people of Judah to prepare for war, and to beat their plowshares into swords and their pruning hooks into spears [*Yes, you heard it right*], and to brag of their strength.

Then he says that he, Yahweh, will be right there in the Valley of Jehoshaphat to pass judgment on the miscreant nations gathered there. The sun and moon will go dark, the stars will cease to shine. He will roar from Zion and thunder from Jerusalem, but the people of Judah will be safe from his wrath.

Then he says that after that, he will dwell on the Hill of Zion, and foreigners will never again invade the land of Judah. There will be no more droughts, and the land will flourish....

But Egypt will be desolate, and Edom will become a desert, because of the way they treated the people of Judah.

Then he says, "Judah will endure forever, and Jerusalem down through the generations, and any guilt on their part that I haven't yet pardoned, I will pardon.
For Yahweh dwells in Zion.!"

And that was that.

....

But I have been concerned about this Valley of Jehoshaphat that will accommodate all nations and be the site of the final armageddon. It would need to be large enough to hold all nations or a good fraction of them

Modern Bible historians identify the "Valley of Jehoshaphat" with the valley of the Kidron or Cedron river. This is a steep, rugged declivity --what in the western US would be called a canyon or gulch rather than a valley, since it contains no flatland-- carved millenia ago by the Kedron river. It runs along the east side of Old Jerusalem, separating the Temple Mount from the Mount of Olives. In Biblical times it was a running river. Today it 's a fetid, sewage-laden waterway to the Dead Sea, similar to our Colorado River by the time it empties itself into the Gulf of California. The Kidron Valley is and was inhospitable. It would not have been a comfortable place for the nations to assemble, even if they would all fit. But it would have been an ideal place for Yahweh to show his wrath at the time of armageddon.

The Bible, Chapter 71

The Book of Amos
part 1

The book of Amos dates from the same period as the book of Hosea: the time when Jeroboam II ruled the Northern Kingdom of Israel, and Uzziah ruled the Southern Kingdom of Judah. His prophecies are similar in vein to those of Hosea. A little back story will help make sense of what is going on.

The reign of Jeroboam II was a time of unparalleled prosperity in the kingdom of Israel. Business and trade flourished, fortunes were made, lands were conquered, a substantial middle and upper class developed, and they enjoyed comfort as well as (by the wealthy) luxury. But as their creature comfort grew, their devotion to spiritual and religious matters diminished. They stopped giving Yahweh their full-time devotion. They ignored his commandments and oppressed the poor. They made sacrifices in non-holy places; they worshiped idols and foreign gods. Ethically and morally (from Yahweh's point of view) they fell into chaos and materialism and sin and degeneracy

The reign of Uzziah in Judah was likewise a time of great prosperity. But unlike their northern neighbor, they remained strongly Yahweh-ist and stuck with the god of Moses. The downfall of Uzziah came not from idolatry but from getting too big for his britches. The more Judah prospered, the more the king's power grew, and the more his power grew, the bigger his head got. One day he marched into the Temple and started burning incense to Yahweh. That was unheard-of effrontery, since the right to burn temple sacrifices to Yahweh had been reserved to the Aaronite priesthood centuries before. Uzziah's arrogance didn't sit well with the priests, and apparently not with Yahweh either, since the king was immediately stricken with leprosy of the face. He was forced to live in seclusion for the rest of his life, while his son took over as regent and ran things in his place.

This is the milieu in and of which Amos finds himself writing, probably before the face-leprosy episode.

Chapter 1
In his first chapter, he takes on neither of the two kingdoms, but rather their surrounding nations, in a repetitive pattern. Quoting Yahweh:

"**Damascus is a nation of habitual sinners, but I won't let them get away with it.** They savagely attacked Gilead. For that, I'll burn down their fortresses, kill their king,and send their people into exile."

"**Gaza [Philistine country] is a nation of habitual sinners, but I won't let them get away with it.** They overran whole communities, and sold their captives to Edom [south of Judah] as slaves. For that, I'll burn down their fortresses, kill their king, and keep bashing them until the last Philistine is dead."

"**Tyre is a nation of habitual sinners, but I won't let them get away with it.** They have sold whole communities to Edom, so for that I'll destroy their walls and burn down their fortresses."

No mention of killing their king or other stuff. He probably wasn't as mad at them as he was at the others.

"**Edom is a nation of habitual sinners, but I won't let them get away with it.** They hunted down their brothers the Israelites without mercy and with anger that had no limits. For that, I will blast them with fire and burn down their fortresses."

"**Ammon is a nation of habitual sinners, but I won't let them get away with it.** While extending their territory, they ripped open the pregnant women of Gilead. For that, I'll do to them what I am going to do to Tyre. There also will be shouts on the day of battle, and the fighting will rage like a storm. The king and his officers will be forced into exile."

Gilead was the Israelite territory east of the Jordan River. It lay between Israel and Ammon. and contained what is now the West Bank. They had a history of antagonism toward each other. Ripping open pregnant women is pretty gruesome stuff, you must admit.

Chapter 2

"**Moab is a nation of habitual sinners, but I won't let them get away with it**. They dug up the bones of the king of Edom and burned them to ashes as a symbol of contempt. For that, they will get fire and burned-down fortresses. I'll send them war, and kill their king and his officials."

This is the only mention in the Bible of the bone-burning episode. You'd think that if it was such a big deal to Yahweh, they would have told us a little more about it.

"**Judah is a nation of habitual sinners, but I won't let them get away with it.** They have rejected the law of the Lord, and haven't kept his decrees. They have been led astray by false gods, so I shall smite them with fire that will consume their fortresses."

I hate to say this about a prophet, even a minor one, but Amos is guilty of a frame-up. Judah did no such thing. By every account, Judah under King Uzziah (and his regent son Jotham, after the leprosy incident) stayed tight with Yahweh. There was never any rejection of Yahweh's laws, no idolatry, and only one transgression by one person: Uzziah. He violated the rules about burning incense in the temple, and was busted for it. Amos' accusation is made up out of whole cloth, and I hope Yahweh recognized it for what it was.

"**Israel is a nation of habitual sinners, but I won't let them get away with it.** [*Here, Amos is on solid ground.*] They have perverted justice by accepting bribes, sold into slavery honorable

358

men unable to repay a debt, They trade them for a pair of sandals. A man and his father both Go In Unto the same temple girl, defiling my holy name. At their religious feasts they lounge around in clothing left by poor people as security for a debt, and drink the wine taken as payment for fines."

"I led you out of Egypt, gave you the land of the Amorites, raised up prophets and Nazirites among you, did I not? But you force the Nazirites [*remember Samson*] to drink wine and prevent the prophets from prophesying. For all of this, I will crush you like an overloaded grain cart. You can't run fast enough to escape me, you can't grow strong enough to prevent me. None of you — archers, warriors, horsemen— will escape my wrath."

Chapter 3
Then Amos carries on some more in the same vein. And then some more threats.

"An enemy will overrun your land and you will be left with nothing. When I punish Israel for her sins, I will destroy the false altar at Bethel, knock off its horns and let them fall on the ground. I will tear down the fancy homes of the wealthy."

Chapter 4
"Listen to me, you fat cows of Bashan, you women who grind the faces of the poor, and say to your menfolk "Hey, bring us some drinks." Before long, you will be dragged away with hooks like fishhooks through your noses and tossed out through the nearest hole in the wall."

And on and on and on...

Chapter 5
More of the same.

Chapter 6
"Those who lounge in comfort and luxury in Zion and Samaria think nothing will happen to them. They are mistaken. They lie on couches of ivory and dine on tender lamb and veal, and play

with their harps as if they were David, and drink wine by the bucketful, caring nothing at all that their brothers need their help. They will be the first to be torn from their luxury and sent into exile when the time comes."

Yahweh detests Israel's pride and will punish them for it. Yada yada yada.

Then, after all this preaching, we get some narrative about Amos.

The Bible, Chapter 72

The Book of Amos
part 2

Chapter 7
Yahweh got together with Amos, and showed him some stuff. First he showed him a swarm of locusts he was preparing to send out just before the second harvest. When Amos saw what the locusts had done, (or would do), he protested: "Lord, you can't do that to poor Jacob, because he is so small." By Jacob, of course he meant Israel, which was Jacob's other name. So Yahweh relented and said, "Okay, I won't do that."

Then Yahweh showed him a wildfire which dried up the streams and devoured everything in its path. Jacob made the same protest. So Yahweh relented again, and said, "Okay I won't do that."

Then Yahweh showed him a wall that had been constructed with the help of a plumb line. Yahweh asked him What do you see? and Amos answered, "A plumb line". Then Yahweh said,"I'm using it to illustrate how my people are out of line, like a wall that's crooked. And this time I'm not going to relent. The places where idols are worshiped will be destroyed along with every other place of worship. I'm going to see to it that the reign of king Jeroboam comes to a violent end."

Chapter 7 continued
Amaziah was the priest of Bethel, which you may recall was one of the alternative centers of worship that Jeroboam I had set up after the northern tribes of Israel were denied access to the temple in Jerusalem down in Judah. Amaziah sent a message to the current Jeroboam (Jeroboam II), saying "Amos is preaching sedition against you in the very heart of Israel. He has to be

stopped, because what he's saying is: You, Jeroboam will die by the sword, and the tribes of Israel will be dragged into exile in foreign lands."

Then the priest ordered Amos to get out of Bethel and out of Israel and go back to Judah where he belonged. "Bethel is the king's sanctuary and temple, and you can't prophecy here any more."

Amos told him, "Look. I didn't start out as a prophet. I don't come from a family of prophets. I was a shepherd and a fig-tree farmer...until Yahweh came to me and commanded me to go preach to his people in Israel."

"You tell me to stop preaching against Israel and against the worship of idols. But here's what I say to you in the name of the Lord:
Your wife will become a whorelady and will ply her trade in the streets of the city. Your sons and daughters will be killed in war. Your land will be taken away from you and divided up. You will die in some pagan country. And the tribes of Israel WILL be driven into exile in a foreign land. So there."

Chapter 8

Then Yahweh got together with Amos again, and showed him a basket of ripe fruit. What do you see, Amos? "A basket of ripe fruit, of course." *(Remember Jeremiah and the basket of figs. This seems to be the living, walking, Yahweh of Abraham, Moses, and Jeremiah, not the transcendental Yahweh of Solomon, et al.)*

Yahweh: "Just as the fruit is ripe, the time is ripe for me to smite Israel. I'm not going to wait any longer. Then the songs will turn to wailing, dead bodies will be strewn everywhere."

"Pay attention, Israel! You trample the needy and abuse the poor. You get impatient for the Sabbath to be over so you can go back to selling wheat...raising the price, giving short measure, and adulterating it with floor sweepings. You buy a poor person for money or for a pair of sandals! I will not forget what you've done."

Then there's a long description of the usual sort, about the desolation and misery to be inflicted on Israel.

Chapter 9

Then Yahweh stands by the altar and repeats his threats to Amos. All will suffer, none will escape, there will be no hiding, the kingdom will be wiped from the face of the earth, yada yada yada.

Then after he's done threatening, he starts talking about the restoration of Israel. He will undo all the damage he has wrought, and will make it as it was before. The exiled people will return, the land will be fruitful, there will be peace and prosperity and all will be nice forever. And Yahweh won't ever send them into exile again.

So says Yahweh.
………………..

But that altar he's standing beside has me wondering. It has to be the one in Bethel, since that's where all this is taking place. But Yahweh doesn't recognize the legitimacy of the altars that Jeroboam I set up in Israel at Dan and Bethel, after the kingdoms split. Those are where he had set up Golden Calves as symbols of the Lord, and commanded his people to worship there and nowhere else.

For Yahweh-ists, the only legitimate altar for sacrifice to Yahweh is the one in the Jerusalem temple, down in Judah. The one in Bethel is a false altar, set up in opposition to Yahweh's laws, flanked with golden images that serve as idols.

So what in the world is Yahweh doing standing next to it? That should be the last place he'd want to be, accompanied by golden calves while giving divine directives to a prophet.

The ways of Yahweh are mysterious.

The Bible, Chapter 73

The Book of Obadiah

Obadiah is the shortest book in the Bible, consisting of one chapter of one verse. Its date is uncertain, but sometime after the Babylonian destruction of Jerusalem and the conquest of Judah. Here is the back story of the tale.
****

ALL ABOUT EDOM
Edom was a largish nation roughly south of Judah, extending all the way to the Red Sea. It was rocky and mountainous, largely desert, with very little arable flatland.

Its people were mountain dwellers, who carved temples and dwellings in its cliffs. Its importance was as a major trade route through the Negev desert to Israel and surrounding nations.

When Moses was leading his people to Canaan, Edom refused them passage, which put them on the on the bad side of the Children of Israel.

Edom's independence came to an end when King David decided to take over its important trade route. He invaded, conquered, slew several thousand, deposed their ruler, turned Edom into a province of his kingdom and appointed a governor to run it. (You can read all about it elsewhere in the Old Testament.) This humiliated and pissed off the Edomites, and they never got over it

The situation remained more or less the same until the fall of Jerusalem under Nebuchadnezzar some centuries later, which provided them with an opportunity to get even. And they took it, eagerly joining the Babylonian forces in the sacking of Jerusalem and Judah.

To the exiled Jews, the Edomites were seen as Quislings who had supported the invading forces against a local kingdom, and were never forgiven. This "treachery" is what Obadiah is fulminating against, some indefinite time after it happened.

Edom is traditionally the nation founded by Esau, who was cheated out of his birthright by his brother Jacob, later renamed "Israel". The names Edom/Esau and Jacob/Israel are used interchangeably in these preachings

****

Chapter Only
Yahweh speaks:

"All nations will come together and make war on Edom."

"You Edomites are a bunch of hillbillies who live in caves and on mountains, and regard yourselves as special for living in the heights. But I'll make you despised and ridiculed by the world. No matter how high among the eagles you make your homes, you will be brought down."

"A robber doesn't take everything he could. A man stealing grapes leaves a few. But when I'm done with you, you'll have nothing. Your allies will turn on you, your friends will deceive and abandon you. Those who eat at your table will plot your downfall, but you won't be aware of it."

"Don't think your Wise Men of understanding will avoid destruction. Your bravest warriors will be too terrified to fight. Everyone in Esau's mountains will be cut down in the slaughter."

"You have attacked your brother Jacob, and for that you will wallow in shame forever. When you watched while invaders carried off his wealth, it was the same as being one of them. You should have stood by your brother in his misfortune, not celebrated it! You should not have joined the enemy in seizing his goods! You should not have ambushed his people and turned them over to the enemy."

"Edom, what you have done to Israel will in turn be done to you. You will drink from the cup of punishment until you are bloated."

"But Mount Zion [in Jerusalem] will remain holy, and the house of Jacob will regain what it has lost. The house of Jacob will be like a fire, and the house of Esau will be like a stubble field consumed and destroyed by that fire. None will survive the conflagration."

"Your lands will be turned over to other tribes. The exiles from the Northern Kingdom will return from Assyria and reclaim their nation. Mount Zion will once again govern Esau."

"And the kingdom will be the Lord."

The Bible, Chapter 74

The Book of Jonah
part 1

The book of Jonah is a narrative, without any preaching. Rather than a prophecy, I would categorize it as a fable, except its moral, if any, is obscure. It is undated, and doesn't seem to fall in any particular place in the time stream of the Old Testament that we have been working with. It contains one of the most famous of all Bible tales.

Chapter 1
Jonah is a prophet living somewhere in the northern kingdom of Israel. One day Yahweh comes to Jonah and directs him to go up to Nineveh to preach to its people and get them to give up their evil ways.

Nineveh was the capital of the Assyrian empire, located way to helandgone up by the Tigris river, hundreds of miles from Israel and not remotely within Israelite territory. It was a difficult trek that would take months. The people there worshiped Ishtar, or Astarte, and had no truck with Yahweh. May not even have heard of him. They would probably not have taken well to some foreigner coming in and talking trash about their god.

This may have been in Jonah's mind as he thought over Yahweh's directive. Finally he said, "I don't think so," and took off to flee the country in the opposite direction. He went to the sea port at Joppa, and bought a ticket on a ship bound for Tarshish, all the way at the western end of the Mediterranean, somewhere around Spain, about as far from Nineveh as he could imagine. It was not an Israelite ship, and its crew were not

Yahweh-ists.

A few days out, Yahweh sent a violent storm that threatened to tear the ship apart. The crew panicked, and called on their various gods to help them out, and started jettisoning cargo to lighten the load. It didn't do much good.

Jonah was zonked out below decks when the captain went to him and said, "Wake up!. And see if you can get this god of yours to do something for us. Our gods aren't doing us much good!"

Meanwhile, the sailors had decided among themselves that some miscreant on board had to have something to do with it. They chose the obvious way to find out who it was, by drawing straws. Jonah got the short straw.

They said, "We need to know who's behind this. Who are you? What do you do? Where do you come from?" He told them he was a Hebrew, and that he worshiped Yahweh, the god that created everything. They hollered, "Why have you done this to us?" because he had told them earlier that he was fleeing from a directive by his god.

As the storm became more violent, they said "What should we do? What *can* we do to get this Yahweh of yours to make the storm go away?" Jonah was conscience-smitten, and said,"It's all my fault, and I'm sorry for doing this to you. Just chuck me overboard and let me drown. That should get Yahweh to relent and call off the storm."

They knew it would be wrong to kill an innocent man, showing they had good moral sense whatever their gods. So they decided to try to row back toward land. But the seas just grew heavier, so in desperation they prayed to Jonah's god, "Dear Yahweh, please don't kill us for taking the life of this innocent man; but it's the only thing we have left to do in the face of this storm you sent us."

Finally, they took Jonah and chucked him overboard. At once the storm went away and the seas grew calm. But they were still worried about what Yahweh might do to them, so they offered a sacrifice and vows to him.

Meanwhile, out in the water, Jonah didn't drown after all. Instead, Yahweh sent a huge fish that swallowed him whole. And he lived inside the fish three days.

At this point, the skeptics start hooting and hollering and saying "That's impossible. No fish is big enough to swallow a man whole. And if a man did get swallowed, he wouldn't last for 3 days. He'd suffocate in a few minutes."

Which shows that these people aren't paying attention. They are straining at this gnat while having swallowed a camel. We have Yahweh, who created everything and who can conjure up storms at a moment's notice, and send fire from the skies, and make dead bones get up and walk. Do they suppose he'd be unable to

come up with a big enough fish, or unable to keep a man alive inside a fish for as long as he wants? Get a grip, folks. This is Yahweh.

In the retelling, Jonah's fish has gotten called a whale. But a whale isn't a fish, and it's probably harder to protect a man from the digestive juices of a mammal. So it was a fish.

My candidate is the whale shark. These beasts are huge, up to 40 feet long with a mouth the size of a Volkswagen A man could probably fit in there sideways.

A minor problem is that the whale shark is a plankton eater, and it's gullet isn't big enough for a man to get through. Also, whale sharks prefer warm oceans and aren't known to frequent the Mediterranean. But since Yahweh can take care of the rest of it, this part would be no problem. Heck, it might not even be a whale shark. It might be a special fish, invented for just this occasion. We're talking Yahweh.

While he's in the fish, Jonah starts meditating on his situation…

The Bible, Chapter 75

The Book of Jonah,
part 2

Chapter 2
From inside the fish, Jonah issues a prayer:
"O Lord, when I was in trouble, I called you and you heard me. I called from the doorstep of death and you heard me… and you answered by casting me into the depths down to the very bottom of the sea!"

"That made me think I was abandoned and could never be in your favor again. The water choked me, the seaweed wrapped around my head, and I thought: This is it!"

"But then you came through at the last minute. As my life slipped away you heard me, from your place in the Holy Temple! You kept me alive!"

"People who worship idols have lost faith in you. But not me! I will praise you and offer sacrifices to you from now on! You were the source of my salvation."

At which point, the fish barfed Jonah up onto dry land.

And presumably Jonah went back home, and carried on his business as if nothing had ever happened, as if three days inside a fish was no big deal. A normal man would have been running around and telling everybody, "Hey! I was swallowed by a fish and lived to tell about it! I was inside him for three damn days, and I hate to tell you what it smelled like! I'll bet nobody else has ever done that!"

But there's no indication he did any of that. Nobody asked "Where've you been? Whatcha been doing?" As if he had never been gone. We are never told about Jonah's post-fish adventures. Which is a shame.

And I have some problems with that inside-the-fish prayer, similar to problems I've had before. It was Yahweh who got him thrown into the water. Jonah admits that. Yahweh didn't send the fish in his beneficence, to rescue Jonah from a misfortune. The fish rescued Jonah from a fate that Yahweh had deliberately caused. Jonah's response is: Thank you for not killing me. For that, you deserve my unending worship.

We've seen this attitude before. I still don't get it.

Chapter 3

Figuring Jonah had learned his lesson, Yahweh once again told him, "Go to Nineveh, and preach to them my message that their wicked practices will lead to their certain destruction." This time Jonah obeyed, and headed off to Nineveh.

Nineveh was a big city; it took three days just to see everything that was there. When Jonah got there, he started preaching: "In 40 more days, Yahweh will overturn Nineveh and destroy it!" To his amazement, they believed him! They declared a fast, and everybody from the King on down dressed themselves in sackcloth. (Sackcloth was a rough fabric something like burlap, quite uncomfortable when worn next to the skin.)

After the king put on his sackcloth, he prostrated himself and wallowed in the dust, and issued a proclamation to his people. He told them nobody was to eat or drink anything. No animals were to eat or drink anything. Everybody was to wear sackcloth. Even the animals were to wear sackcloth. Everybody was to give up their evil ways and everybody was to pray to Yahweh.

Maybe that would get him to relent, and not destroy Nineveh.

And it worked! Yahweh saw that the people of the great city of Nineveh, capital of the Assyrian empire, had abandoned their evil ways and converted to Yahwehism. So he relented, and didn't destroy them as he had threatened.

Chapter 4
Which really pissed Jonah off. It made him look like a fool, after all the doom he had predicted, then have it not happen. He told Yahweh, "See! I knew it would go like this. That's why I headed for Tarshish the first time! I knew that after all the threats and preaching, you'd chicken out! You wouldn't crush them the way you said you would. After I'd done your bidding, and prophesied disaster, I knew you'd leave me hung out to dry this way! I knew it! Please kill me now. I'd be better off dead."

Yahweh told him, "What right to you have to be angry about this?"

Jonah didn't answer. He stomped off out of the city, and sat down to see what would happen next. Yahweh sent a magic vine that grew quickly beside Jonah, so that its leaves shaded him from the hot sun and made him comfortable. Jonah liked that a lot.

Next day, Yahweh sent a worm of some sort to chew off the vine, which quickly withered and died, taking away Jonah's shade. Yahweh sent a hot wind along with the blazing sun, to help Jonah's discomfort along. Jonah pissed and moaned and whined and complained and said "It would be better for me to die than to live."

Yahweh asked, "Do you have a right to be angry about the death of the vine?"

"Damn right I do," said Jonah. "I'm angry enough to die."

Then Yahweh said, "You numbskull. You're in a lather about

that stupid vine dying! You didn't make it grow, you had nothing to do with it. It wasn't anything you deserved; it just grew one day and died the next."

"But there are a hundred and twenty thousand of people in Nineveh, ordinary souls who don't know their right hand from their left, not to mention all the cattle. Those were the ones I had threatened to destroy, and relented. Why shouldn't I have been concerned about them?"

On the whole, I do not find Jonah an admirable person.

The Bible, Chapter 80

The Book of Micah

Micah was a native of Judea (Judah), contemporary with the prophet Isaiah, roughly 737-686 BC. Hezekiah was king of Judah most of that time. During much of King Hezekiah's reign, Judah was under the thumb of the Assyrians, and paid tribute to them. Micah was around to witness the destruction and dissolution of the (northern) Kingdom of Israel by the Assyrians in 722 BC, and was worried that Judea might suffer the same fate. Samaria had been the capital of the Kingdom of Israel, as Jerusalem was capital of the Kingdom of Judah.

Chapter 1
During the period when Jotham, Ahaz, and Hezekiah were kings of Judah, Yahweh spoke through Micah, giving his vision of Samaria and Jerusalem.

"Listen up, Nations! Yahweh is about to speak to you. He is coming down from his holy place to walk the earth. He will walk the mountaintops and they will erupt in fire and melt like wax! They will run down the valleys like a flowing stream."

"This is because of the sins of Israel. Only Samaria is responsible for Israel's rebellion against Yahweh; only Jerusalem is responsible for Judah's."

"Samaria will be reduced to an open field strewn with rubble, fit only for planting grapes. The rubble will roll down into the valley. Its idols will get smashed, its temple gifts reduced to ashes, its images crushed to pieces. Those things were part of their lewd fertility rites; now their enemies will take them for use elsewhere."

Micah speaks of this in the future tense, but I have a hunch he is describing much of what he has already seen happen to Israel. Outlining his fears of what may be in store for Judah.

"Because of Israel, I, Micah, will weep and wail in mourning. I shall go about barefoot, naked, howling like a jackal and hooting like an owl. Israel's wound is incurable, and now Judah is on the same path...destruction is at the gates of Jerusalem in my homeland."

Then Micah lists the outlying towns in the path of advancing invaders, telling what will happen when the time comes. He tells them they will live in anxiety as they await their fate. "Shave your heads in mourning for your beloved children. Make yourselves as bald as a buzzard, as they are taken from you in exile."

Chapter 2
And then there's a lot more in the same vein, about the dreadful fate awaiting Israel.

Followed by one of the usual assurances that, in the end, all will be well. The Israelite survivors will come together once again, like a flock led by a shepherd, with Yahweh at their head.

Chapter 3
Micah rebukes the wicked leaders and prophets of Israel, at considerable length. He accuses them of corrupting Judah. "They despise all that is right, they build Jerusalem on a foundation of bloodshed and wickedness. Their judges take bribes, their priests charge a fee for teaching, her prophets tell fortunes for money. Yet they say, 'Yahweh is on our side. Nothing will happen to us'."

Chapter 4

Micah prophesies:
"In the last days, the Temple Mount in Jerusalem will be recognized as the highest of all. People will flock to it. Nations will come to climb to the Temple, to learn the ways of Yahweh. His law will go out from Jerusalem, he will judge peoples and settle disputes among nations. They will beat their swords into plowshares and their spears into pruning hooks. [*You my recall that Joel prophesied just the opposite.*] Nations will no longer make war. Every man will live in peace among his own vineyards and orchards. Each nation may worship its own god, but we will worship Yahweh forever."

Yahweh speaks:
"The time will come when I will bring back together all those I have punished or sent into exile. They are crippled and far from home, but I will bring them back. I will turn them into a strong nation, and I will rule over them on Mount Zion from that day onward."

"Jerusalem, which is my watchtower, will once again govern Judah..."

And then some strange stuff that I do not understand, as if he's saying "That will happen...but not yet."

"What are you whining about, moaning in pain like a woman in labor? Is it because you have no king? Keep on moaning, because you will be forced out of the city to live in open fields, and you will be taken away to Babylon...But eventually I will rescue you from your captors."

"Nations will assault you, saying 'Now is the time for Jerusalem to fall.' But they have no idea what I Yahweh have in mind. They don't realize that I have gathered them in a bunch, to be treated like wheat on the threshing floor."

"I will turn you, Zion, into a mighty nation of power, with iron horns and hooves of bronze, to trample and conquer many nations."

Notice how the mood changes between the peaceful beginning of this chapter, and the militant end.

Chapter 5
Micah preaches:
"Gather your forces, people of Jerusalem, for your leader is under attack!"

Then he predicts that a new leader of Judah, one of ancient ancestry, will be produced by Bethlehem, one of its smallest hamlets. But Yahweh will abandon the people until that leader shows up. That's when the coming-back-together stuff will take place. He will rule with strength that comes from the Lord, and peace will prevail. *Later New Testament writers will make much of this.*

"When the Assyrians invade the land", he says, "we will marshal our strongest fighters. We will recruit help from the surviving remnant of Israel. We will get allies from the land of Nimrod. They will kick the enemy's butt, and save us from the invaders."

But at that point, Yahweh will step in and snatch away their victory. He will kill their horses and destroy their chariots. He will raze their cities and tear down their fortifications. He will eradicate their witchcraft and magic and destroy their idols and images. He will vent his anger and wrath on those who have disobeyed him.
....

Here I need to pause for a moment. I no longer know whether Micah is talking about Israel or Judah. Some years before the fall of Israel (722 BC), Judah was ruled by king Ahaz. During his reign, paganism and idolatry abounded. This was on Micah's watch, so he was familiar with it. But Ahaz was soon (728 BC) replaced by Hezekiah, who was a reformer. He abolished the paganism and idolatry, and put the country back on the good side of Yahweh. This was the situation in Judah at the time Israel fell to the Assyrians.

At that time there were no idols or witchcraft or any of that sort of thing in Judah. Hezekiah had done away with it. So when Micah talks about idols and images, either he's talking about Israel, where that stuff used to go on...but in the future tense to make it look more prophetic... or he's talking about Judah under Ahaz, pre-Hezekiah. But that would mean that this was written when he was not yet in his teens. Or it was written later, during Hezekiah's time, but looking back to a state of affairs that no longer existed and worrying about that.

Is he talking about his homeland Judah, that he's worried about, or Israel, whose fate his worry is based on?

I don't know, so I'll let it pass. Micah rambles on and on, first speaking as himself, then without transition speaking as Yahweh's mouthpiece—"I will do such-and-such", or as the voice of Israel—"We have done such-and-such", then as the narrator —"They have done such-and-such",then as himself again, preaching away. Hard to get a grasp on what he's referring to.

....

Chapter 6
Micah/Yahweh is hollering about Israel again. The Lord brought you out of Egypt, and did all this stuff for you, and what does he expect back from you? Not elaborate sacrifices and burnt offerings... only that you live justly and mercifully, and follow the Lord.

Then there's a litany of Israel's offenses, which are familiar and I won't go into them.

Chapter 7
More of the same. On and on. Yahweh will punish the people.

....

Israel speaks through Micah: She is optimistic that things will work out alright in the end. There will be no reason for her enemies to gloat over her downfall. Yahweh will restore her; then her enemies will see that, and be mortified.

"As in the days when Yahweh delivered you from Egypt, he will show his power. Other nations will see, and be embarrassed, and become weak. They will cover their mouths and plug their ears. They will crawl in the dust like snakes, and will come slithering out of their dens. They will fear Yahweh, and be terrified of you."

"There is no god like Yahweh, who pardons and shows forgiveness. His anger passes, and he is pleased to show mercy. You, Lord, will again have compassion on us. You will throw out and discard all the bad things we've done. You will show faith and love to your people, the descendants of Abraham and Jacob, as you promised our ancestors long ago."

And the book ends.

The Bible, Chapter 81

The Book of Nahum

The book of Nahum is a long poem celebrating the destruction of the Assyrian capital of Nineveh in 612 BC. Not much is known about Nahum himself, and the date of the writing is uncertain. Assyria had been a thorn in the side of Judah for a long time, squeezing them for tribute and generally being unpleasant. Pretty clearly, when Jonah converted them to Yahwehism under threat of disaster, after the fish episode, it didn't last.

In the 600's BC, the Assyrian Empire was the most powerful in the region, and had a lot of enemies. Eventually, the Babylonians got together with the Medes and attacked the Assyrian capital, razing it to the ground and putting an end to the empire. In Judah, this was a cause for celebration. Some see the book as a prophecy, written a hundred or more years before the event.

Others, I think more plausibly, see it as a history written around the time of the destruction of Niniveh.

The first chapter concentrates on telling us what Yahweh is like.

Chapter 1
Yahweh is a jealous, vengeful god, that crushes all who oppose him. He's not short-tempered, but when he gets angry, watch out. He can control the weather, creating storms, drying up lakes and rivers, and making life unbearable. He causes earthquakes that shake down the mountains. His anger is fierce, and when he's mad, he pours out his wrath like fire.

Yahweh's usually a good god. He cares for his people, and gives them refuge in time of trouble. *[I find this a bit of a stretch, but never mind.]*

But NINEVEH! is another matter. Them, he will destroy and leave without trace. No matter what they do, they can't avoid it. He will bust their chops hard, and they won't ever have another chance to cause trouble.

NINEVEH spawns enemies of Yahweh, who commit and teach evil stuff. They are big and powerful and have allies, but that won't matter. He will whack them as hard as he can..

In the past Yahweh has laid a share of grief on Judah, but now that comes to a stop. Now he's going to go after the ones oppressing them, and give them what they have coming. Nineveh will have no progeny to carry their line. When Yahweh gets done with them, all their idols will be smashed, and they will be ready for the grave, because they are vile!

"Judah, it's celebration time! Peace is at hand. You'll have no more evil invaders. Yahweh will have fixed them for good."

The next chapter gets down to the gritty details of what's in store for Nineveh. You can almost see Nahum licking his chops as he recites them.

Chapter 2
Yahweh is going to restore the splendor of Jacob's Israel, that was taken away by these wicked people. [*Remember, a century or two back, Assyria had decimated and destroyed the Kingdom of Israel, and hauled its people off to exile.*]

"Bolster up your defenses, Nineveh; an attacking force is headed your way."

Then we get a graphic description of the approaching attackers: their uniforms, their weapons, their chariots that thunder through the city streets. Nineveh's troops rush to the fortifications, but it doesn't do them any good. Yahweh has decided that the city will crumble, its slave girls beating their breasts in terror. Nineveh's resources are draining away.

The attackers overrun the city, plundering it of its wealth. Yahweh has it in for the city, and they are doomed.

Chapter 3
I can't do justice to the poetry here except by quoting it:

"Woe to the city of blood, full of lies, full of plunder, never without victims!
The crack of whips, the clatter of wheels, galloping horses and jolting chariots!
Charging cavalry, flashing swords, and glittering spears!
Many casualties, piles of dead, bodies without number, people stumbling over the corpses —
All because of the wanton lust of a harlot, alluring, the mistress of sorceries,
Who enslaved nations by her prostitution and peoples by her witchcraft."

Yahweh is going to humiliate them and pelt them with dung and whatever. Thebes was overrun and destroyed, little bitty babies had their brains dashed out. Nineveh can expect no better.

And so on and so on and so on.

"Everybody who hears about your fall claps their hands in glee and celebrates. They've all felt your endless cruelty. So there."

And that was that.

The Bible, Chapter 82

The Book of Habakkuk

The Book of Habakkuk was written around the time when the Babylonian Empire was becoming ascendant, and invading countries and killing everybody and taking their stuff, but before they got around to Jerusalem. Nothing is known about him except that he wrote this book. However, there is a tradition (don't ask me from where) that Habakkuk was the son of the woman that Elisha "miraculously" got pregnant (see Ch. 31 of this series) a couple of centuries before Babylon arose as a major power. That seems unlikely.

The book begins with a conversation between Habakkuk and Yahweh.

Chapter 1
Habakkuk: Lord, how long must I call for help before I get your attention? How can you just stand and ignore the terrible things that are going on? Destruction and violence and fighting and quarreling seems to be everywhere. The laws don't protect us, and there's no justice anywhere. Evil men prevail over good men. When are you going to do something about it?

Yahweh: Pay attention to what's going on and you'll be amazed at what I'm going to do. I'm bringing the Chaldeans [Babylonians] to power —yes, those ruthless and cruel people— who are marching across the earth and taking over other peoples' territories. They are a law unto themselves. Their warriors are the mightiest in the world. Their armies advance like a storm. They are contemptuous of kings and any other high officials. They overrun a territory and move on. The only thing they worship is their own power.

This clearly is not what Habakkuk was hoping to hear.

Habakkuk: Okay Lord, you are the god I worship, and you are supposed to be my protector. Yet you have ordained these horrid people to conquer and punish us! Your eyes are "too holy to look at evil", so how can you stand to have anything to do with them? How can you not do anything while they are busy destroying righteous people? How can you treat your people like a school of fish or a swarm of insects, a grouping with no worth, no direction and no leader?

The Chaldeans are like fishermen, snagging people with hooks, scooping them up in their nets, and bragging about their catch! They worship their hooks and their nets, because those are the things that allow them to live in luxury.

Is that what you intend? For them to keep emptying and filling their nets, destroying nations without mercy?

Chapter 2
I await your reply.

Yahweh: Write this down clearly, so that it may easily be read by anyone. You need to write it down to preserve it, because it isn't going to happen yet. But it will happen in time. It may seem slow to you, but just be patient. It will definitely happen in due time.

Note this: **Wicked men trust only themselves and they will perish; but righteous men trust in me and live.**

I say to the Chaldeans, you are drunkards, sotted with wine. You are always greedy for conquest, but like death you are never satisfied.

But the time will come when your captives will taunt you, saying "Justice has caught up with you at last. Now you will get what's coming to you!" Your debtors will turn on you and take all your stuff, while you stand unable to stop them. The survivors of the nations you have plundered will now plunder you!

Woe awaits you who get rich by cheating and dishonesty!
Woe awaits you who build cities with money gotten through murder and bloodshed and robbery!
Woe awaits you who get your neighbors drunk, so you can peek at their nakedness and shame them! Soon your arrogance will be replaced by shame.
You terrified those caught in your nets. Now terror will strike you because of your murdering and cruelty everywhere.

The time will come when the whole world is aware of my glory, as the waters fill the sea.

What good is an idol? It's just something someone has made out of wood. It tells you nothing, and those who say it does lie. What good does it do for him who made it to trust it and worship it? Can you say to the stick of wood, "Come to life!" and have it happen? Can you say to a lifeless carving of stone, "Wake up!" and have it happen? These idols may be covered with silver and gold, but there is no life in them. They are just fancy sticks and stones.

But I am in my holy temple. Let the world be silent in my presence.

This is all very well and good, but it does nothing to answer Habakkuk's piercing questions. Eventually Yahweh will bring disaster on the Chaldeans, and give them their comeuppance for all the bad stuff they have done. Eventually.

But Habakkuk was asking: Why are you empowering and encouraging these evil people in the first place? It's no good to say, "Never mind. I'm eventually going to smite them for all the evil things I empowered them and encouraged them to do."
These people Yahweh has empowered have inflicted (or will

inflict) incalculable misery on Yahweh's own people. That's not excused or compensated for by punishing the inflicters afterwards. I find this whole response of Yahweh's unsatisfying.

Chapter 3

This chapter is just silly. Habakkuk, in despair, has asked Yahweh for help, or at least for an explanation of why he's not providing any help. He hasn't received an explanation, and he hasn't received any promise of help. What he's gotten is assurance that the misery to be inflicted on him will eventually be avenged: the evildoers will be punished. THAT'S NOT HELP! It relieves no misery, dispels no fears, does nothing to answer Habakkuk's concern. If I'm being tortured, it's no relief to be told "Don't worry. The guy applying hot irons to your body will eventually go to jail." Relief is when the guy is stopped from applying the irons, not when he's punished for having done it.

This is where we're at at the end of Chapter 2. And what is Habakkuk's response in Chapter 3? It's to change the subject, and deliver a long-winded hymn of praise for Yahweh, and what a wonderful god he is. No mention of Chaldeans or any of that stuff. No mention of the misery the Children of Israel have suffered or are suffering.

He ends by saying,

"The Lord gives me strength. He makes me as sure-footed as a deer, and keeps me safe in the mountains."

All I can say is: Go figure.

The Bible, Chapter 83

The Book of Zephaniah

According to his introduction, Zephaniah wrote this book during the reign of King Josiah of Judah. A bit of history: Josiah was the son of King Amon, an idolatrous wretch who was assassinated by his household. When Josiah took the throne, he immediately started a program of reform, getting rid of the idols and their worshipers and getting back to Yahweh. This was accelerated when, in the course of revamping the Temple, they discovered a copy of Deuteronomy which contained all the dreary details of Yahweh's laws. With the laws in hand, they no longer had to rely on guesswork and memory to know what was needed, and the reform proceeded apace. So throughout Josiah's reign, Judah was (or should have been) in Yahweh's good graces. Zephaniah didn't think so.

Chapter 1
Yahweh announces his intention clean house and sweep away everything from the face of the earth: humans, animals, birds, fish. None will survive. *[Here, Yahweh is in a snit and pitching a hissy-fit, offering to destroy everything on earth because of what's going on in the little kingdom of Judah. As we move along, he seems sometimes to get over that and become more selective.]*

"I will punish the people of Judah and Jerusalem. I will eradicate the last traces of Baal-worship and Molech-worship. I will destroy those who worship the moon and stars. I will destroy those who claim to worship me, but swear oaths to other gods, and those who have turned away and no longer follow me."

This is hard to fathom, given the facts mentioned above. While Josiah is king, none of that stuff is going on any more. He has gotten rid of it without the need for Zephaniah's threats, or Yahweh's, or anybody else's. Zeph is addressing a non-existent problem.

Then there's a long rap describing the slaughter that will take place on Yahweh's day of judgment, which is just around the corner, and re-inventorying who the victims will be, and what he's going to do to them, and so on. "Their blood will be poured out like water, and their entrails like filth." Nothing can save them from the Lord's wrath. In his anger at them, he will cleanse the earth of every person and every thing.

Just one comment. Since Yahweh is going to destroy everybody, there was really no need for him to enumerate specific ones as targets of punishment. They will be included in the "everybody". Maybe he just wants us to know which ones are to blame for the general destruction to come. Not that that knowledge is going to do us very much good for very long, since we're going to be eliminated along with everybody else.

Chapter 2

Here Yahweh tells us that it's not certain and inevitable after all. Those who repent and turn to Yahweh before the day of destruction may survive on that day.

Then Yahweh starts hollering about the Philistines. He vows to eradicate them entirely, and turn their land over to the survivors in Judah. He, Yahweh, will take care of those survivors and see to it that their fortunes are restored

Then he starts hollering about Moab and Ammon. He's mad at them for taunting and insulting his people, and threatening to come take their land. They will be beaten, and the surviving remnant of Judah will plunder them and take their stuff.

Then he promises that the Cushites [Ethiopians] will be slain by the sword.

There's no reason for that; the land of Cush was a long ways from Judah and not hurting anybody. Maybe he was still mad because the Cushites had attacked Judah back during the days of king Asa, 250 years before. Or maybe he just wanted to get rid of them because of their black skins; but that doesn't seem likely.

Then he lashes out at Assyria. making all the familiar threats.

Chapter 3

Then he starts in on Jerusalem again. *And I can't help but think he must have written this earlier than he says; back during the kingships of Manasseh and Amon, when his accusations would have made sense.* He calls it a doomed and corrupt city that oppresses its own people. He says they haven't listened to him or accepted his discipline. *Which is a crock. They were following their recently-found copy of Deuteronomy, for crying out loud.* He goes on and on in the same vein, inveighing against practices that didn't exist. And threatening the usual punishments.

Since Judah refuses to repent and mend their ways, Yahweh intends to assemble the nations and royally chew them out. *But he doesn't mention the Valley of Jehoshaphat, as Joel did.* Then he will use his powers to reform the people, cleanse them of their wickedness, and turn them all into devout Yahwehists. And after that, the surviving remnant of Judah will be safe and never have anything more to fear.

And then he breaks into a hymn of celebration and joy for how everything has gotten better. But we must suppose it is meant to be sung AFTER everything has gotten better; not at present when things are fixing to get worse.

"Rejoice, Israel! The Lord has taken away your punishment and repelled your enemies. Yahweh is with you, and nothing bad will ever happen to you again. He will take delight in you, and engage in sing-alongs with you."

"He will remove your sorrows, deal with your enemies, heal the lame, and reassemble all the Children of Israel who have been taken away and scattered. He will make you honored throughout the world, as he restores your prosperity before your very eyes."

And that's where the book ends.

As you can tell, I don't take much stock in Zephaniah. He doesn't seem to know what he's talking about. He's just making up a story about a divine tantrum, in order to give it a happy ending.

The Bible, Chapter 84

The Book of Haggai

The time frame of the book of Haggai is the interregnum in the rebuilding of the temple that Ezra tells about. After Cyrus the Great of Persia told the exiled Jews that they could go back home to Judah if they wanted to, a substantial number took him up on it. When they got there, they started rebuilding the temple on the footprint of the old one. But they only got as far as constructing the sanctuary when political events involving Samaritans and others brought the project to a halt. It remained stalled for eighteen years before work resumed. Haggai is writing during that period when construction was stalled.

Haggai's account reveals a venal side of Yahweh we hadn't seen before.

Chapter 1
Yahweh gives a revelation to Haggai, to be relayed to Zerubbabel the governor of Judah, and Joshua, the high priest. The revelation is a complaint about the delay in getting the temple built so Yahweh can live in it.

The people are saying, "The time isn't yet ripe to start on the temple again." But Yahweh says, "Is the time right, then, for you to be living in nice houses while my house lies in ruins?"

"Pay attention now: You plant much, but barely harvest enough to keep you alive. Your vineyards don't produce enough wine to do you any good. You don't have enough clothing to keep you warm. The little money you earn disappears as through holes in your pockets. Now why do you think that is? It's because you're stiffing me."

"Get up off your butts, go up into the mountains and cut timber, and get to work building my house so I can take pleasure in it and be honored properly.

"You strive for much and gain little. When you brought your harvest home, I blew it away. Why do you think I did that? Because you busy yourselves with your own affairs while my house remains in ruins, that's why. Because of that, I've withheld nature's bounty from you. I brought you a drought, to undercut the work you were doing to benefit yourselves."

So Zerubbabel and Joshua and everybody else understood the threat, and commenced obeying. They went back to work rebuilding the temple.

Chapter 2
A month later, Haggai delivered another prophecy to Zerubbabel and Joshua.
Yahweh asked, "Are there any of you people who remember what the old temple was like before it was destroyed? Right now it's a dump, but I want it even grander and finer than it was before. That was part of the bargain in my covenant with you when I brought you out of Egypt. I was with you then and I'm with you now."

"Before I'm done, all the nations will be overthrown and their treasures will be brought here to adorn my temple. All the silver and gold of the world is mine!!
The glory of my new house will be greater than it ever was before! Once it's all fixed up for me, I will bring peace."

Two months later, Haggai delivered yet another prophecy. "Ask the priests what the law says. Can consecration pass from one thing to another? If a man is carrying consecrated meat in his cloak, and it touches a jar of oil or a loaf or bread, do the oil or bread become consecrated?"

The answer: "No, of course not."

"Then can defilement pass from one thing to another? If a man is defiled from having touched a dead body, and then he touches the wine or bread, does it become defiled?"

The answer: "Yes, of course it does."

"Then the same thing holds true of the people of this nation: whatever they produce is defiled, and so everything they offer on the altar is defiled. They contaminated their offerings with their selfish attitudes and behavior. They gave no thought to my needs, but only to their own."

"Can you now see what has happened to you? Before you started work on the temple, you would go to a pile of grain expecting twenty bushels and find only ten. I did that. You would go to the wine cask to draw out fifty bottles of wine, and only find twenty. I did that. I struck your works with blight, mildew and hail, but did you repent your selfish ways and come to me? You did not!"

"Today the foundation of my temple has been completed. See how things go from now on. You may not have any grain or wine or figs, but you will have my blessing."

That same day, Haggai got a final revelation:
"I m fixing to shake the heaven and the earth and overthrow kingdoms and shatter their power and overturn chariots so their drivers will kill each other with their swords."

"On that day, I will take you Zerubbable and make you like my signet ring. I have appointed you to rule!" says Yahweh.

Thus ends the book.

One thing that strikes me, among many, is Yahweh's claim, "**I** want it even grander and finer than it was before. That was part of the bargain in my covenant with you when I brought you out of Egypt. I was with you then and I'm with you now."

I'm trying to find the place where Yahweh, as part of his covenant with the Children of Israel, demanded an ornate temple filled with gold and silver and other fancy stuff. I haven't been able to find it. In fact, until David came up with the idea of a temple, Yahweh was perfectly happy living in a tent, as he always had. David didn't start to build a temple because he was obligated to do so as part of a covenant; he came up with the idea on his own, as a special way of honoring Yahweh.

The whole "part of the covenant" thing is bogus. Yahweh is laying a guilt trip on the people that they do not deserve. Yahweh had demanded a lot of things from them, but an ornate palace wasn't one. Until now. They may have done bad things, but they can't be accused of welshing on a covenant.

And they haven't returned to the temple-rebuilding as part of an ancient covenant. They're doing it because Yahweh busted their chops until they did. Yahweh was ticked off that they took care of their own affairs and families instead of constructing him a Stately Pleasure Dome, so he systematically made their lives miserable.

And in the end, after they went back to work on his palace, did he make them less miserable? Nope; he left them without grain or fruit or wine. Instead he gave them a blessing! You can't eat, drink, or wear a blessing; but that's what he gave them.

This book paints Yahweh as a ruthless, greedy, bling-hungry tyrant. He has shown himself to be mean and ruthless in the past. But never because of a lust for fancy possessions..

I'm not sure Haggai got it right. He may just have wanted to be a cheer-leader for getting the temple rebuilt, so he made this stuff up. I'm not going to buy this sudden, new, character facet for

Yahweh that springs out of nothing in the past. I think the author made it up.

The Bible, Chapter 81

The Book of Zechariah
part 1

Zechariah was a contemporary of Haggai, and both date their works to the same year: "The second year of Darius I", which would be 519 BC. Their interest is the same —the rebuilding of the temple— but their styles and approaches are dramatically different. In particular, Zechariah's prophecy involves a lot of dreams or visions, while Haggai's had none.

Chapter 1
In the eighth month of that year, Zechariah has a revelation from Yahweh. He is addressing the people of Jerusalem. Yahweh is angry about their ancestors; so he tells them to get right with him and he will get right with them. Those ancestors had refused to listen to the prophets who tried to bring them to the way of the Lord. But they and those prophets are long dead. Your ancestors disregarded my warnings, and suffered the consequences, but they finally admitted they had it coming to them.

Three months later, Zechariah has a vision in his sleep. In a grove in a ravine, he saw a man riding a red horse. Other colored horses were in the background. Zech asked a nearby angel, "What're these horses all about?" and the angel said "I'll show you what they're about." Then the man on the red horse said, "The Lord sent these horses to go throughout the world, and report back." Then the horses spoke up and said to the angel (who apparently was not the man on the red horse, although the horseman was probably an angel too),"Throughout the world we have found calm and peace."

Then the angel addressed Yahweh: "Lord, how much longer are you going to stay mad at the people of Judah and Jerusalem? It's already been seventy years."
Yahweh spoke some comforting words to the angel, and the angel told Zech what Yahweh had said: "I have high regard for the people of Jerusalem and Zion. But am pissed off about those nations that are enjoying peace and quiet; because I was only slightly annoyed with my people, but those nations caused them to suffer far more than I had Intended. "

"I have returned to Jerusalem to await the rebuilding of my temple, and Judah will return to prosperity."

Then Zechariah either has another vision or has a continuation of the first one. He looks up and sees four horns, like those of oxen. He asks the angel what they are and the angel says, "Those are the world powers that have scattered the people of Judah, Israel, and Jerusalem." Then Zech sees four guys carrying hammers, and asks what they are. The angel says, "They are the forces that are going to crush those horns."

Chapter 2
Another vision: Zech sees a man with a measuring line who is fixing to measure Jerusalem. Then another angel comes up to the first angel, and tells him, "Go tell that guy with the measuring line that Jerusalem isn't going to have any walls. There will be too many people and too much livestock. Yahweh will protect it in lieu of walls."

Then Yahweh issues instructions: "You who've been exiled in Babylonia for the last 70 years, now is the time for you to escape and return to Jerusalem!"

I don't think so. King Cyrus had released the exiles from captivity and allowed them to return to Judah some 17 or 18 years earlier. Yahweh may be addressing the Jews who elected to stay in Babylon rather than emigrate...but they were no longer in captivity to escape from.

Then there's some stuff about how Zechariah has been sent against the nations that plundered Judah, to threaten them for attacking Yahweh's favorite people. As punishment, those nations will be plundered by their captives.

Then Yahweh tells the people to sing for joy, because he's coming to live among them and will adopt other nations to be part of Judah, and Jerusalem will again be his favorite city. Then he tells them to be silent in his presence. These seem to be conflicting instructions.

Chapter 3
Another vision: Zech sees the high priest Joshua standing with an angel, while Satan stands alongside them, ready to accuse Joshua of something or other.
The angel tells Satan, "Yahweh says Shame on you! This man has been rescued like a burning stick snatched from the fire."

Joshua is standing in filthy clothes. The angel has his assistant remove them, and tells Joshua, "I've removed your sins, and will dress you in finery." Then he has the assistant dress Joshua in nice clean clothes, and tells Joshua, "If you follow Yahweh's commands, he'll let you be in charge of the temple and will treat you the same as these angels here."

Then Yahweh says something about one of his assistants called The Branch, which may be an angel or something else, and puts a stone with a bunch of eyes in front of Joshua, and says he will inscribe something on the stone with eyes, and that will immediately absolve the sins of Judah and Jerusalem.

Chapter 4
Another vision: Then the angel aroused Zech from his reverie, and asked him, "What do you see?" Zech says, "I see a golden lamp stand, topped by a bowl full of lamps. There are seven of them, and each one has seven wicks. There's an olive tree on each side of the lamp stand." He asks what the vision means. The angel tells him, "It is Yahweh's message to Zerubbabel [the governor of Judah]. He says, 'You won't govern by might, but by

my spirit and guidance.'."

Then there's some stuff about how mountains will become level ground before Zerubbabel. Yahweh predicts that Zerubbabel will start the reconstruction of the temple, and will complete it.

As for the stone with eyes, "Those are the seven eyes of Yahweh, which see everything in the world." [*This bothers me. It seems to destroy the image of Yahweh as man-like (or man as Yahweh-like) and presents him as one of the freaky creatures in Daniel's nightmares. "The Thing With Seven Eyes." Creepy.*]

And then the vision takes a strange turn: Zech asks the angel about the meaning of the olive trees flanking the golden lamp stand, and gets no answer. So he asks a different question:

"What is the meaning of these two olive branches beside the two golden pipes that pour out the golden oil?"

This is the first , and the last, we have heard of golden pipes pouring out oil. In Zech's hallucination, did the trees and lamp stand somehow morph into branches and pipes, without Zech noticing the change? Did the branches and oil pipes emerge as a new element in the vision? Were they there all along, but Zech forgot to tell us? I guess we'll never know.

Anyhow, the angel says, "You really don't know what they are?" Zechariah says No.

"Those are the two men Yahweh has chosen to serve him as Lord of everything."

Two problems here. First, using golden oil pipes to represent divine helpers strikes me as unintelligible symbolism. But I'll let that go, since I suppose anything can symbolize anything when you're in the business of interpreting visions. Think of Freud.

Second, the chapter ends right here, with no inkling of who the two men might be. Does he mean Zerubbabel and Joshua? Does he mean somebody else? Maybe the man on the red horse and the man standing in the grove? Again, I guess we'll never know.

Chapter 5
Another vision: Zechariah sees a flying scroll, approximately the size of your living room, with writing on both sides. The angel tells him the scroll bears a curse that is going out over the whole world. On one side it says all thieves will be sent into exile. On the other side it says all who lie under oath will be sent into exile.

Yahweh says, "I will send it into the house of every thief and every perjurer. It will remain in the house and reduce the house to rubble." *Which makes no sense to me at all.*

Zech looks up and sees a measuring basket approaching from the air. The angel tells him, "That contains the sins of the whole world." The lid to the basket is made out of lead. It opens and a woman sits up inside! The angel pushes her back down and slams the leaden lid shut, saying "That woman is wickedness."

Then two women with wings like a stork swoop down, grab the basket, and fly off with it. They angel says, "They're taking it to Babylonia. They'll build a house for it and leave it there, because that's where she belongs."

Chapter 6
Another vision: Zechariah seems to be on an acid trip. He sees four chariots come roaring out from between two mountains made of bronze! Each of them has different colored horses. The angel tells him, "Those are the four spirits of heaven, heading out from Yahweh's presence. The one with the black horses will head north, the one with the white horses will head west, and the one will the dappled horses will head south." The fourth one had red horses; we're not told where it was headed, but east would be a likely candidate.

As the horses were straining to get where they were going, the angel hollered, "Look! The ones headed north have quieted my spirit in the north country."

I *don't get this at all. The only things north of Judah were the territory once occupied by the Kingdom of Israel, then Syria, and then some remnants of the old Assyrian empire. Why would they quiet the angel's spirit? And why would an* angel's *spirit ever be unquiet?*

A revelation: Yahweh instructs Zechariah to go get the gold and silver from some of the exiles, and make it into a crown, and put it on the head of Joshua the high priest. Then tell him he is (or may be, or somebody else may be) the man called "The Branch", who will branch out from his place and build the temple of the Lord, which was previously predicted of Zerubbabel. He will be richly clothed, and will rule from his throne. There will be a priest alongside him, and the two will get along. It's all very confusing. Then after the coronation, the crown will be given back to the ones who supplied the gold and silver.

Let us pause in our narrative.

The Bible, Chapter 82

The Book of Zechariah,
part 2.

Chapter 7
Two years later, a contingent from the people of Bethel came to the priest and asked, "Should we mourn and fast in the fifth month, as we always have?"

Yahweh issues a non- answer: "When you did all that fasting and mourning for the past 70 years, were you really doing it for me? And when you were eating and drinking, weren't you just doing it for yourselves?" That's the same thing he had said back when Jerusalem was peaceful and prosperous. It didn't answer the question then, either.

Then he gave Zechariah a message: " Long ago I told my people to be merciful and compassionate toward one another, to administer justly, to care for the needy and the widows and those far from their native land. But they wouldn't do it. They were hard-hearted and refused to follow my instructions. And that made me mad. They wouldn't listen to me, so I wouldn't listen to them. I scattered them among nations and made their land desolate."

Which hardly provided an answer to the question that the people asked. A simple Yes or No would have sufficed, instead of re-hashing ancient offenses. As it stood, they had no idea what they were supposed to do. THEY weren't the ones Yahweh was inveighing against; those people were long dead.

Chapter 8
Zechariah gets another revelation. Yahweh tells him he cares

405

deeply for the people of Zion, so he repeats his intention to live in Jerusalem, which will then be renowned as the City of Truth. "Once again, old people will be safe to sit in the streets and visit each other. Boys and girls will again be able to play." Then he will protect them from foreign invaders and reassemble all those exiled in foreign countries, and so on.

Then Yahweh recounts how he had punished everybody, and says he won't do it again, and Judah will prosper and so on. He re-issues his instructions to the people: "Be just in your judgments and honest with each other. Don't plot against your neighbors. Be good. Then the fasts of months 4, 5, 7, and 10 will be joyous celebrations." Then he goes on some more about how people will gather to Jerusalem for all nations to pray to him.

Chapter 9
Yahweh prophesies how he will handle the enemies of Israel, in much gory detail that I won't relate. Then he tells how a king for Judah will show up riding on a donkey, or a colt, or some other small beast of burden. *[Later, New Testament writers will find this prophetic.]* Yahweh will rid the surrounding nations of their war-making stuff, and the new king will proclaim peace yada yada yada.

Then Yaweh will equip Judah to make war on the Greeks. The Greeks will get their butts kicked while Yahwah oversees the action. Their blood will flow as from a sacrifice, where the blood is caught in a bucket and splashed on the altar. And the Lord will see it, and call it beautiful.

Chapter 10
More of the same sort of carrying on.

Chapter 11
Yahweh will destroy the forests of Lebanon. We aren't told why.

Then there are more inexplicable threats of punishment, in a long complicated parable about sheep destined for slaughter and their own shepherds not protecting them, which is odd since, after all, the sheep were raised to be eaten. I won't attempt to report on it.

Chapter 12

Yahweh prophesies: "I'm going to make Jerusalem like a cup of wine, that makes the surrounding nations drunk. Jerusalem will come under attack, but I will make her like an immovable rock. Those who try to move her will just injure themselves. The day they attack, I will make their horses panic and their riders go mad. Then I will blind all the horses. Then the people of Judah will realize that Jerusalem is strong because they worship Me."

"At that time, I will make the leaders of Judah like a torch in a woodpile. They will consume everything, but Jerusalem will be unharmed."

And then there's a passage I don't know what to make of. Yahweh is quoted as saying, **"I will pour out the spirit of mercy and prayer on the house of David and the people of Jerusalem. They will look on me, the one they have pierced, and they will mourn for him the way one mourns for an only child, and they will grieve bitterly as one losing a first-born. On that day every clan will mourn."**

Two problems here. The first is the notion that Yahweh himself has been physically stabbed or pierced (and killed!) by the people of Jerusalem. The second is the juxtaposition of pronouns. "They will look to me... and they will mourn him." Why would Yahweh switch from first person to third person if he's talking about himself? Why would he use first person if he's not talking about himself? Zechariah 12:10 has received a lot of attention from Bible scholars, but nothing conclusive has emerged. So here's my take on it.

Someone will be "stabbed", and will be mourned as for the dead. Yahweh cannot literally be stabbed to death with a knife or spear. Yet he claims to be the one who was pierced, and he claims that the one who was pierced is mourned as for the dead. First of all, since he's Yahweh, the fatal stabbing can't be literal; it has to be metaphorical. The people have hurt him --"stabbed

407

him to the heart"--by their misbehavior. Later, after they have received the spirit of mercy and prayer, they realized what they have done. They hurt his feelings, betrayed his trust, and lost his grace. They are mourning the death of the relationship to him that they have lost. Yahweh, having identified himself as the injured party, moves to the position of one of the observers who are mourning "him". They are mourning out of regret.

Well, it makes as much sense as anything else.

Chapter 13

When that happens [*mourning in regret for their past sins*], a fountain will be opened to cleanse them from sin and impurity. Then Yahweh will banish the very names of the idols from national memory. Then he'll get rid of the prophets. "Then if anybody still claims to be a prophet and keeps on prophesying, his own parents will condemn him to death for prophesying lies, and will stab him."

I'm going to understand this the same way I understand the other stabbing business: the parents won't take a spear and impale him; rather, they'll "stab him to the heart" by disowning him and rejecting him from their family and their confidence. He will be "dead to them". I like that better. Moses probably wouldn't.

Then all the prophets will throw away their prophet outfits, and reject any claim to be prophets. If somebody asks them, "What do you do?" they'll say, "I'm a farmer and always have been."

Then another unfathomable bit. I suspect Zechariah was suffering from a toothache or the cramps when he wrote this.

Yahweh throws a tantrum, and says "Wake up Sword, and attack the shepherds who work in my name! Kill them so their sheep will be scattered! Then I will attack my people and annihilate two thirds of them! The remainder I will test through trial, as silver is refined in fire! When I get done with them, they'll acknowledge me as their god and I'll call them my people."

There's nothing in the text to explain this outburst. Make of it what you will.

Chapter 14

Zechariah's apocalyptic vision. Yahweh is going to bring all the nations together to attack Jerusalem. They will overrun the city and ransack the houses and rape the women. "You'll see them dividing up the plunder before your very eyes. Half of the city will be taken into exile; the other half won't."

Then Yahweh will jump in and fight those nations he brought in, and will defend Jerusalem! He will stand on the Mount of Olives to the east of the city, and the mountain will split down the middle forming a valley. "You will escape through this valley, fleeing as you fled from the earthquake when Uzziah was king [two centuries earlier]. Then the Lord will come, bringing his angels with him."

"That will be a unique day in the history of the world. There will be no cold or frost, no distinction between night and day —it will always be light. Then miraculous water will flood out of Jerusalem, half flowing south toward the Dead Sea, half flowing west toward the Great Sea. It will continue to flow steadily all year. Then Yahweh will rule over the whole earth, and will be recognized as the only god."

"The whole surrounding territory will be leveled, but Jerusalem will rise up and remain in prominence. It will be re-inhabited, and thereafter will always be secure. Yahweh will strike the attacking nations with a plague, as follows: Their flesh will rot off while they are still standing. Their eyes will rot away and then their tongues. There will be a general panic, and they will begin attacking each other. The armies of Judah will come to Jerusalem's defense, and will take back the stolen loot from the attackers"

"Those of the attackers who survive this will return, year after year, to worship Yahweh. Those who fail to come will suffer drought and other disasters. The harness bells of the horses will be inscribed, DEDICATED TO THE LORD. Every cooking pot throughout Judah will be consecrated to the Lord. Those who come to perform sacrifice will use the pots to cook in. And all merchants will be banished from the temple of the Lord."

And that is that.

The Bible, Chapter 87

The Book Malachi

Nothing is known of the person Malachi, or even if that is a name rather than a title. The book was written some time after the return of the exiles from Babylon, and after the restoration of the second temple (516 BC). It is the last book of the Old Testament, and probably the latest in writing; later than both Ezra and Nehemiah. Yahweh comes off as whiney and petulant.

Here as elsewhere, 'Jacob' and 'Esau' refer to the twin brothers, sons of Isaac, and also to the kingdoms they founded: Israel and Edom. The book of Obadiah tells something about the relationship between the two.

Chapter 1
Yahweh says he loves his people, and he loves Jacob, but he hates Esau, whose kingdom he has turned into a desolate hill country. The Edomites may vow to recover, but Yahweh says, "Whatever they build, I'll tear down again. They'll be known as the Evil Country, the Wicked Land, a people I shall hate forever."

A little back story here. Of the two brothers, Esau was clearly the good guy and Jacob the bad guy, who twice cheated his brother Esau out of his birthright. That alone should have put Jacob on Yahweh's bad side. But we're actually talking about something else. Centuries down the line, Jacob, renamed 'Israel', had been the progenitor of the kingdom of Israel, the land of Yahweh's chosen people, while Esau had been the founder of the rival kingdom of Edom. The two had been on bad terms for a long time, and when Nebuchadnezzar came to destroy Jerusalem, the Edomites chipped in and gave him a hand. That, for Yahweh, was unforgivable.

....

Then he changes the subject and starts ripping on the priests for disrespecting him.

"You priests obviously have contempt for me. You put defiled food on my altar. Instead of young healthy animals, you bring ones that are old or sick or crippled. If you offered those to your governor, he'd throw you out. When you offer such stuff to me, how do you expect me to respond?"

"Somebody should lock the temple doors, to keep you guys from lighting your useless fires on my altar! I'm mad at you, and I won't accept any of your offerings! Everywhere in the world, from east to west, people honor my name by burning incense and bringing worthy offerings to me. But you guys insult me with food you wouldn't eat yourself! Do you think I'll accept these miserable, diseased creatures you try to foist off on me? I curse those who bring me this crap, when they could have brought a young healthy animal instead! I'm a Great King, and all nations fear me...but you bring me this crap!"

Chapter 2
"And another thing. You're supposed to honor me in what you do. If you won't listen to me, I'll put a curse on you! In fact, I've already cursed you and the horse you rode in on, for not taking my commands seriously! "

"Because of you, I'm going to punish your descendants. I'm going to rub your faces in the dung of these worthless animals you bring me, and then have you thrown into the dung heap! Then you'll know that I've told you this in order to keep my covenant with Levi and his tribe." [*Levites were the designated priests.*]

I don't get it. How is cussing them out keeping a covenant with Levi?

"I promised them life and well-being, and I gave it to them. Back in those days, they gave me respect. They taught what was right, not what was wrong. They got along with me. They preserved true knowledge, as priests are supposed to. But you guys! You teach stuff that makes people go bad. When you do that, YOU violate and nullify my covenant with Levi!"

"So for that, I'm going to make you despised among the people of Israel...for that, and for not judging cases fairly and impartially."

"We all have the same father; the same god created us all. So why do we break our covenant with him by cheating and lying to one another?" [*At this point, Malachi is no longer speaking as Yahweh, but as himself.*] "The people of Judah have violated their bargain with Yahweh. They've done horrible things throughout the land. They've even married women who worship other gods! I hope Yahweh kicks such men out of the community and forbids them to participate in temple sacrifices."

"And another thing! You drown Yahweh's altar in your tears, because he no longer accepts your offering. Do you know why that is? It's because you have broken your commitment to the wife you first married when young. You promised Yahweh you would stick with her, but now you've broken with her. Yahweh joined you in body and spirit to allow you to have legitimate children. How can you break that bond?"

"Yahweh hates divorce! [*Malachi needs to take this up with Ezra.*] He also hates it when you are mean to people. So don't do that!"

"You have tired the Lord out with your yapping about how he loves evildoers the same as good people, or by questioning whether there is a god of justice."

Chapter 3

"A messenger will prepare the way. Then the Lord you question will show up in his temple. The messenger will proclaim Yahweh's covenant...but who will be able to endure that day when the Lord comes? He will be like a strong soap that cleanses, like the fire that refines metal, and he will come to judge and purify his people. Then the offerings of the people of Judah will again be acceptable."

"Yahweh will be quick to punish sorcerers, adulterers, perjurers, those who cheat their workers out of their wages, those who mistreat widows and orphans, and those who give unfair treatment to foreigners. He says so."

"I am the Lord, and I never change." [*Malachi is again speaking for Yahweh.*] "So I won't leave you descendants of Jacob completely lost and cast out as you deserve. For generations you have ignored my commands and wishes...but if you repent, I'll take you back in."

"You ask, 'What must I do to repent?' I ask: Is it right for a man to cheat his god? You ask, 'How are we cheating you?' In tithes and offerings! You are robbing me!
Bring the whole tithe to the temple, not just part of it, so there will be ample food in my house. Do right be me, and see if I don't do right by you. I'll keep pests from eating your crops, and keep your vines from dropping their fruit. Then all nations will recognize your well-being because your land will be a good place to live."

"You've been trash-talking me, saying there's no point and no gain in serving me, or in following my commands. No point in showing sorrow for what you've been doing. The way you see it, the wicked prosper and those who defy me don't get punished."

"But there are others, who have stuck with me, and I have heard them and listened. I have written on a scroll, a record of those who have remained faithful. When the time comes to settle matters, I'll spare them just as a father spares a faithful son. Then those saying 'There's no point in being good' will see the difference between what happens to the righteous and what happens to the wicked."

Chapter 4

"The day is coming when the arrogant and the wicked will get what's coming to them. They will burn like straw. Nothing will be left to them. But for those who have honored my name, my power will shine like the sun over them. Then they will be happy and will frisk about like calves let out of the pen. They will overcome the bad people, and will trample them like dust under their feet."

"So remember the laws I gave to Moses on Mount Sinai for the people of Israel to obey."

"But before the day I mentioned comes, I will send the prophet Elijah to minister to you. He will bring fathers and children together again."

"And if he can't succeed in doing that, I'll have to come and destroy your country."

....

And that's that for the Old Testament.

Here's what I think. Malachi is a doofus who can't follow a coherent train of thought before jumping to a new topic, and who can't keep his stories straight about what's going to happen to Jerusalem. He is going to ring in a prophet who's been dead and gone for 300 years? This isn't meaningful prophecy full of hidden meanings. It's just rambling. Is what I think.

Some Apocrypha

About the Apocrypha

There are a number of ancient writings on topics found in the Old Testament that are regarded as important enough to include along with the Bible, but not agreed to be carrying the same divine imprimatur as the books of the Old Testament. These are called the Apocryphal Books, or the Apocrypha.

Many editions of The Bible include some or all of the Apocrypha in a separate section, between the two Testaments. But since they are not officially part of The Bible, many editions omit them altogether. The familiar King James Version does not contain them. The Catholic Bible includes seven Apocrypha in the listing of books of the Old Testament.

There are about fourteen apocryphal books altogether. Two of the historical Apocryphal books, Tobit and Judith, are included here, with a brief salute to Maccabees.

=======

These chapters were written after the chapters of the New Testament. That explains why their numbers aren't consecutive with those of the Old Testament

The Bible, Chapter 151

The Book of Tobit

Introduction

Overall, the book of Tobit reads more like a fairy tale than a gospel. The only aspects that make it gospel-y are the occasional prayers, and the long moral advisory Tobit gives to his son Tobiah. Otherwise, it's just a tale, and a not very exciting one. It is highly episodic, as I shall note. It was written (probably) in the second century bc.

The first part is written in the first person. The setting is Nineveh, capital of Assyria, not too long after the Assyrian Captivity (ca. 722 bc), when most of the population of the northern kingdom of Israel had been carted off into exile by the Assyrians. It was written (probably) in the second century bc.

Before the Assyrians came down like a wolf on the fold, the situation in Israel was this: the United Kingdom of Judah and Israel had separated with the death of Solomon. The northern kingdom had rejected the bid of Solomon's boy Rehoboam to rule the United Kingdom, and had chosen the non-Davidic Jeroboam to be the king of Israel. With the two kingdoms on not very good terms, it became difficult for the Israelites to worship at the Temple in Jerusalem, deep into Judean territory, even though that was the only place specified by Mosaic law.

To make it easier for the people to carry out their religious practices, Jeroboam set up a couple of local (Israelite) shrines where people could conduct their sacrifices. These shrines were to be dwelling places of Yahweh, just like the Jerusalem temple. They were guarded by two golden statues of bulls. But apparently, some people missed the symbolism and started doing

418

their sacrifices to the Golden Bulls, rather than to Yahweh. (Probably why Yahweh let the Assyrians haul them away in captivity.)

However a number of devout Israelites avoided the substitute shrines, and continued to trek all the way to Jerusalem to worship at the Temple. One of them was Tobit.

Here Beginneth Tobit

Tobit starts out by telling us what virtuous man he is. In Israel before the exile, he had been one who regularly went to Jerusalem to sacrifice at the true Temple, unlike the Bull-worshipers. He took loads of food and goods, for the sacrifices and for the priests, and paid tithes two or three times a year. He also did good works for widows and orphans, and was a paragon of virtue.

Among devout Israelites, it was demanded that a man not only avoid marriage to a Gentile woman, but that he marry a woman of his own tribe, and indeed of his own lineage. They were required to marry kinfolks. So Tobit married a kinswoman named Anna, and sired a boy named Tobiah, and raised him to be a good boy.

In captivity in Nineveh, he refused to follow his kinfolks in eating the food of heathens; he stuck with kosher. Yahweh appreciated that, and fixed it so he became an aide to the king Shalmaneser. This gained him privilege of going wherever he liked.

Episode 1
Periodically, he traveled to the city of Rages in Medea with a large bag of money paid him by the king. In that city lived a kinsman, Gabelus, or Gabael; Tobit then deposited the money with him to hold. *This would be no small journey. Rages, or Rhagae, was approximately 500 miles from Nineveh. Traveling on foot, it would take several weeks. And he did this many times.*

419

This gives some notion of the time-line of this story.

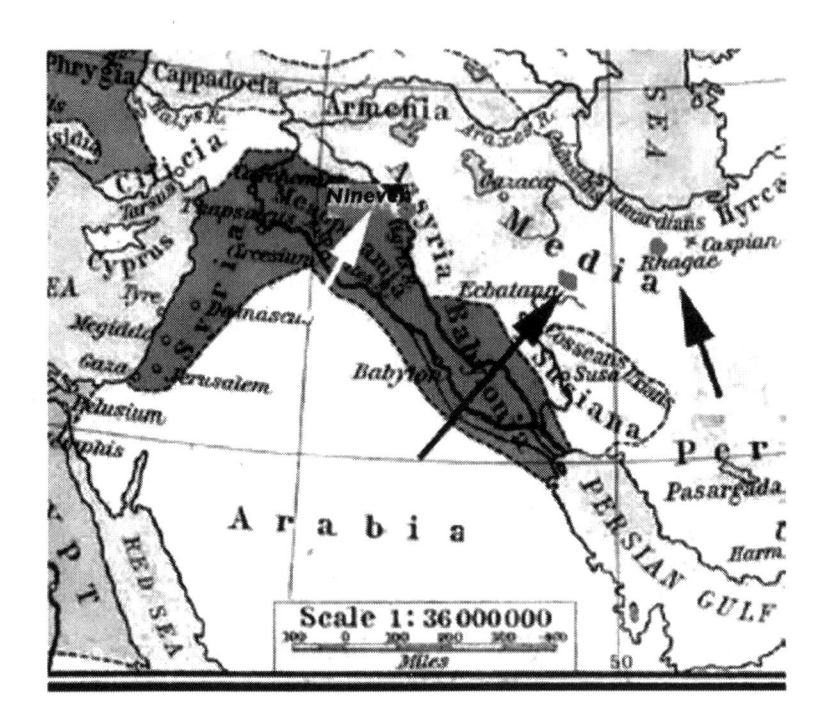

Episode 2

Back in Nineveh, Tobit continued to do good works for his people. But the king died and was replaced by his son Sennacherib, a tyrannical wretch who hated Jews. He wouldn't even allow them a decent burial. Their dead were simply flung outside the city walls for the buzzards. Tobit did his best to secretly bury every dead Israelite that he could, despite the king's ruling.

When Sennacherib got back from a campaign, and heard about the burials, he had a cow. He levied a death sentence on Tobit, and confiscated his stuff. Tobit hit the road with his wife and son, and hid out among friends.

In a month or so, Sennacherib was done in by his own sons. Tobit came out of hiding, and his stuff was returned to him, and he went on as before.

Episode 3
There was a festival of some sort, with a lot of food prepared at Tobias' house. Tobit told his son to go out and invite some fellow tribesmen to share the dinner. Tobiah went out, but came running back hollering that there was a dead Israelite lying out in the street. Tobit ran out and carried the corpse back into the house for later burial. Then he went back and finished his dinner.

After dark, he went out and buried the body. The neighbors saw him and said, 'You numskull, you got a death sentence for doing that before, but you keep on doing it!"
But no matter, he kept on doing it as a religious duty.

And that's enough for this chapter.

The Bible, Chapter 152

The Book of Tobit
Part 2

Episode 4
One day, Tobit lay down outdoors to take a nap. As he lay there, a swallow in a tree overhead took a poop, which landed square on Tobit's eyes. It struck him stone blind. Must have been Some Poop. Wonder what the bird had been eating.

Tobit didn't blame Yahweh for his misfortune, for which reason the writer compares him to Job. I don't buy the comparison. Tobit was blinded by birdshit, because he napped in the wrong place. Job was deliberately subjected to a cataract of misfortunes, in order to settle a bet between Yahweh and Satan: Namely, whether a wholly righteous man like Job could be made to recant his faith in the face of unremitting misfortune. The only similarity between Tobit and Job is their failure to renounce Yahweh.

Episode 5
Tobit's wife Anna worked as a weaver of goods for the upper classes. One day, as a bonus for her work, they awarded her a young goat for their dinner. When Tobit saw it, he thought it was stolen. He threw a hissy-fit, and told her to take it back. He wouldn't listen to her explanation, and she finally told him, "You hypocritical jerk! Where's that tolerance and understanding you've pretended to?"

Episode 6
Then Tobit issued a long prayer, asking Yahweh to grant him death and release from the travail of his blindness by birdpoo. Yahweh didn't come through.

Episode 7
Meanwhile, the scene shifts back to Rages in Media. Tobit's

422

kinsman Raguel had a hot young daughter named Sarah, with a really unfortunate background. She had been married seven times, and still had not been Gone In Unto. On each wedding night, about the time the groom was fixing to jump on her bones, a jealous evil spirit named Asmodeus had struck him dead. Sarah remained a reluctant virgin.

A household servant bugged her about it, saying she had probably murdered each of them on her wedding nights. This left Sarah in such a bout of blue depression that she first decided to commit suicide by hanging, then changed her mind and (like Tobit) prayed to Yahweh to just let her die.

She proclaimed that she had never sought to be Gone In Unto out of lust --far from it --but by the purest of motives. But it seems she had been "found unworthy" of it and so on yadda yadda yadda. (Asmodeus not mentioned.)

Apparently, for these people, the normal sex drive was impure, and so the only permissible excuse for wanting to Do It was something else. "He and I aren't fixing to do it because we have the hots for each other... we reluctantly join our bodies through some totally pure motive or other." So in acknowledgement of her purity, the Angel Raphael was sent to take a hand in the matter.

Anyhow, the reluctant virgin prayed for death...but didn't get it . Neither did Tobit.

Episode 8
Meanwhile, back in Nineveh, Tobit mistakenly thought that death was imminent, so he called his son Tobiah in for some last minute advice:

•Take care of your mother after I'm gone, and when she dies, bury her alongside me.
•Always keep Yahweh in mind, and don't do anything he wouldn't like.
•Support those less fortunate than you.

- Abjure fornication.
- Be not proud.
- Pay your workers promptly.
...and so on.

Then he told him about the money he had deposited with Gabelus many years before, and that he had a signed promissory note for it. He instructed Tobiah to head off to Rages in Media, with the promissory note, and get the money from Gabelus.

Tobiah said that was all well and good, but he had no idea where Rages in Media was, or how to get there. Tobit said, go find an honest man who knows the way, and pay him to guide you.

Episode 9
Here's where the fairy tale aspects begin to emerge. Tobiah sets out and immediately runs into a young dude who looks like he's suited up to go on a journey. The dude is really the angel Raphael, in disguise, but he claims to be an Israelite named Azariah, and to know the way to Rages, and to be a friend of Gabelus. I guess it's okay for an angel to lie, if it's for a worthy cause like helping someone collect on a debt.

After an interview with Tobit, the angel/dude agrees to be Tobiah's guide. Tobit says, "May an angel of the lord go with you," (not knowing how close he is to the facts); and off they go on a 500-mile trip.

And that's enough for this chapter.

The Bible, Chapter 153

The Book of Tobit
Part 3

Episode 10
As soon as they were out the door, Tobit's missus started weeping and wailing and hollering at Tobit, "You've just sent away our only source of support in our old age, and he's going to get killed and won't ever come back! We need our son more than that money!"

Tobit told her, "Tut. He will arrive there safe and return home safe; I have faith that an angel of the Lord is watching over him." The wife felt assured, and quit crying. Maybe Tobit had guessed the truth about the angel/dude.

Episode 11
Tobiah and the dude set out, and the dog followed them. *[A curious detail. No further mention of the dog.]* The first night ,they camped by the river Tigris. Tobiah went down to wash his feet, and an enormous fish grabbed him by the foot. He hollered, "Help! this fish is attacking me!" The angel/dude said, "Attack him back. Grab him by the gill and drag him up on the bank." When they had the fish out of the water, they started to gut him, but the dude said "Save the heart and liver and gall. They have medicinal properties." They cut the fish up and cooked and ate part of it. The rest they salted, to take with them on their trip. They still had a long ways to go.

Tobiah asked the dude, "You made me keep these fish innards. What are they good for, really?" The angel/dude said, "If you put a piece of the heart on the embers of the fire, the smoke will drive away evil spirits. And the gall is good for curing blindness caused by cataracts."

Episode 12

As they approached the city of Ecbatana, about 2/3 of the way on their journey, Azariah/Raphael grabbed Tobiah and told him, "Guess what? There's a kinsman of yours named Raguel living in Ecbatana. He has a hot young daughter named Sarah. Since you are her nearest relative, you have first dibs on marrying her...and you are in line to inherit from Raguel. You're obliged to make her your wife. I'll make the deal with her father. Then when we get back from Rages, you'll marry up with her. But tonight, we'll get you engaged."

Tobiah said, "Wait a minute. I think I've heard of this woman. She's been married seven times, and each time the groom was killed by some evil spirit. on the wedding night before he could Go In Unto her. I don't think I want to be the eighth."

The angel told him, "Here's the full story you haven't heard. Each of those seven was a horn-dog devoid of holy thoughts or motives. Their immediate goal was to get Sarah into the sack and Go In Unto her as soon and as often as possible. They gave in to Lust as a horse or mule *[Mule? Mules are sterile females.]* would. And that made them susceptible to the power of the devil. He's what killed them."

"Here's how you avoid being the eighth victim. After the wedding, you are not to touch her for three days, but spend the time doing nothing but praying with her. On the first night, put the fish's liver on the coals of the fire to drive away the devil. After the third night, on the fourth day, you may Go In Unto her with the fear of the Lord, motivated not by lust but by doing what is necessary to procreate children in the lineage of Abraham."

I begin to understand why Catholics want to include this book in their Bible.

Episode 13

When they arrived at Raguel's house in Ecbatana, Raguel looked at Tobiah and thought: My! He looks a lot like my cousin. He asked where they were from, and when they told him, he said, "Do you know my brother Tobit?" They said they did. Then the angel/dude said "Tobit is this man's father."

Raguel went into a paroxysm of joy, kissing and hugging and laughing and I don't know what-all. Wife Edna and daughter Sarah joined in. Raguel ordered that a sheep be slaughtered, and dinner was prepared. But Tobiah said, "I won't eat a bit until you promise me the hand of Sarah in marriage." *[These Bible people don't understand the notion of allowing a slaughtered animal to hang for a couple of days, to age and become more tender. They kill it and cook it while it's still warm, as if it were a chicken. Civilized cooking is still in the future.]*

When Raguel heard this, he thought: Uh oh, here comes the eighth one. I don't like the look of this. He didn't respond. The angel told him, "Don't be hesitant; this man is Yahweh-fearing, and nothing can happen to him when he marries your daughter."

So Raguel gave his approval, and they didn't wait to finish their journey to Rages; they held the marriage ceremony right there and then. Apparently in those days they didn't need a clergyman or Justice of the Peace. The bride's father had the couple join hands, and said "The God of Abraham, and of Isaac, and of Jacob, be with you." And they wrote out a certificate of marriage, and that was that. Then they had a big dinner party in celebration.

By and by, Raguel told his wife Edna to go prepare a bridal chamber for the couple. She did, but when she brought Sarah in, Sarah burst into tears. We are not told why. Maybe she too was afraid this would be number eight. Or maybe they were tears of joy at the prospect that she might finally get laid.

Episode 14
When Tobiah and Sarah were finally alone together, he took a piece of the magic fish liver and laid it on the embers of the fire. At that moment, Raphael (the angel/dude) took hold of the evil spirit, and tied him up, and magically hauled him off to the

boondocks of Upper Egypt and dumped him there. Then the angel made his way back. (*So maybe the smoke from the fish liver was just a smoke screen. All the real work was done by Raphael.*)

Episode 15
Back in the nuptial chamber, Tobiah told his reluctant virgin bride, "Let's hold off on Doing It for a few days, and pray about it. During those days we will be joined to Yahweh. After the third day, we will be truly joined to each other, not like the heathens who jump right in and slake their lust." We are not told what Sarah thought of this arrangement. But she spent the next 3 days with him, praying and praying. And Tobiah prayed, "Lord, not for fleshly lust do I take my sister to wife, but only for the love of posterity, in which thy name may be blessed for ever and ever." And Sarah prayed, "Lord have mercy on us." She said nothing about not giving in to lust.

This whole "anti-lust" business leaves me flabbergasted. I don't recall anything similar in the Old Testament that I have read. Apparently, if you engage in sex because you enjoy it, giving no thought at the moment to procreation, you are a wicked person. The only time to Get It On is when you don't feel like it. Then you can be sure you're not doing it out of lust, but out of duty. I suppose, to be really pure, you both need to be reciting prayers to Yahweh the whole time during the act, and grimly dreading the finish.

The Bible, Chapter 154

The Book of Tobit
concluded.

Episode 16
Early next morning before sunup of the first day, Raguel gathered his servants, and they went out to dig a grave, just in case Tobiah turned out to be Number 8. Then he told his wife "Go have one of the maidservants peek in and see if he's dead, so we can bury him before daybreak." The maidservant returned with the news that they were sleeping peacefully. Raguel issued a long prayer of thanks to Yahweh. Then he had the servants go fill in the grave before anybody saw it.

Episode 17
Raguel prepared a wedding party feast, and swore that Tobiah wouldn't leave for at least two weeks. When he did leave, as son-in-law he'd be taking with him one half of Raguel's fortune, and would inherit the other half after Raguel and Edna died.

Episode 18
Tobiah then told Azariah/Raphael to take some men and camels and go to Rages to retrieve the money that Tobit had deposited with cousin Gabiel. Then to bring the money and Gabiel back, so he could enjoy the wedding feast too. Raphael did it. (*The distance was about 175 miles each way, so it would have taken a couple of weeks at least.*) When Raphael fetched Gabiel in the door of Raguel's house, Tobiah jumped up and hugged him and carried on for a long time about how good it was to see him.

Episode 19
The scene shifts back to Tobit in Nineveh. Tobit had made up an itinerary of the number of days it should take Tobiah to go and

return, and he was keeping track.

Tobiah was of course way behind schedule because of the wedding business, and on the day he should have shown up, but didn't, Tobit started wondering what could have happened. He wasn't worried, just wondering.

His wife Anna started keening a wailing, and hollering "I knew it! He's been killed, just as I told you!" and carrying on and making a spectacle of herself. Tobit tried to calm her: "Look, he's probably been delayed by a piece of business. Azariah is a good guy, and Tobiah is okay."

It didn't work. She kept hollering, "Don't lie! My son is a goner!" Every day, she would go out and sit and watch up the road where he had gone, and wouldn't eat. Then at night she'd go home and weep and wail all night, never getting any sleep and not letting others get any, either.

Episode 20
Meanwhile, back at Raguel's place. The two weeks were up, and Tobiah told Raguel, "Please let my go home. My folks are going to be frantic because I've been gone so long." Raguel tried to get him to stay a little longer, saying he'd send messengers to tell Tobit his son was OK. Tobiah said, "No, I've got to go."

Raguel said alright, and handed over 1/2 of everything he owned, including money, livestock, slaves, clothing, and so on, for Tobiah to take back with him. Herding this retinue back to Nineveh was likely to cause further delay, but there was nothing to be done about it. He then handed over Sarah, Tobiah's bride, wished them well, and hoped to see grandkids some day.

Time passed. They traveled.

Episode 21
As they neared Nineveh, Raphael/Azariah told Tobiah, "Let's you and me go on ahead, and prepare things for the arrival of the

others...and be sure to have the fish gall in your pocket." So they went.

When mama Anna spotted him coming down the road, she started whooping and hollering "Tobit! here comes our son and his friend!." She had a thing for hollering.

Just before they got there, Raphael told Tobiah, "When you see your father, smear the fish gall on his eyes. That will make his cataracts peel off, and he will see again." *(These bird-poop cataracts apparently were some kind of a coating, unlike regular cataracts which are cloudings inside the eye. I still wonder what that bird had been eating.)*

Anna ran out and hollered with joy, and hugged Tobiah and carried on. When Tobit blindly stumbled through the gate, Tobiah grabbed him and told him "Hold still and watch this." Then he smeared the fish goo in Tobit's eyes, which stung. Then, with his fingers, Tobiah started at the corners and peeled off the cataracts from his Daddy's eyes. Now that Tobit could see him, he threw his arms around his son and loudly praised Yahweh for everything.

Episode 22
Tobiah told his dad the story, about getting the money from Gabael, and getting married to Raguel's daughter Sarah, and bringing half of Raguel's stuff back with him as a wedding present.

Tobit then struck out down the road to greet his daughter-in-law and the accompanying caravan. When the neighbors saw his striding along, without being led, they hardly knew what to say.

When Tobit reached Sarah, he welcomed her and blessed her and thanked Yahweh a bunch of times. The word spread among all the Jews living in Nineveh, and everybody celebrated. They had a wedding feast that lasted a week. People brought them presents.

At this point, Tobiah was probably the richest Israelite in Nineveh: He had the bags of money from Gabael, plus half of Raguel's riches, plus the wedding presents garnered at the feast. Raphael had done right well by his ward Tobiah.

Episode 23
After the feast, Tobit and Tobiah discussed what would be appropriate payment to Azariah for guiding Tobiah through the journey. They agreed that he should get half of what Tobiah had received from Raguel, since he had played such a major role in the unfolding of events. So they called Azariah in and told him their decision.

Episode 24
Azariah took them aside. First, he preached them a long sermon, exhorting them to praise Yahweh, and to continue Tobit's good works of almsgiving and charity.

Then he told them who he really was. "Tobit, when you prayed, it was I who delivered your prayers to Yahweh. When you buried the dead Jews, I did the same. Yahweh commissioned me to heal you, and your daughter-in-law Sarah. I am **Raphael**, one of the seven angels who serve the glory of the Lord."

This scared the crap out of them, and they flung themselves on the ground before him. He told them, "No no; get up. You've got nothing to fear. When I came to you, it was under Yahweh's direction. Praise him every day. When you thought you saw me eating and drinking, it was a hallucination to make you believe I was human. While you're praising the Lord, I will be ascending to him."

Then Raphael ascended into the heavens. Long after he was out of sight, Tobit and Tobiah continued singing the praises of Yahweh.

Episode 25
Then Tobit composed a great long poem, part sermon and part prophecy. The sermon part is the usual exaltation and praise of

Yahweh

The prophecy is about the future of Jerusalem.

Remember, this is written several centuries AFTER the time frame of the story itself. So the time the prophecies are ABOUT should be the writer's present. The "prophecies" should be confirmed by "present day" facts. Alas, not so.

I*t predicts a bright and glorious future for Jerusalem, when it will be the focal point of the entire world. Nations will come to honor her, bearing gifts for Yahweh, and she will be the chosen city of nations forever.*

Those who set out to overthrow you will be forever accursed. Your lives will be filled with joy and happiness. Your gates will be built of precious stones; your towers will be made of gold; your streets will be paved with rubies and jewels. And all will cry their worship of Yahweh, for bringing this all about.

Thus ends Tobit's poem.

Episode 26
Tobit died at the age of 112, fifty years after the bird rendered him blind. On his deathbed he called his son and grandsons together, and gave them a prophecy.

He told them, as soon as he and Edna were dead, they were to get the hell out of Nineveh and move to somewhere in Media. Assyria was about to be overrun by hostile forces. They would also overrun Israel and Jerusalem.

The Temple would be destroyed. But the Israelites would rebound, and rebuild the Temple. All the nations would gather to worship Yahweh there.

They should always conduct themselves in accordance with The Law. But as soon as Tobit andEdna were in the ground, Tobiah and his crew should hightail it out of there. Bad things were fixing to happen to Nineveh, and Tobiah shouldn't be around when they happened.

Episode 27
When Anna died, she was buried next to her husband Tobit. Then Tobiah pulled up stakes, and re-settled in Ecbatana with his father-in-law Rageul. When Raguel and Edna died, he inherited their estate.

Tobiah died at the age of 117. But he lived long enough to witness the destruction of Nineveh. He praised Yahweh for its destruction, and rejoiced about it. He was a man to carry a grudge.

The Bible, Chapter 155

THE BOOK OF JUDITH

All four of these Apocryphal books are narratives, rather than sermons or prophecies. My favorite book in the Old Testament is Esther. It is a gripping tale, without preaching. The religious element, the faith and victory of Judaism, comes out through the story rather than on top of it. From my preliminary survey, I expect Judith to be similar.

Written a couple of centuries B.C., Judith has no claim to historicity. Historically, the names of the principals,, and periods of the events, cannot be correlated with the known history of the period. It's fiction, based on half-remembered stories of the past. That doesn't diminish the worth of the story, or fable, one bit.

Part 1

We begin with the war between the Assyrians and the Medes, the former, under Nebuchadnezzar centered in Nineveh , and the latter, under the leadership of Arphaxad, centered in Ecbatana. (*This is not the historical Nebuchadnezzar of the Book of Ezra, et al. That one was the king of Babylon.*)

Neb decided to extend his empire. He sent emissaries to every kingdom he could think of, from Persia to Egypt, to drum up support for his armies.

He got no takers. They saw no reason to go along, and didn't see him as a threat to them. A serious error on their part.

This refusal REALLY busted Neb's chops. He flew into a rage, and vowed to teach them a lesson by invading and killing everybody, and taking their stuff. Neb wasn't one to take an insult lightly. Any kingdom that had refused to join him was

435

dead meat.

Then we are given a long account of how Neb's armies, led by general Holofernes, raged through the territory, killing everybody and taking their stuff.

News of this scared the jeepers out of the people in his path. They sent messengers to suck up to Holofernes, vowing loyalty to Nebuchadnezzar, and surrendering everything to Holofernes' disposal. The people of the cities welcomed his armies with garlands and dancing.

It did them no good. Holofernes sacked their cities and cut down their sacred groves and destroyed their temples. He was under orders to see to it that nobody worshiped anybody but Nebuchadnezzar, who saw himself as a god. He also burned their grain fields, and killed a lot of people and took their stuff, and took their women as booty.

Eventually, Holofernes set up camp near the hills of Judea, and settled down for R&R and refurbishing his equipment.

I shall stop here, since we are at the end of the preliminaries and are about to get into the meat of the story.

....

The Bible, Chapter 156

The Book of Judith
part 2

Holofernes has set up his garrison near the hills east of Judea. He had an army of almost 140,000 soldiers & cavalry, which presented an impressive, and ominous display.

When the Judeans heard how Holofernes had treated the peoples he had overrun, killing everybody and destroying their temples and whatnot, they were more than a little bit scared.

They had only recently returned from exile, and put the altars and the Temple back in order. So they sent word to all their outlying regions, to alert them to the danger. The people there posted lookouts on the high mountain tops, fortified their villages, stockpiled provisions, and prepared for the worst. Joakim, the High Priest in Jerusalem, sent word to guard the mountain passes that gave access to Judea. They were easily defended, since they were only wide enough to allow two abreast. The people followed his instructions.

Then everybody went into a religious fervor, petitioning Yahweh for help. All the men, women, kids, and domestic animals were clothed in sack-cloth. They prostrated themselves in front of the Temple, and dumped ashes on their heads, and did the same to the altar. *This sort of humbling and self-abasement was supposed to curry favor with Yahweh.* They prayed fervently, and constantly, for Yahweh to protect them from the fate of the kingdoms Holofernes had overrun, seizing their women and profaning their holy sites and killing everybody and taking their stuff.

The Lord heard their plea, and was sympathetic to their plight. But he didn't do anything about it just yet.

When Holofernes learned that the Israelites had armed themselves, and prepared for his attack, and guarded the mountain passes, he had a cow. He called up all the leaders of the Moabites, Ammonites and others, and demanded information from them. "What kind of people are these mountain-dwellers? What are their main cities? How large are their armies? What is the main source of their strength? Who are their leaders? Why have they refused to welcome me like the other leaders of the west?" This last shows a certain cluelessness on the part of Holofernes. Did he suppose they hadn't heard what he was up to?

Achior's Testimony
One Achior, leader of the Ammonites, stepped forward and offered to tell what he knew.

He started by giving a condensed, but complete, history of the Israelites, from Abraham in Chaldea, to settling in Canaan, to emigrating to Egypt during the famine, to leaving Egypt under Moses leadership, to their program of conquest across Sinai and to Canaan, where they killed everybody and took their stuff.

As long as they were faithful to their god Yahweh, everything went well for them. But when they fell away and sinned, they were ground down by their enemies and hauled off to foreign lands as captives. Their temple was destroyed, their cities were overrun.

But when they returned to their god Yahweh, they were allowed to return and prosper.

So their source of power lies in their faithfulness to their god Yahweh. So long as they keep free from sin, he will protect them. But if they've been being naughty, he'll turn his back on them. So if you can establish that they are doing things against what

Yahweh wants, they'll be at your mercy and you can whip their butts.

But if they have Yahweh on their side, you'd be wise to avoid attacking them. Otherwise, Yahweh will protect them and you'll get your butts whipped.

…………..

When Achior had finished his speech, the Assyrians started fuming and fussing that he could DARE suggest that they might get whipped by a puny lot like the Israelites. Let's cut this insulting wretch up into dog meat, and go attack them right away.

Holofernes got them calmed down, and told Achior, "Who do you think you are, presuming to tell us not to attack the Israelites because their god Yahweh protects them? There is no god other than Nebuchadnezzar. His forces will wipe them from the face of the earth, and nothing can protect them! Nebuchadnezzar has decreed that they will perish, and so they shall!"

"As for you, you Ammonite hireling… for saying these insulting perverse things, you won't see my face again until I have eradicated these expatriates from Egypt. You'll see how wrong you were. Then we'll retrieve you, take you there, and skewer you along with them. You won't die until I smash you along with them. I promise that."

 He ordered his men to take Achior to Bethulia and turn him him over to the Israelites. When the Israelites saw them coming, they started slinging rocks; so the soldiers tied up Achior and dumped him and left.

After the soldiers left, the Israelites came and untied Achior, and brought him to the rulers of the city. They asked him what's going on. He recounted everything that had taken place between him and Holofernes, including Holofernes' threats and boasting.

439

This put the people into a dither. They went running around and prostrating themselves and hollering "Lord, see how uppity and arrogant they are compared with our meekness and lowliness. Look on us with favor, when need be." They praised Achior, and had a big dinner, and spent the rest of the night calling on Yahweh to be on their side.

…………..

Holofernes Displays His Troops
The next day, Holofernes ordered his entire army of foot soldiers and supporting troops, to attack Bethulia, and seize the mountain passes. In the valley near Bethulia, there was a spring which provided the water supply for the city. They camped at the spring, and spread out covering several miles.

When the Israelites saw the size of the force, they began to despair. "Holy Cow! That swarm can eat up the whole country —mountains, valleys, cities! There's so MANY!" But they went ahead and grabbed their weapons, and set signal fires on the hilltops, and a nighttime watch in case of surprise attacks.

Next morning, Holofernes brought in and showed off several thousand cavalry, to further intimidate the Israelites. He scoped out and seized their water sources.

A New Strategy
The leaders of the surrounding kingdoms who had aligned themselves with Holofernes told him, "Look. There's a way for you to take the city without suffering a single casualty. These Israelites don't base their security on a strong offensive military force, but on the mountains where they live, which allow them to mount a solid defense."

"But there is no constant source of water in the city. They have to come down to the springs in the valley. You now control those. All you have to do is wait them out. Thirst and hunger will eventually decimate them to where they'll no longer be able to fight. We will take our troops and establish a perimeter, so they can't escape. By and by you can just march in and kill them and take their stuff, as punishment for refusing to meet you peacefully."

Holofernes thought that was a splendid idea, so they immediately acted on it. They secured their control of the water sources, the perimeter was established, and they settled down and waited.

And on this cliff-hanging note, let us stop for now.

==================

…………..

The Bible, Chapter 157

The Book of Judith
Part 3

Bethulia is under siege. There's no way out, and they're running out of water.

The siege has been going on for over a month. The cisterns have run dry, and the reservoirs are about to. Water is rationed. Women and children are collapsing and dying from thirst. Everybody prays to Yahweh for relief, but none comes.

A Proposal to Surrender
The people descended on Uzziah and the city council, and raised up a howl. "Look what you've got us into. You didn't make peace with the Assyrians, and now we're dying! Yahweh has sold us into their power, through thirst and exhaustion. We demand that you submit, and deliver the city over to Holofernes! We'll be slaves, but at least we won't be watching our children die before our eyes! Yahweh is punishing us for our sins, and those of our ancestors!" *[Note that there have been no deviations from Yahweh for them to be punished for. But that's the only way they can make sense of what's happening.]*

Uzziah told them, "Let's not rush into things. We'll give Yahweh five more days to rescue us. If he hasn't by then, I'll do as you say." Then he sent everybody on home.

Enter Judith
There was a prominent woman of the town named Judith. We are given her genealogy back 16 generations all the way to Jacob aka Israel. She was a widow. Her husband Manassech had died of sunstroke during the barley harvest. Judith went into mourning. Instead of living in their house, she pitched a simple tent on its

442

roof, and lived there, except on sabbaths and holidays. She wore widow's weeds, and sack cloth and ashes. She fasted every day except for sabbaths and holidays. In short, she was a thoroughly righteous woman.

She was also a woman of rare beauty. Her face could have launched a thousand ships, and her figure was a lecher's dream. Also, she was rich. Her husband had left her a sizable estate — money, servants, house and goods, livestock, and agricultural fields which she maintained. She had a lot going for her.

You would have expected the local populace to be green with envy; but they weren't. They looked up to her as a woman of intelligence and wisdom, and nobody had anything bad to say about her. She was an important community figure.

When Judith heard what was going on up at the city council, she sent her housemaid to ask them to come to her tent and visit her. They came, to hear what she had to say.

What she did was give them a royal chewing out.

Judith's Speech

"This business of setting a timetable for Yahweh to rescue us, or you surrender to the Assyrians, is ridiculous. It's not your place to lay down conditions for the Lord! Your proposals are more likely to annoy him, than to get him to do what you want."

"He doesn't need to meet your five-day deadline. He has his own schedule. All we can do is wait for him to rescue us when he's ready. We have good reason to think that he will. Unlike other tribes in other times, we have never worshiped idols, nor done anything else to get on his bad side

"if we surrender to the Assyrians, they'll soon take over all of Judea. They'll destroy our holy places, slaughter our people, and bring ruin. And who do you think will be held responsible? Us! It will all be on our heads, for surrendering ourselves and our city to them. When we're enslaved, we'll be a mockery in the eyes of our slave masters, and Judah will be disgraced in the eyes of the world."

"Instead, we need to set an example for all Judeans. Their lives, and the defense of all of Judea, depend on what we do now. Yahweh didn't let us get into this situation as punishment for sins; he's done it as a test of our will and our faith. Don't let him down."

Uzziah was convinced: "What you said sounds right. You're well known for your wisdom and righteousness. People can hear what you've said and see that it's correct. But they've been so tortured by thirst they convinced us to agree to do as they demanded. Please, as the Yahweh-fearing woman that you are, pray for the Lord to at least send us some rain, to fill up our cisterns."

A Secret Plan

She said, "I have a better plan, that may go down in the history of our people. But don't ask me what it is. I won't tell you until afterwards. Tonight, let me and my maid out through the city gate, and before your deadline, Yahweh will, through me, rescue Israel."

She doesn't say, "If it works," or anything like that. She's mighty sure of herself. I suspect that Yahweh ought to regard that as prideful arrogance, but he didn't.

She then went home, put on sack cloth and ashes, and started praying in a loud voice. "Oh Lord! Remember when you put a sword in the hand of my ancestor Simeon, to take revenge on those who had ravished his sister! Through him, you slaughtered the menfolk, and their princes, and their slaves, and handed over their womenfolk as booty. Do the same for me as you did for Simeon."

The Rape of Dinah
The incident she's talking about is recounted in chapter 34 of Genesis. To my mind, it's a tale of treachery, deceit and cruelty. But she didn't see it that way.

Here's the tale, briefly. Jacob had a daughter, Dinah, and the prince of the territory got the hots for her, and Had his Way with her. This outraged her brothers, one being Simeon. The prince decided he really loved Dinah, and asked permission to marry her. His father thought the alliance with the Israelites would be a good thing. When he put it to Jacob, Jacob said, only on the condition you convert to Yahwehism and get your menfolks circumcised.

So all the men got circumcised at once. And while they were laid up from the surgery, Simeon and his brothers roared in and killed the prince who had violated Dinah, and all his family, and servants, and all the other males in the city, and took the womenfolk as booty. This left a lot of dead people who had nothing to do with what happened to Dinah, a lot of women husbandless and in bondage, a sister no longer virgin, and the one guy eager to marry her dead in the streets. This is supposed to be a warm tale of retributive justice.

Then she carried on about the Assyrians, and how they were out to defile Yahweh's holy places and slaughter his chosen people. Yahweh has the power to defeat them. Please allow her, a widow, to use that power to carry out her plan. "Let my guileful speech bring wound and wale on those who have planned dire things against your covenant, your holy temple, Moun Zion, and the homes your children have inherited." And on and on in that vein.

Judith Pretties Herself Up
When she was done, she went down to the house with her maid. They got her cleaned up from the sack cloth and ashes, and got rid of her widow's weeds. Then she bathed, anointed her body with perfumed ointment, and received an attractive hair-do. She

put on her best party outfit, sandals, and anklets, bracelets, rings, and other jewelry. By the time she got herself done, she was heartbreakingly lovely.

She had her maid put together a supply of kosher provisions, and they left the city and headed down toward the camp of Holofernes.

As this seems as good a place as any to stop and rest. *She had seduction in mind..*

The Bible, Chapter 158

The Book of Judith
part 4

They soon arrived at an outpost of the camp, where they were arrested and questioned. Judith told them she was from the Hebrews in the city, but she had left them and come to join up with Holofernes, because she was certain the city would soon be overrun. She knew of a route he could use to go up and take over not only the city, but the entire mountain region. *She lied, of course. As with Tobit's angel, it's okay to lie for a good cause.*

Because she was such a hottie, they bought her story and conducted her to the camp, and to the tent of Holofernes. When the crowd saw her, they thought "Wow. If those Israelites can produce women like this one, they're a real threat. They could beguile the whole world if they had the chance." *If they only knew.*

Judith Meets Holofernes
She was ushered into Holofernes' tent. When he saw her he was knocked out by her beauty. She flopped down and prostrated herself before him, but the servants immediately put her back on her feet. Holo told her not to be afraid, that he'd never harm anyone who had come to serve the cause of the great Nebuchadnezzar, King of the World.

She said, "Hey, I'm your handmaid, and tonight everything I'm going to tell you will be the truth. Follow my advice, and fortune will smile on you." She followed up with a string of praises of the great Nebuchadnezzar, and buttered up Holofernes, calling him just about the smartest man alive, and a military genius. He ate it up.

She reminded them of the story Achior had told them: The first part of what he said was absolutely true, she said, and should be paid attention to.

The Israelites are Yahweh's chosen people. They're under his protection, and can't be harmed or conquered, so long as they are faithful to him and don't sin against his laws. He will always protect them, under that condition.

Judith Reveals Her Supposed Plan
Then Judith spun an implausible tale about how the Israelites were about to lose that protection.

Obedience is the condition for Yahweh's protection. But In their hunger, they were fixing to violate it; and when they did, they'd be ripe for the plucking. They had decided to slaughter and eat forbidden unclean animals contrary to the Law, in order to have anything to eat. They also planned to take back the tithes of grain and wine and oil they had consecrated for the priests — things no layman is permitted to touch. They had sent a messenger to Jerusalem to get the okay to do this. They expected to get it, because Jerusalem was also corrupt. As soon as they got the permission, they'd follow through with their plan....and piss Yahweh off, and lose his protection. That's when Holofernes could wade in.

I pause for comment. Holofernes had seen to it that Bethulia was completely hemmed in, so tightly that nobody could escape. So how could they have sent a messenger to Jerusalem? Holofernes should have known this. For that matter, the whole story was suspicious on its face. Apparently, the only reason Holofernes bought her story was that he was enchanted by this wickedly beautiful hottie. Just a few days before, when Achior was there, he had ridiculed the idea that there could be a god greater than Nebuchadnezzar. Now he was swallowing it hook, line, and sinker.

Judith's plan was working.

"As soon as I heard of the plans I ran away. Yahweh has sent me here, to do things that will astonish the people of the world when they hear about them."

The Plot Thickens
Then she told him, "I'm a holy woman, and I worship Yahweh night and day. While I'm here, every night my servant and I will leave the camp, and go down to the ravine to pray to Yahweh in private. The Lord will tell me when the Israelites have begun to ignore his laws and have earned his wrath. Then I'll pass the news on to you, and the rest will be easy."

Another bit of the plan.

"After you've taken Bethulia, I'll lead you across Judea all the way to Jerusalem. You can drive the Israelites before you like sheep, and make Jerusalem your capital."

Holofernes Takes the Bait
She got him. Says Holofernes, "No other woman in the world looks so beautiful or speaks so wisely." *Feminine wiles are working.* "Your Yahweh did the right thing, sending you to help us. You are so DAMN good looking! And you speak as beautifully when you talk to me. If this comes off as you say, I'll accept your Yahweh as my god. You'll live in honor in Nebuchadnezzar's palace, and you'll be famous everywhere in the world."

Then he ordered a banquet to be served, but she said ""I'd be sinning against Yahweh to eat your Assyrian food, so my servant and I will eat the permitted stuff we brought with us. It wouldn't do, for me to get on Yahweh's bad side at this point."

Holofernes: "But when the kosher supplies you brought with you are gone, where do we get more? We don't have access to your people up there." Judith: "Don't worry. We won't run out of supplies before Yahweh accomplishes, through me, what he's determined." *No doubt in her mind.*

Judith and her maid found accommodations in Holo's tent. About dawn, she sent a servant to tell the guards to let them out of the camp to do their prayers to Yahweh. And so they did. Each night for three days she left the camp to do her prayers. After offering prayers to Yahweh, she bathed in the spring, and returned to the camp. And things were copacetic between her and Holo and his crew.

.

Here I shall take pause.

The Bible, Chapter 159

The Book of Judith
Part 5

On the fourth day, Holofernes threw a party for his servants alone. No officers were invited. He sent his eunuch Bagoas to invite Judith to come. "It would be a shame to have such a woman with us, and not socialize with her."

Bagoas went and told her that a beautiful babe like herself should have no hesitation in joining the household for eating and drinking, just like the Assyrian women who live with Nebuchadnezzar.

Judith: "How can I refuse my lord anything? I'll do whatever pleases him, and will remember it with joy until the day I die."

Then she got her maid to dress her in her finest gown, and the rest of her trinkets and adornments, and make her as sexy as possible, to get ready for the party. She had seduction in mind.

I insert a point of information here. In those days, they didn't take their meals sitting on chairs at a table; they ate reclining, before a low table holding the food and beverages. When Judith first arrived at the camp, Bagoas had furnished her with a fleece to lie on while taking her meals. He now took the fleece and carried it to Holofernes tent, where he spread it out before him.

Then the lovely Judith came and reclined on it. When Holofernes saw her lying there, his hormones leapt. He had been itching to jump on her bones first chance he got, and he figured that the chance was going to occur that night.

He announced, "Let's eat and drink and be merry!" Judith said, "I certainly shall. I've never had as much fun in my life, as I'm having today." Then the feast commenced. Judith ate the kosher fare her maid had set for her.

Holofernes ate, and partied, and drank. And drank some more, in celebration. He was anticipating a hot time later in the evening. So he drank some more. He ended up drinking more wine that night than he had ever drunk at one sitting. In the end, he was drunk as a skunk.

When the party broke up, all the other partiers went back to their own tents, to sleep it off. Judith was alone with Holofernes in his tent. Her maid, as always, waited outside, to accompany her to their evening prayers later on.

But Alas, Holofernes couldn't follow through with his plans for the evening. Instead, he flopped down on his bed and passed out. There was nobody else around. This was the moment Judith had been leading up to.

She prayed to Yahweh, to approve what she was about to do. "I'm doing it for the glory of Jerusalem and to further your heritage, and to foil the enemies against us."
Holofernes' sword was hanging on the bedpost. Judith took it up, said "Strengthen me this day, god of Israel". Then grabbed Holofernes' hair, and proceeded to hack his Assyrian head off!

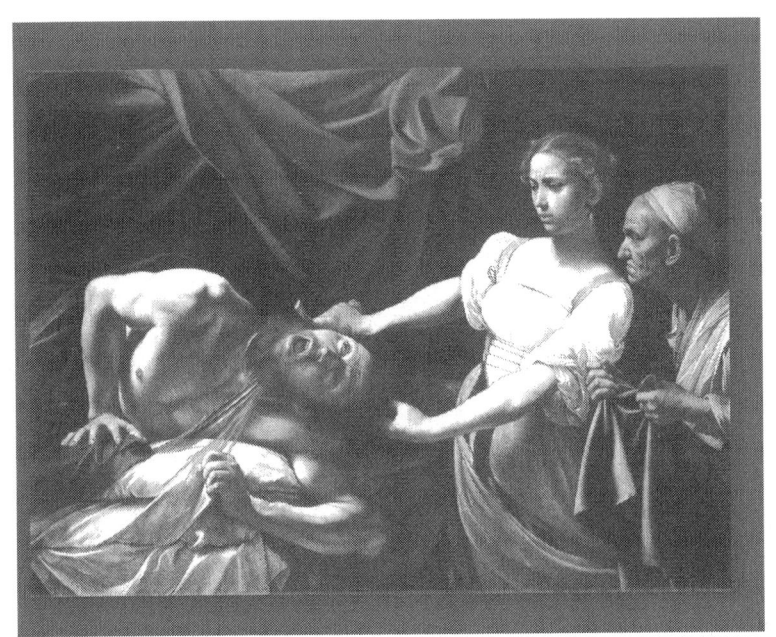

She rolled the body off the bed, pulled down its ornate, jeweled canopy and folded it up to take with her. Then she went to the door of the tent, and handed the head to her maid, who hid it in her food pouch. Then the two of them headed toward the ravine, as if for their evening prayers.

I can't help but mention that when a head is hacked off, there is a phenomenal gush of blood. It must have taken Judith some fancy footwork to avoid getting drenched and drawing attention to herself.

But instead of going to the ravine, they headed for Bethulia. When they got within earshot, Judith hollered, "Open the gates! Yahweh has manifested his power against our enemies!" They opened the gates, and let her in, and built a bonfire for light to see by. As they gathered round, Judith proclaimed, "Praise Yahweh! He hasn't withheld his mercy from us, but tonight has destroyed our enemies by my hand!"

I can't let this pass without commentary. So far as I can see, Yahweh had no hand in the matter. All of the credit goes to

Judith. Anytime Yahweh inserts himself into human affairs, it shows up in some untoward event like a plague of frogs, or an earthquake, or a volcanic eruption, or the appearance of an angel, or an attack of leprosy: things that can't be explained through human agency. We have none of that here. Judith formulated the plan, and carried it out by herself. She made herself irresistible, in order to seduce Holofernes into trusting her, and get him aching to Go In Unto her. Devine influence wasn't needed to get him hot for her; it was a natural and anticipated outcome. Perhaps, Yahweh prompted him to get drunk. But that's idle speculation, since things turned out as they did with no hint of Yahweh taking a hand in the matter.

Here's what I think. Judith was a brilliant strategist. She invented the plan, and she executed it. But being a creature of her culture, she couldn't bring herself to believe that a "mere woman" could do it on her own. And she probably couldn't expect others to believe it, either. So she lays the credit on Yahweh, in order that the people wouldn't accuse her of gettin' above her raisin' and taking credit a woman couldn't be entitled to.

Then she pulled out the bloody head of Holofernes and said "Ta Daa!" and showed it to them, along with the canopy from his bed. And she assured them that it was her beauty alone that let her overcome him; she never had to get into the sack with him to pull it off. On that score, she was pure as could be.

And then she related the entire sequence of events to them. The people bowed down before her, and worshiped Yahweh, and thanked him for what she had done. Then Uzziah acknowledged Judith's role in the affair, calling her the most blessed of women, and proclaiming that her deed would live in memory forever. The people hollered "Amen!"

....

This seems as good a place as any to take a recess.

The Bible, Chapter 160

The Book of Judith
Part 6

Judith has shown off the head of Holofernes and gained the praise of the people. But the main goal —to get rid of the Assyrian army— is yet to be achieved. From here on, the plausibility-quotient of the story takes a downturn.

The people regarded Judith as a kind of superwoman, and were eager for her to tell them what to do next.

Judith says, "Now here's my plan."
"Hang Holofernes' head from the parapet, where it can be seen. Then at daybreak, each man is to take up his weapons and assemble at the gate. They will rush out under the command of an officer, as if they're about to go down and engage the Assyrians, but won't really go down."

"When the Assyrians see them, they will grab their armor and prepare for battle. But when they go to Holofernes' tent for leadership and don't find him, the whole army will panic and run away. THEN our troops will go down and slay them as they retreat."

"But first, go get Achior the Ammonite and bring him here, so he can watch it unfold."

When they brought Achior out, he didn't know what was up.

455

When he saw the head of Holofernes held by one of the men, he promptly fainted. When they revived him, he began praising Judith, and asked how this had come about. She related the tale, and when Achior heard what Yahweh had done, he immediately converted to Yahwehism and had himself circumcised.

Judith's plan came off exactly as she had predicted. The men of Bethulia roared out as if fixing to attack. The Assyrians saw them, notified their officers, and waited for orders what to do next. When Holofernes didn't show up, they figured he was still in his tent humping Judith, so they sent Bagoas to roust him out.

When Bagoas knocked and got no answer, he went in and saw Holofernes, headless and dead. He started hollering and screaming and tearing his clothes, and rushed over to look in Judith's tent. Nobody was there. That's when he understood. He went out and shouted, "People, we've been diddled! A single Hebrew woman has brought disgrace on the house of Nebuchadnezzar and killed our leader! Here you see Holofernes, headless and dead."

When the officers heard this, they started hollering and screaming and tearing their clothes. When the troops heard them and found out what was going on, they were "overcome with fear and trembling." Discipline collapsed. They ran off in all directions, in a panic and leaderless.

Then the Israelites swarmed after them and cut them down as they fled. Other tribes in the area soon joined them,chasing and killing the Assyrian soldiers in their panic-driven flight.

Meanwhile, the remaining people in Bethulia descended on the abandoned camp and began stripping it of everything worth taking. By the end of a month, the amount of loot was enormous.

Here I must pause and say: Give me a break. We are to suppose that a gazllion battle-hardened troops, with a well-established command structure, are going to fly into a tizzy and scatter like a

456

flock of pigeons when they hear that their commanding general has been assassinated. And that they will abandon their weapons and their armor, and forget how to fight, and become easy pickings for a band of weekend warriors from Bethulia. Really?

I don't think so. In a normal world, what would have happened is that the Assyrians would have been, not frightened, but mad as hell , and the second in command would have taken charge, and the army would have invaded Bethulia and killed everybody and taken their stuff, in revenge for the assassination. A story plausible until now has turned into a fairy tale where the three little pigs eat the big bad wolf.

It would at least have made sense if we had been told that Yahweh interfered and turned their spines to jelly, the way he hardened pharaoh's heart back in Moses' day, so that Judith's plan would work. But we are not told that. It was their own craven natures, these erstwhile conquerers of everything in their path, that made them turn tail and run. That's the story, and I don't buy it.

Nevertheless, the story is what it is, so let us continue to the end.

All the bigwigs from Jerusalem came down to see things for themselves, and to congratulate Judith. Then they collectively gave her their blessing for what she had done for Israel. And the people all hollered, "Amen".

By the end of the month, they had plundered Holofernes' camp of everything valuable. And they gave a lot of it to Judith, including Holo's tent and all its furnishings, his dinnerware, his silverware, and his couches. Judith harnessed up her mules, hitched them to her wagon, and loaded up all of her stuff.

If it seems odd that Judith would know how to harness a mule, remember that she was just a farm wife and was no doubt familiar with such everyday things.

Then there was a big celebration by the women of Israel, with

457

dancing and garlands and singing and carrying on. Judith led them in a song she had written:

    Break out the instruments, and play a serenade to Yahweh
    He is the Lord, who crushes warfare and sides with his people
        He snatched me from the hands of my persecutors

        The Assyrians came from the north in huge numbers
      Their forces clogged up the streams and covered the hills

  They threatened to burn our land, to slaughter our young men.
            To trample our babies into the ground,
              To hunt our children as prey,
      And to take our virgins as the spoils of war

    But Yahweh thwarted them, by the hand of a woman
    Their mighty leader was not struck down by young men,
                Nor by Titans,
                Nor by Giants,
        But by Judith, daughter of Merari

     She conquered him not by force, but by her beauty.
  She shed her widow's weeds and did everything to make herself
              beautiful and desirable.
 Her beauty caught his eye, captured his mind, and put him in her
                    power
         Then the sword cut through his neck.

The Persians trembled at her boldness,   the Medes were daunted
                  at her daring.

           Then our people shouted in victory.
        They had once been weak and oppressed,
But then our citizen army drove the enemy to retreat in panic and
                    fear

  We are only the descendants of slaves, but still the soldiers
                 turned and ran

> Sons of slaves chased them down and massacred them
> They were defeated by the ranks of my Lord's people
> ....
> Woe to any nations who attack our people
> Yahweh will smash them
> In the day of judgment he will send fire and worms into their flesh
> And they will burn in hell, forever

The claim that Yahweh "snatched her from the hands of her persecutors" has no basis in the story that I can find. She never had any persecutors to be snatched from the hands of.

Judith is exaggerating about the business with the Medes and the Persians. The setting of her story is Judea and surroundings. The Medes and Persians were located about a thousand miles to the east. I seriously doubt that the Bethulian national guard ventured that far; and there was no telegraph to spread alarm among the Persians. The author is piecing together half-remembered bits in order to make a good story.

After Judith finished her song, everybody headed off to Jerusalem to do their religious business. As an offering to Yahweh, Judith dedicated all of Holofernes' belongings she had been given, including the ornate bed canopy she had taken after dispatching Holofernes. They stayed in Jerusalem for three months, celebrating. Then everybody went to their respective cities.

Judith went back to Bethulia She remained a famous woman all her life. A lot of men were eager to marry her [*no wonder; she was both beautiful and rich*] but she rejected all of them and remained celebate for the rest of her days. She lived in the house she had shared with her husband, and died at the age of a hundred and five. She was buried in the tomb of her husband.

Before she died, she distributed her wealth among her husband's relatives, and her own. The maid, who had accompanied Judith on her sojourn with Holofernes, was released from bondage and given her freedom.

Thus ends the book of Judith.

The first book of Maccabees is an account of the doings of the Jewish revolutionary Judas Maccabaeus. It begins with some historical background.
=============

The First Book of MACCABEES

Alexander the Great conquered every place he could get to, and carried the Greek culture with him. Then he died, and his empire was parcelled out among his various officers. They appointed themselves kings, and their sons after them.

A couple of centuries down the road from Alexander, two hundred years of imported Greek culture had infected a substantial Israelite population, who hid their circumcisions, and followed the ways of the Greeks. (But not all did.)

Antiochus, King of the territory that included Judea, took over Jerusalem and looted the temple of all of its goodies. Then he took his loot and went back home.

A couple of years later, the army came back. They sacked Jerusalem, took everybody's stuff, put the city to the torch, and took all the women and children as booty. Across the river from the Temple Mount, they built a huge fortress dubbed the City of David, and settled in for a long stay.

Antiochus issued a decree that everybody had to abandon their local ways, religious practices, and customs, and follow the Greek way. Gentiles had no problem with it; neither did the fallen-away Jews. Enforcers were sent to the cities to make sure the law was obeyed. They desecrated the holy places, slaughtered unclean animals (pigs) for sacrifice, and outlawed the practice of circumcision.

Those who disobeyed, died. Any copy of the scroll of the Law that they found, got burned. The person that had it got executed. Mothers who went ahead and had their sons circumcised were put to death, along with their families. The circumcised babies were hanged by the neck. Nevertheless, a lot of Jews refused to go along. Many left the cities and hid out in the hills.

Enter Matthias
One of them was a priest named Matthias, who couldn't abide what was going on in Jerusalem and took himself and his family of five sons away from Jerusalem to settle in a tiny village a few miles away. The names of his sons are important: John (Gaddi), Simon (Thassi), Judas (Maccabeus), Eleazar (Avaran) and Jonathan (Apphus).

Moving didn't help. The Enforcers showed up at his village, and urged everyone to obey the King's law. Matthias declined. He said, "The Gentiles may give up their gods of their fathers and follow the Greeks; but we won't. We'll keep the covenant of our fathers, thank you, and will follow the laws and commandments of Yahweh. And that's that."

Just then, a fallen-away Jew stepped up to the pagan altar the troops had erected, and was fixing to offer a sacrifice. Matthias threw a tantrum, grabbed a sword, and killed the guy. He also killed the Enforcer in charge, and tore down the pagan altar. Then he raged through the town sowing rebellion: "All of you who intend to stay faithful to Yahew's covenant, follow me!"

He and his sons beat it for the hills, and plotted rebellion. Some followed him there, others decided to go settle in the desert, and got annihilated..

This is as much of I Maccabees as I have managed to relate, and it's all I'm going to relate. I have read the whole of 1 Maccabees, and the first half of II Maccabees, and I won't burden you with their retelling.

Each is a repetitious chronicle of wars and killings, one after another, with little filler plot to make them interesting. They also have a vast Dramatis Personae that is almost impossible to keep track of.

If you want the dreary details, read them yourownself.

The Bible, Chapter 88

Final Commentary

In writing these accounts, I have treated the Old Testament as if it were a book of fiction, to be taken on its own terms, not a historical document to be refuted. Within the book, Elijah really rose to heaven in a fiery chariot, the same way Tom Sawyer really whitewashed a fence.

The Bible is the most important written work in the history of western civilization. It tells stories that have guided peoples' beliefs and activities for centuries. I have read it, to find out what it says.

The Old Testament is at least this: a blending of legends and myths and folk history written a long time ago by a primitive people in a small sector of Asia Minor. It has been regarded as a guide to the conduct of life. However, I deplore the way it's been used to justify cruelty and injustice in the name of a god whom it does not present as admirable, and whose main claim for obedience is the power to destroy.

.

Here are a few things I have learned from reading the Old Testament:.

In the Old Testament there is no mention of heaven or hell as destinations for those who have died. There's no mention of "immortal souls" at all. All punishments and rewards are earthly, and physical. Individuals are punished with leprosy or other diseases or personal misfortunes. Groups are punished with natural disasters: drought, famine, plagues of locusts or frogs, earthquakes, etc. Individual are rewarded (from on high) with things like prosperity and positions of power and many descendants. Groups are rewarded with bounty, and peace, and victory in war, and so on.

In the O.T., "survival after death" doesn't come from an immortal soul; it comes through a man's descendants –his sons and their sons and their sons, and so on. A man is a link in part of a dynasty, a family line, a "house". He cares as much about a continuing family line as he does about himself. One of the greatest misfortunes a man can suffer is to have no sons to carry on his family line. Onan was slain for failing to provide his dead brother with a surrogate family line People are punished by inflicting disaster on their descendants. A man and his family line are one.

Ezekiel, and so far as I can remember, nobody else, talks of bringing the dead back to life. Dried out skeletons are re-clothed in flesh and made to walk about. At the end of days, all of the dead people or a large subset of them will be resurrected into living, breathing human beings. No persisting souls of the dead are involved. These are straight-ahead corpses or skeletons or skeletal fragments that get re-animated.
....

Nobody today, and possibly not even then, takes the whole of the laws of Leviticus and Deuteronomy seriously. Not Christians, not Jews. People pick and choose among them, to suit their prejudices and preferences, and ignore the rest. That's because the rest are too bizarre for a sensible person, even a devout one, to accept. We don't condemn disobedient sons to be stoned to death. It's okay to weave different kinds of yarn together, and to crossbreed animals —that's how we get mules. If anyone cites the bible as authority for some grotesque practice or belief, tell him to go read the whole of Leviticus, and and see if he's willing to swallow all of it.

....

These bible people understand and observe a principle I find weird: the notion of inherited or group or collective guilt. Whole peoples —usually the Israelites or Judeans— are punished with plagues and whatnot for the "sins of the people", even though the sinning was certainly done by only a portion of individuals within the people. "The people stopped following Yahweh;" the people were struck with a blight of some sort . Sodom and Gomorrah were dissolute; the cities were destroyed including old people, children, little bitty babies who had done nothing wrong. Didn't matter; they were part of wicked group and suffered the group's punishment.

A man who did wrong had disaster inflicted not upon himself, but upon his descendants for many generations. Even though they had done nothing wicked themselves, they had the misfortune to have a sinful ancestor. Yahweh judges whole peoples, not the individuals in them. A people retains its identity, and its guilt, over centuries, even though its population changes entirely.

This isn't as foreign to 21st century attitudes as it might be. Think Ireland: Catholic vs. Protestant. Think the Middle East: Sunni vs. Shiite. Think the U.S. political scene: Those Evil Liberals vs. Those Evil Conservatives. Think most everywhere: Us vs. Them.

....

The Promised Land that Yahweh gave to the Children of Israel wasn't his to give. it was occupied by people collectively called Canaanites who had lived there and worked the land for generations. The Children of Israel didn't arrive there as immigrants. They arrived as a conquering force that invaded, killed everybody, took their stuff, and occupied their land. Which was okay, because Yahweh told them to do it...and helped them to do it. Do you know why? Because Ham inadvertently saw his drunken daddy Noah naked. So Noah cursed Ham and all his descendants, who turned out to be the Canaanites that the

Children of Israel therefore had permission to overrun and massacre and take their stuff. All because Noah didn't like being seen with his clothes off.

....

Exclusionism was rampant among the Children of Israel, no different in kind from that of the Aryan Brotherhood. The C. of I. were **Yahweh's chosen people**, a breed apart from and superior to all others. They were allowed to have no intercourse, social, sexual, or commercial, with the wretched heathens around them. No friendships, no alliances, nothin'. When they overran a country, they killed everybody. The ones they didn't manage to kill they took as slaves. If they started intermixing with other cultures, Yahweh came down on them like a bucket of rocks. They were supposed to keep their racial strain pure and unsullied.

Probably related to this is the scorched-earth approach to conquest. When they overran a nation and got it to surrender, they didn't make it into a vassal state and move on; they killed everybody and took their stuff. That left no temptation to intermingle.

....

The morality in the O.T. is based on rules and punishment and fear. The only reason to do or not do something was to avoid getting bashed. Officially at least, there was no recognition of right and wrong except in terms of The Law and in terms of avoiding getting stomped on by Yahweh. Why care for the poor and infirm? Not because it's the right thing to do, but because Yahweh demands it and will bust you if you don't.

As you can tell, I find that moral framework both cynical and deplorable. You gain no points with me if you behave yourself only because you can't get away with not behaving yourself. Virtue practiced under threat isn't virtue; it's capitulation.

....

In the Old Testament, God/Yahweh isn't the loving shepherd father-figure sweetly overseeing his people as mentioned in various psalms. He is a ruthless, ego-driven tyrant whose main activity is to hand out terrible punishments when people go against his wishes. He is not one you would call Daddy. The proper attitude toward him is fear and trembling, since he is capricious and you can never be sure what's going to set him off next. He's not a paragon of any recognized human virtue, not even forgiveness, since his is selective. He governs not by example, but by unfettered power, and he loves to unleash that power when people cross him.

In the Bible the people are told to love God and also to fear God. Those are incompatible commands; the latter is the one that carries the day.

....

Don't believe that guff about the Song of Solomon being some kind of a hymn to Yahweh, because it isn't. It's a love song pure and simple, and the love it's talking about is the carnal kind between a guy and a gal. And it's a rather nice love song.

....

I've learned that Old Testament history (after Genesis) is actual history, filtered through folklore. The kings and events it mentions are real kings and real events, taking place at real times in real places identifiable today. I've found it both entertaining and instructive to locate the biblical events within the broad panorama of the history of the middle east in the centuries B.C. Knowing the actual history makes the Bible stories easier to understand.

....

I've learned that the Bible has a lot of cool stories that haven't yet been made into movies.

....

I've learned that Biblical heroes, like modern-day heroes, are often jerks.

....

Of course there's more. But that's all I'm going to mention. You want more, learn it yourself.

Appendix I:

A BRIEF EARLY HISTORY OF THE JEWISH PEOPLE

(Compiled From the Old Testament Together with Other Sources.)

The patriarch and progenitor of the Jewish race is Abraham. Every genuine Jew is descended from him. Abraham (né Abram) was born in a place called Ur of the Chaldees, which was either over by the mouth of the Euphrates, near the Persian Gulf, or else up north somewhere in Syria. At any rate, it was a long ways away from Canaan's land. He traveled to Canaan, where Yahweh promised him that one day, that whole territory would be owned and ruled by his descendants. At that time there were no Jews and wouldn't be for a long time: just Hebrews.

When Abraham was 99, his aged wife was allowed by Yahweh to give Abraham a son, whom he named Isaac. Abraham also had an illegitimate son named Ishmael by a servant girl, but that's another story. Abraham had no other children.

When Isaac grew up he had two sons, Esau and Jacob. Esau was a burly outdoor type who brought home venison for the family. Jacob was a mama's boy who stayed home and, with mama's connivance, cheated his elder brother out of his birthright. Everybody was still living in Canaan, which consisted of the Jordan river Valley and parts of Sinai and Lebanon.

When Jacob grew up he had a wrestling match with an angel, and was given the name Israel. He went on to have twelve sons:

Reuben, Simeon, Levi, Judah, Dan, Naphtali, Gad, Asher, Issachar, Zebulun, Joseph, and Benjamen. Each would, a long ways down the road, become the patriarch of one of the 12 Tribes of Israel, which is to say the 12 Tribes of Jacob.

All were jealous of Joseph, because they thought he was daddy's favorite, so they arranged to sell him to a slave merchant who was passing through Canaan on his way to Egypt. They also arranged for daddy to think he had been killed by wild animals.

So Joseph became a slave in Egypt. But he was a resourceful lad, and eventually worked his way up to become the second in command under the Pharaoh.

In the years this was happening, a famine came along and struck Canaan. Eventually, there was little to eat. Jacob heard rumors that there was lots of grain in Egypt, so he sent his boys there to see if they could get some to bring back.

When they got there, at first they didn't recognize Joseph. But he finally revealed who he was, and after some adventures, sent his brothers back to Canaan, to collect the rest of the family and bring them to Egypt where there was food.

With Jacob's whole family there, they waxed and multiplied. But since they were Hebrews, they were always subservient to the Egyptians. After 40 years, they numbered many thousands. Then Moses came along and led the whole bunch...every one of them a descendant of Jacob and therefore of Abraham...back toward Canaan, which Yahweh had promised to the descendants of Abraham.

So they got to Canaan, where they killed everybody and took their stuff, then settled in and made it home. Each of the sons had a ton of descendants of his own, constituting his Tribe. Each Tribe was given hegemony over a piece of the territory.
They continued to wax and multiply.

For a long time there was no central government. Things were administered by tribal administrators called Judges. But eventually a strong-man named Saul came along and established himself as King over the whole territory.

Saul was a demented paranoiac, who eventually was killed in war and was succeeded as King of the territory by David the Goliath-slayer. Although the Kingdom was united under a single ruler, there was a *de facto* rivalry between the two lower tribedoms —Benjamin and Judah, home of King David — and the remaining tribedoms to the North.

David ruled for many years, and was succeeded by his son King Solomon. King Solomon ruled for many more years. He was a rather dictatorial ruler. When he died, his heir-apparent was his son Rehoboam. Rehoboam's advisors urged him to go easier on the people than Solomon had. Rehoboam said, Not a chance. He'd be even harsher than Solomon. When the northern tribes heard this, they refused to recognize Rehoboam as their king, and chose someone else (Jeroboam) who was not of the Davidic line.

Judah (where Jerusalem was) along with Benjamin, elected to go with Rehoboam from David's line because he was their local boy.

So they split in two: the Northern Kingdom of Israel, and the Southern Kingdom of Judah. The two kingdoms went their own ways for a couple of hundred years, quibbling back and forth and each forming and dissolving their own alliances. Both remained nominally Yahweh-ist, but with periodic deviations, especially in the North.

The Northern Kingdom's last alliance was with the Assyrian Empire to the north. After spotty relations under various Israelite kings, the Assyrians finally got fed up, captured most of the population of the Northern Kingdom of Israel, and hauled them off into captivity in Assyria. From there, they dispersed throughout the world and became the Ten Lost Tribes of Israel.

The Southern Kingdom of Judah, or Judea, carried on for another century and a half under various kings. Finally, the Babylonian King Nebuchadnezzar invaded Judea, razed the city of Jerusalem with it's Temple, and carried everybody who was anybody back to the Babylonian Captivity. This was around 560 BC.

That lasted 50 or 60 years, until the Persians came and conquered Babylon. The Persian King Cyrus allowed a bunch of the people to return to Judea and rebuild Jerusalem and the Temple. A bunch more, who had made their home in Babylon, decided to stay there. Esther was one of them. Because they were all Judeans, they were called "Jews", directly descended from Abraham.

Then a bunch more stuff happened and various empires took over and were taken over. That part of history has little to do with the Bible. Look it up yourself, if you're interested.

.

Appendix II:

Kings of Israel and Judah

Kingdom: United Kingdom of Israel and Judah

King	Reign
1. Saul	1052-1010
2. David	1025-970
3. Solomon	970-931

Kingdom of Israel (Ten Northern Tribes)

King	Reign	Religion
1. Jeroboam I	931-910	H
2. Nadab	910-909	H
3. Baasha	909-886	H
4. Elah	886-885	H
5. Zimri	885	?
6. Omri	885-874	B
7. Ahab	874-853	B
8. Ahaziah	853-852	B
9. Joram	852-841	H
10. Jehu	841-814	Y
11. Jehoahaz	814-798	H
12. Jehoash	798-782	H
13. Jeroboam II	782-753*	H
14. Zechariah	753-752	?
15. Shallum	752	?
16. Menahem	752-742	H
17. Pekahiah	742-740	H
18. Pekah	740-732*	H
19. Hoshea	732-712	H

722 BC Fall of Samaria to Assyria

Kingdom of Judah (and Benjamin)

King	Reign	Religion
1. Rehoboam	931-913	Y
2. Abijah	913-911	Y
3. Asa	911-870	Y
4. Jehoshaphat	870-848	Y
5. Jehoram	848-841	B
6. Ahaziah	841	
7. Athaliah	841-835	B
8. Joash	835-796	Y/B
9. Amaziah	796-767	Y/I
10. Uzziah (Azariah)	767-740	Y
11. Jotham	740-732	Y
12. Ahaz	732-716	B
13. Hezekiah	716-687	Y
14. Manasseh	687-642	B
15. Amon	642-640	B
16. Josiah	640-608	Y
17. Jehoahaz	608	B
18. Jehoiakim	608-597	B
19. Jehoiachin	597	B
20. Zedekiah	597-586	U

Destruction of Jerusalem, 586 BC, Babylonian Captivity

H = Jeroboam's heretical version of Yahweh-ism.
B = Baal et al. Other gods
Y = Yahweh-ism
I = Idolatry
U = who knows

Appendix III:

Prophets of the Old Testament

Prophet	*Approx. Date*	*Ruler*
Ahijah	931 BC	Solomon, Jeroboam
Jehu	909 BC	Baasha, Elah, Jehoshafat
Elijah	874 BC	Ahab
Micaiah	870 BC	Ahab
Elisha	853 BC	Jeoram, Jehu, Jehoahaz, Jehoahash
Joel	unknown	
Jonah 7	96 BC	Jeroboam II
Amos, Hosea	782 BC	Jeroboam II
Isaiah	767 BC	Uzziah, Jotham, Ahaz, Hezekiah
Micah	740 BC	Jotham, Ahaz, Hezekiah

Assyrian Conquest of Israel 722 BC

Nahum	642 BC	Josiah
Zephaniah,	640 BC	Josiah
Jeremiah	640 BC	Josiah
Habakkuk	609 BC	Jehoahaz
Ezekiel	592 BC	Zedekiah
Daniel	592 BC	Nebuchadnezzar
Obadiah	587 BC (?)	unknown

Babylonian Captivity of Judea 586 BC

Haggai	520 BC	Cyrus
Zechariah	520 BC	Cyrus
Esther	478 BC	Xerxes
Ezra	458 BC	Cyrus
Nehemiah	445 BC	Artaxerxes
Malachi	433 BC	Cyrus

Made in the USA
Lexington, KY
02 September 2018